The Essentials of Financial Modeling in Excel

THE ESSENTIALS OF FINANCIAL MODELING IN EXCEL

A CONCISE GUIDE TO CONCEPTS AND METHODS

Michael Rees

WILEY

Registered Offices
John Wiley & Sons, Inc., 111 River Street, Hoboken, NJ 07030, USA

John Wiley & Sons Ltd, The Atrium, Southern Gate, Chichester, West Sussex, PO19 8SQ, UK

Editorial Office
The Atrium, Southern Gate, Chichester, West Sussex, PO19 8SQ, UK

For details of our global editorial offices, customer services, and more information about Wiley products visit us at www.wiley.com.

Wiley also publishes its books in a variety of electronic formats and by print-on-demand. Some content that appears in standard print versions of this book may not be available in other formats.

Library of Congress Cataloging-in-Publication Data

Names: Rees, Michael, 1964- author.
Title: The essentials of financial modeling in Excel: a concise guide to
  concepts and methods / Michael Rees.
Description: Hoboken, NJ: John Wiley & Sons, Inc., 2023. | Includes index.
Identifiers: LCCN 2022043302 (print) | LCCN 2022043303 (ebook) | ISBN
  9781394157785 (paperback) | ISBN 9781394157792 (adobe pdf) | ISBN
  9781394157808 (epub)
Subjects: LCSH: Finance—Mathematical models. |
  Corporations—Finance—Mathematical models. | Microsoft Excel (Computer file)
Classification: LCC HG106. R439 2023 (print) | LCC HG106 (ebook) | DDC
  332.0285/554—dc23/eng/20220908
LC record available at https://lccn.loc.gov/2022043302
LC ebook record available at https://lccn.loc.gov/2022043303

Cover Design: Wiley
Cover Image: © Skylines/Shutterstock

Set in 10.5/13pt Palatino LT Std by Straive, Chennai, India

SKY10040317_122122

This book is dedicated to Elsa and Raphael.

Contents

About This Book

This book provides a concise introduction to financial modeling in Excel. It aims to provide readers with a well-structured and practical tool kit to learn modeling "from the ground up." It is unique in that it focuses on the concepts and structures that are commonly required within Excel models, rather than on Excel per se.

The book is structured into six parts (containing twenty-one chapters in total):

- Part I introduces financial modeling and the general factors to consider when designing, building, and using models.

- Part II discusses the core features of Excel that are needed to build and use models. It covers operations and functionality, calculations and functions, and sensitivity and scenario analysis.

- Part III covers the fundamental structures and calculations that are very frequently used in modeling. This includes growth-based forecasting, ratio-driven calculations, corkscrew structures, waterfalls, allocations, triangles, and variations of these.

- Part IV discusses economic modeling, measurement, and evaluation. It covers the analysis of investments, interest calculations and compounding, loan calculations, returns analysis, discounting, and present values.

- Part V treats the core applications of modeling within corporate finance. It covers the cost of capital, the modeling of financial statements, cash flow valuation, and ratio analysis.

- Part VI covers statistical analysis, as well as data preparation, manipulation, and integration.

Readers will generally obtain the maximum benefit by studying the text from the beginning and working through it in order. It is intended that the reader builds from scratch the models that are shown, to reinforce the learning experience and to enhance practical skills. Of course, there may be areas which are already familiar to some readers, and which can be skim-read. Nevertheless, the text is intended to be concise and practical, and to contain information that is potentially useful even to readers who may have some familiarity with the subject.

Although the text is focused on the essentials, at various places it briefly highlights some aspects of more advanced topics. These are described in Further Topics sections, which are situated at the end of some chapters. These sections can be skipped at the reader's discretion without affecting the comprehension of the subsequent text. Note that another of the author's works (*Principles of Financial Modelling: Model Design and Best Practices Using Excel and VBA*, John Wiley & Sons, 2018) discusses in detail some topics that are only briefly (or not) covered in this text (notably VBA macros, optimization, circularities, named ranges, and others). For convenience, in the current text this other text is occasionally mentioned at specific places where it contains significant additional materials related to the discussion, and is subsequently referred to as *PFM*.

The Author

Dr. Michael Rees is a leading expert in quantitative modeling and analysis for applications in business economics, finance, valuation, and risk assessment. He is Professor of Finance at Audencia Business School in Nantes (France), where he teaches subjects related to valuation, financial engineering, optimization, risk assessment, modeling, and business strategy. His earlier academic credentials include a Doctorate in Mathematical Modelling and Numerical Algorithms, and a BA with First Class Honours in Mathematics, both from Oxford University in the UK. He has an MBA with Distinction from INSEAD in France. He also studied for the Certificate of Quantitative Finance, graduating top of the class for course work, and receiving the Wilmott Award for the highest final exam mark. Prior to his academic career, he gained over 30 years' practical experience, including in senior roles at leading firms in finance and strategy consulting (JP Morgan, Mercer Management Consulting, and Braxton Associates), as well as working as an independent consultant and trainer. His clients included companies and entrepreneurs in private equity; auditing and consulting; finance; banking and insurance; pharmaceuticals and biotechnology; oil, gas, and resources; construction; chemicals; engineering; telecommunications; transportation; the public sector; software; and training providers. In addition to this text, he is the author of *Principles of Financial Modelling: Model Design and Best Practices Using Excel and VBA* (2018); *Business Risk and Simulation Modelling in Practice: Using Excel, VBA and @RISK* (2015); and *Financial Modelling in Practice: A Concise Guide for Intermediate and Advanced Level* (2008).

The Essentials of Financial Modeling in Excel

Part One
Introduction to Modeling

1

Modeling and Its Uses

1.1 WHAT IS A MODEL?

A financial model is a representation of a real-life situation in business, economics, or finance. That is, it identifies the items that represent the core properties of the situation and expresses the relationships between these. For example, there is a relationship between the price per unit, the volume sold, and the sales revenue of a business. This can be captured visually in an influence diagram (Figure 1.1).

From a pure theoretical perspective, the relationship can be defined more precisely using a formula:

$$S = P \cdot V$$

(Where V is the volume sold, P is the average price achieved per unit, and S is the sales revenue.)

It is worth noting that the arrows in Figure 1.1 indicate the directionality of the logic. (For convenience, such diagrams would use the "natural" left-to-right flow wherever possible.) On the other hand, in the formula,

Figure 1.1 **Influence Diagram of a Simple Revenue Model**

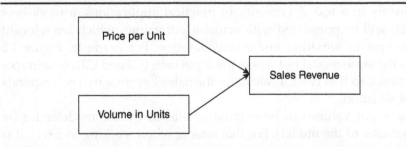

3

the logic is "right-to-left": In the context of numerical computations (and modeling), the = sign is used to mean that the item on the left (called the output) is calculated from those on the right (called the inputs). In other words, although from a purely mathematical perspective the left- and right-sides of the formula could be reversed, this would not be possible from the perspective of modeling, where formulas act not only as a statement of mathematical equality, but also of directionality.

An Excel worksheet can be used to represent the situation in a very similar way (i.e. to capture only the relationships). For example, Figure 1.2 shows the formula (in cell C4) that calculates Sales Revenue by multiplying the value of the Price per Unit (cell C2) with that of the Volume in Units (cell C3), even as the input cells (i.e. C2 and C3) are currently blank.

Figure 1.2 **Excel Model That Contains Formulas but No Values**

	A	B	C
1			
2		Price Per Unit	
3		Volume in Units	
4		Sales Revenue	=C2*C3

In Excel, the * symbol is used for multiplication, so that the formula can be thought of as:

$$C4 = C2 * C3$$

The presentation of the value of cell C4 reinforces that C2 and C3 are the inputs (on the right), with C4 being the output (on the left).

Of course, if one were interested in representing the relationships from a theoretical perspective only, then Excel would be a relatively ineffective way to do so (i.e. one would be better using mathematical formulas directly in a text document). In practical applications, a worksheet (model) will be populated with actual input values, which are relevant for the specific situation under consideration. For example, Figure 1.3 shows the same model but where the input cells (C2 and C3) contain specific values, so that cell C4 calculates the Sales Revenue that corresponds to that situation.

The input values can be entered or altered by the modeler (or by another user of the model). For this reason, when working in Excel, it is

Figure 1.3 **Excel Model with Input Cells Populated with Values**

	A	B	C
1			
2		Price Per Unit	10
3		Volume in Units	1000
4		Sales Revenue	10000
5			

Figure 1.4 **Input Cells with Color-Coding**

	A	B	C
1			
2		Price Per Unit	10
3		Volume in Units	1000
4		Sales Revenue	10000
5			

good practice to make a clear distinction between inputs and calculations (formulas), so that a user knows which items can be changed (and which should not be). Figure 1.4 shows an example of using the shading of a cell to make such a distinction (while perhaps less clear in the black and white image, in addition to the background shading, the font of such a cell can be a different color to that of the font used of a calculated cell, in order to increase the distinction further).

Note that in mathematical formulas, each item (such as P, V, or S) represents both the name and the value of that variable. However, in Excel, by default a formula is "stand-alone," and is created directly with reference to the values of the items. That is, a formula is given meaning (or context) by the labels that are used in other cells. For example, in Figure 1.4, cell C2 contains a value (10), but we know that this represents the price because of the label that is entered in cell B2. Similarly, we know that the value in C3 represents the volume by reference to the label in B3. Similarly, the label in B4 for the sales revenue is an appropriate label for the value in C4 simply because the value is calculated by multiplying price with volume (rather than, say, adding them). In fact, in Excel, it is possible to combine these roles (i.e. of the label and the value) by naming the cells (such as naming cell C2 "Price," cell C3 "Volume" and C4 "Sales Revenue"). This is discussed in Chapter 3 in more detail.

Of course, the input values should be appropriate for the situation that is being addressed. Further – as an entry into a cell of Excel – each input value is a single number (in principle). The output is also a single number that is calculated from the inputs. The terms "base case" or "central case" are often used to refer to this single core "reference" case, which in principle should represent a realistic scenario for the values that may arise (other scenarios can be defined and stored in the model, such as optimistic or pessimistic cases; see Chapter 4).

In fact, very often, the value used for an input is simply a best estimate or a judgment, or a figure that is derived from a comparable situation, or from analyzing historical data. Therefore, there may be some uncertainty as to the true value. Similarly, some inputs may represent items over which a decision-maker has some control in real-life and therefore relate to a decision or choice (rather than being uncertain). These situations can be captured by using various values for the input assumptions to create scenarios, meaning also that there will be a range in values for the output. In fact, the creation and analysis of the possible range of outcomes is an important part of using modeling in decision support. The methods to do so range from the simplest (e.g. copying the model several times, using different input values for each), to specific sensitivity-analysis functionality within Excel (covered in Chapter 4), as well as to more advanced approaches, including risk analysis, simulation, and optimization analysis (which are mentioned in the Further Topics Sections in Chapter 4 and Chapter 20).

1.2 WHAT ARE MODELS USED FOR?

Models can be used to try to gain a better understanding of (or insight about) a real-life situation, with the aim of making a more informed decision in relation to it. For example, one may be deciding whether to launch a business or not. Within the overall decision, there may be several sub-options:

- A mid-market "base" business design (reasonable prices and volumes)
- A "premium" focus (higher prices but achieving lower volumes)
- A "mass-market" approach (lower prices and achieving higher volumes)

Figure 1.5 **Using a Model to Compare Sales Revenues for Business Design Options**

	A	B	C	D	E
1			Base	Premium	Mass Market
2		Price Per Unit	10	15	2
3		Volume in Units	1000	800	8000
4		Sales Revenue	10000	12000	16000

Assuming that one can estimate the volume of consumers' purchases that are likely at each price point (or use market research to do so), the model could be used to capture the effect (on sales revenues) of each option. Figure 1.5 shows an example.

(Note that for simplicity of presentation at this stage, the model has been created three times, i.e. in each column C, D, and E, using the common set of labels in column B. However, in practice the model would typically be created only once, and a sensitivity or scenario analysis would be used to show the different cases.)

Also, of course, in a real-life situation, there would almost certainly be more factors to consider. For example, the decision to launch the business (and with which design) would no doubt also need to reflect the costs and the potential to make a profit (not just the sales revenue). Models should therefore be designed so that they include and evaluate the key decision criteria (as discussed in depth in Chapter 2).

The set of applications of modeling is too numerous to list fully, but includes forecasting, business planning, investment analysis, valuation, target setting, credit assessment, portfolio selection, and optimization, and risk analysis. Within each of these, there are many variations, since most businesses or decision contexts have specific features that need to be captured. Nevertheless, there are numerous concepts which are common to many situations, as well as calculations and types of structures that are frequently used in Excel to implement these. The focus of this text is to treat these essentials in detail.

2

Principles of Model Design

2.1 INTRODUCTION

Modeling activity takes place within an overall context and a wider set of business processes. At a high level, the main steps to consider when planning and building a financial model for decision support are:

- Identifying the decision and its structure, options, and criteria.
- Mapping the elements of real-life that should be captured, including the variables and logic flow.
- Building and testing the model.
- Using relevant external data.
- Using the results, including presentation, graphics, sensitivity analysis, reports, and documentation.

This chapter explores these topics, discussing the core principles of each point and the main practical issues. Note that in this chapter, the discussion is still quite generic; in fact, most of the principles apply whether a model is to be built in Excel or in some other platform. However, the rest of the book (from Chapter 3 onwards) is devoted to implementing these within the Excel environment.

2.2 DECISION IDENTIFICATION, FRAMING, AND STRUCTURE

A model is generally used to support a decision process in some way. Therefore, it is important to establish what decision is being addressed, what are the objectives, and what are the constraints or limitations that must be respected.

A common failing of decision processes is known as the "fallacy of choice": This is where what would have been the best decision option is not considered at all. Clearly, for a model to be most useful, it must also reflect the relevant decision and the most appropriate or best option(s).

Generically, one may think of a decision as having a binary structure ("go or no go?"). Most commonly, Excel models reflect this: The model represents the "go" option, whereas the "no go" option is not modeled explicitly (i.e. it is implicitly considered as being neutral or evaluating to zero).

It is also frequently the case that (within the "go" option) there are set of sub-options which each have the same structure. That is, there is only one model, and the sub-options are captured as scenarios (each simply using different input values). If there were major structural differences between the sub-options then a different model would be required for each (and, in that case, they are strictly speaking not sub-options at all). Figure 2.1 illustrates this for the situation discussed in Chapter 1 (see Figure 1.5 and the associated discussion).

Other types of decision structures include allocations or optimizations (e.g. how much capital shall we allocate to project A, and how much to project B?), multiple structurally different options (such as whether to renovate one's house, buy a new car, or go on vacation), and decision sequences (e.g. using a phased approach rather than making a single up-front decision). These may require more advanced models and tools to properly address them. However, the core points are that the appropriate decision needs to be identified and that the model should reflect the structure of the decision situation.

Figure 2.1 **Basic "Go/No Go" Decision with Sub-Options**

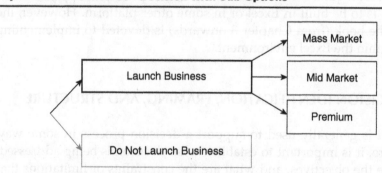

2.3 DECISION CRITERIA AND INFORMATION NEEDS

There are many ways that a decision could be made, or a decision option selected. The least structured is using "gut feel," which is essentially a subjective method. A more robust process is to make the criteria explicit and to evaluate these as objectively as possible (often quantitatively).

In principle it should be self-evident that a model should be designed so that it calculates (or contains) the values of the decision criteria (or metrics) that are to be used by the decision-maker. Figure 2.2 depicts the idealized modeling process. It starts with identifying the decision, with the nature of the decision then determining the decision criteria (metrics). These are used to determine the design requirements, allowing the model to be built so that it evaluates the criteria, with the results used to support the decision.

It is also worth noting that a "gut feel" decision process is often one where the process of decision identification is incomplete and potentially subject to the fallacy of choice. In addition, it may be considered as one in which there is a direct route from decision identification to decision-making (i.e. a route directly downwards from the top-left box to the bottom-left one in Figure 2.2).

Common decision criteria used in economic analysis include measures relating to:

- Breakeven analysis (such as time-to-breakeven and payback periods).

Figure 2.2 **Using the Decision to Design the Model That Supports the Decision**

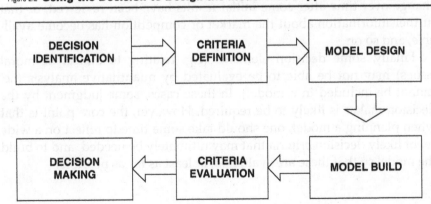

- Returns (such as the internal rate-of-return, the return-on-capital) and net present values).
- Ratios (such as profit/sales, or sales/assets, and so on).

In some cases, one may wish to focus on a specific item only and maximize or minimize this. For example, one may wish to choose the option which has the maximum revenues, that which has the minimum cost, or that with the minimum risk, and so on. Clearly, these criteria could lead to different decision choices. For example, in day-to-day life, the choice to go on the cheapest vacation possible would likely lead to a different selected vacation than if one sought to choose the vacation option by considering both the costs and benefits (such as the quality of the hotel one is staying in). Similarly, in a business context, the option that maximizes revenues may require making significant up-front investments that would not be acceptable if criteria such as profitability or financing constraints were considered.

Note that while one may initially interpret "decision criteria" in a pure economic sense, the term should be thought of in a wider context (i.e. the full information needs of decision-makers). These would typically also include that a sensitivity or scenario analysis (or a full risk assessment) be conducted. That is, one would aim to establish the likely ranges for the decision criteria (such as the range of value for the time-to-breakeven, or for the return-on-capital, and so on). This is discussed further in the next section.

Similarly, in practice, some decision criteria may initially be overlooked when a model is first built: It is possible that the criteria are not understood initially, or that the information needs of decision-makers change over time after some initial results have been reviewed, or that further information about the market or competition has become available, and so on.

Finally, some decision elements (e.g. relating to ethical or moral issues) may not be able to be evaluated by quantitative analysis (i.e. cannot be included in a model). In these cases, some judgment by the decision-maker is likely to be required. However, the core point is that when planning a model, one should take some time to reflect on a wide set of likely decision criteria that may ultimately be needed, and to build the model so that these are evaluated, at least as far as possible.

2.4 SENSITIVITY-BASED DESIGN

Sensitivity analysis is the exploration of the changes that occur to the value of a calculated item when one or more of the input value(s) is changed. It is a key part of decision support, as it can:

- Help to understand the conditions under which a decision makes sense (or not). For example, while a base case may indicate that a "go" decision is preferable (to "no go"), a sensitivity analysis could identify that this is true only if costs do not rise by more than 10%.
- Establish the range of likely outcomes and generally to assess the potential upsides and downsides.
- Identify the relative importance of the key input variables, and hence the effectiveness of potential management actions that could be used to maximize (or optimize) the overall result while mitigating or reducing risk.

A seemingly obvious – but often overlooked – point is that sensitivity analysis should be considered before the model is built (i.e. as a planning and design tool): If it is considered only afterwards, the model may have been built in a way which does not allow the necessary sensitivities to be run! The approach to implementing sensitivity techniques varies according to the stage within the modeling process:

- At the design and planning stage, it revolves around identifying as precisely as possible the sensitivities that will need to be run later. This can help to define the variables that should be included in the model, their roles as inputs or outputs (i.e. the logic flow), as well as the level of detail or granularity that is needed.
- When a model is being built, it can be used to verify and test its general behavior, notably by checking that the relationships that are present in the real-life situation are reflected properly. It can also be used to develop and check complex calculations, by testing their results at various values (ideally a combination of simple values, extreme values, and values which are critical in how the formulas would evaluate).

Figure 2.3 **Using a Sensitivity-Based Thought Process to Define Model Variables**

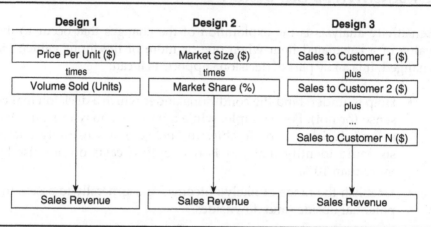

Figure 2.3 shows a simple illustration of the use of a sensitivity thought process in model design and planning. When creating a model forecast of Sales Revenue, there could be several fundamentally different approaches to the choice of variables and the logic used. These include:

- Volume multiplied by Price.
- Market Size multiplied by Market Share.
- Sum of the Sales Revenue per Customer (or per product, geographic region, etc.).

By considering the nature of the sensitivity analysis that will be needed when the model is complete, one should be able to see which of these is most appropriate or what variations of one of them may be required. (The process could also highlight that none of these options are suitable and that other modeling approaches should be considered.)

2.5 DATA AND DATA SOURCES

As noted in Chapter 1, models almost always not only capture the relationships between items, but also have input fields that are populated with relevant values or actual data. In some cases, the values used for the inputs may simply be a best estimate or a judgment made by an expert (e.g. for a bespoke or unusual project where little historical or comparable information is available). In such a case, the process of data integration may be so simple that it may barely be thought of as one that requires specific consideration or techniques. On the other hand, in very advanced applications (such as machine learning), one may need to automate the sourcing, manipulation, integration, and analysis of large data sets that are stored on external servers, and which are being frequently updated. Therefore, while some data analysis is usually required as part of the overall modeling activity, its nature could range from simple to complex, highly advanced analytics. In general, one is commonly faced with a situation that is in between these two extremes: Frequently, some data is available and needs to be analyzed or summarized to inform the values used for the model assumptions. For example, when building a forecasting model to value a business based on its expected profitability over the next 5 to 10 years, it may be sufficient to forecast the operating costs at an aggregate level only (e.g. the total cost by category in each quarter or year), even as the business's IT and accounting systems may be able to provide a much more detailed breakdown of the historical cost of every line item. Similarly, regression or correlation analysis may be needed to explore or determine relationships between variables that may be needed within the model.

From the point of view of model planning and design, when faced with a modeling situation, it is useful to ask questions such as:

- The overall role and importance of data to the model. How much data is available, and from what types of sources? What would the data be used for?
- How is the data structured? How many data sets are there? Where are they located? How can they be accessed? How large are they?
- Is the data "clean" and consistent? How accurate is it? Could it contain errors, or need correction? Would some form of manipulation or integration be required?
- How often will the data be updated, and will the model also need to be updated as often?

The answers to these questions will help to form a clear picture of the data and logical structures and of the techniques that are required to implement a model. These are discussed in detail in Part VI.

2.6   MODEL MAPPING AND APPROXIMATIONS

The term "mapping" refers to the translation of the core aspects of the real-life situation (and the relationships within it) into the model. This requires one to define:

- The variables to be used and their role (inputs, calculations, outputs).
- The overall logic and flow.
- The level of detail (granularity) of these, such as whether the revenues are broken down for each individual product, whether the time axis is annual or monthly, and so on.

From a practical point of view, it is often best to start with items that relate to operational and investment issues (such as prices, volume, revenues, operating costs, investment needs, and so on) before capturing the full impact of these on cash flows and on the consequences for the financing.

The mapping process is not to be done in isolation: It should consider the issues mentioned earlier (notably the decision structure and criteria, the use of sensitivity analysis as a thought-process, and the availability and use of data sets). The process also requires that the modeler has an adequate knowledge of the area of application, in order to understand the behavior and relationships within the real-life situation. For this reason, this text aims to provide some core elements of this for a range of common application areas. (However, in a specific case that one is faced with, it may be necessary to do extra research or study specific concepts in economics, finance, or accounting in more depth.)

A model is usually an approximation or a simplification: There are typically aspects of a situation that cannot be captured in full detail or rare scenarios that may occur in real life that are not reflected in the model. For example, if a model uses price and volume as its underlying inputs (with revenues calculated as an output), then it provides no tracing back (explanation or causality) of the fundamental factors that themselves determine the price or volume. For example, in the case of a hotel business, an increase in interest rates may reduce business activity and hence reduce both the price and the volume that may be able to achieve (as well as increasing its cost of borrowing). By extending the logic of the model further "backwards" in the causality chain, one would create a larger, more complex, and more detailed model. However, the inputs for the new model are still only potential "starting points" for a yet larger model, and so on. Thus, even the most detailed model is unlikely to ever be able to capture the full behavior of the real-life situation in every possible situation that could arise, while the creation of such a detailed model may involve significant work, and not necessarily be more accurate, nor provide additional benefit or insight. A key skill (and objective) is to capture the key elements in a way that is sufficient to fulfill the particular purpose at hand, notably to support the needs of decision-makers. The phrases "Every model should be as simple as possible, but no simpler" (adapted from a quote by Einstein), and "Every model is wrong, some are useful" should also be kept in mind as potentially helpful guidelines.

2.7 BUILDING AND TESTING

There are several principles involved in building models in accordance with "best practices." These include to:

- Name the variables clearly.
- Separate inputs from calculations.
- Create transparency and clear logical flows.
- Break complex calculations into components.
- Use modular structures (largely self-contained that contain closely related items, and which are linked together with a relatively small set of links to create a whole).
- Test the model robustly before applying it.

The implementation of these principles is often specific to the modeling platform used and are therefore discussed in detail in the context of Excel in Chapter 3.

2.8 RESULTS PRESENTATION

The core principles of using model results for decision support include:

- Presenting the situation and assumptions clearly.
- Highlighting the key information needs that decision-makers have, notably the evaluation of the decision criteria and related reporting needs.
- Showing the range of possible outcomes (e.g. through sensitivity, scenario, or risk analysis), and the levers by which the outcome can be influenced.

- Using graphical output as appropriate. Care should be taken to ensure that the most appropriate type of graph is chosen and that the message that the chart is intended to convey is easy to see directly on the chart.
- Providing adequate documentation. This should note the context in which the model is valid, or whether adaptations are necessary as the decision situation or criteria changes.
- Trying to minimize the effect of biases.

(Once again, most of these principles are covered in more detail in Chapter 3, to show their implementation in the Excel environment.)

2.9 BIASES

Biases can impact decision identification and selection even if the right information has been given to decision-makers from a technical or objective perspective. The topic of biases is linked to human psychology (at the individual and group level) and to evolution. While its scope is very large, important examples of biases include:

- The bias of "framing." This means that – for the same situation – one would make a different decision depending on how the information is presented.
- The bias of "loss aversion." This means that people are typically risk-seeking to avoid losses, but risk-averse in the face of gains.

These biases can interact or overlap in their effects. For example, one may be reluctant to sell an investment (such as a stock) that has decreased in value (i.e. to retain the investment rather than realizing its value by turning it into cash). At the same time, if asked to increase one's holding of the same investment, one may also be reluctant to do so. That is, one simultaneously prefers holding the investment rather than cash and holding cash rather than the investment. Similarly, a business decision about whether to continue to invest in a poor project can be affected by whether the focus is on loss-avoidance ("We have invested so much that we can't stop now.") rather than potential gains ("Let's invest in the future of this highly uncertain project – after all, it could turn out well in the end."). An awareness of potential biases can be important to minimizing their effect. However, a full treatment of this rich topic (and related aspects such as behavioral finance) is beyond the scope of this text.

Part Two

Essentials of Excel

3

Menus, Operations, Functions, and Features

3.1 INTRODUCTION

Excel is generally an excellent platform for most common financial modeling applications. It is easy to learn at a basic level and can provide a transparent and flexible environment (if used well). It has many functions and features, and new functionality is added regularly. In cases where one may need to conduct operations that are not present in the default versions of Excel, these can often be found in the free shipped add-ins or by using VBA macros. (However, most of the applications where these would be needed are beyond the scope of this text.) Finally, although there are areas of application where Excel may not be a practical tool for the final implementation of a solution (such as if very high computational intensity is required to manipulate huge data sets extremely quickly), it can often be a convenient platform to communicate and test the concepts or to develop prototypes for these solutions.

This chapter aims to highlight the features of Excel that are indispensable to any modeler working in common areas of application. It is intended to be a structured summary, not only to act as a guide for readers who are less familiar with Excel, but also to form a checklist of core competences for those who already have some experience. The topics covered relate to:

- The structure and menus.
- The creation of calculations.
- The most important and frequently used functions (around 100 are highlighted; these are the functions used later in the text).

- The core operations that are needed to build, test, and use a model.
- Calculation options and settings.
- The use of shortcuts and KeyTips.
- Best practices and the creation of transparency.
- Auditing, testing, and the tracing of logic.
- Using graphs and charts.

3.2 STRUCTURE AND MENUS

Some of the key points about the structure of Excel are:

- An Excel workbook contains one or more worksheets. Each worksheet is made up of a tabular set of cells, which are identified by a column-row reference address (such as C5, to indicate the cell in the third column and fifth row).
- Each cell may be blank or have content entered into it, such as a number or text. Formulas or functions may instead be entered; these conduct calculations that generally return numbers (but can return text, logical items, or errors).
- Typically, to create a calculation in a cell, the inputs are the values that are present in other cells. (Fixed numbers can be embedded within formulas, but it is in general not good practice to do so.)
- A set of cells that forms a rectangular structure (or range) can be referred to by using the cell address of the first and last cells. For example, C5:E9 refers to the rectangular range which starts at cell C5 and ends at E9. This allows for multiple cells to be referred to simultaneously.
- As well as its value or content, a cell or range has other properties. These include the size and color of the font, the type of shading (if any), and the type of border placed around it (if any).

The Excel toolbar contains several tabs, each of which has a descriptive title that relates to the types of menu operations that are offered by the items on the tab. The core tabs are present by default when Excel is first installed (see Figure 3.1).

Figure 3.2 shows the left-hand-side of the Home tab, which contains many frequently required operations.

Figure 3.1 **Core Menu Tabs**

File	Home	Insert	Page Layout	Formulas	Data	Review	View	Help

Figure 3.2 **The Home Tab (left-hand-side only)**

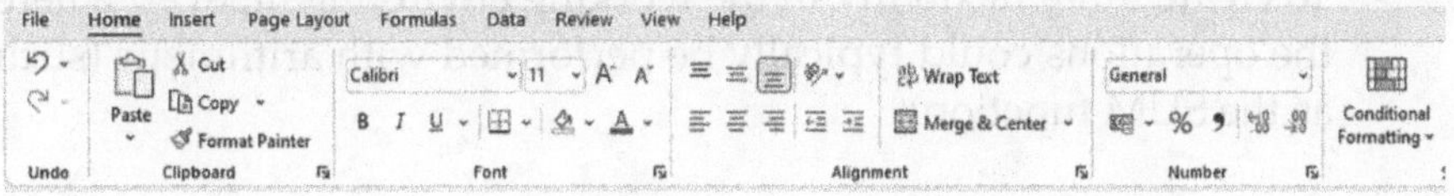

Important operations available on the Home tab include:

- Using Copy/Paste to copy the content of one cell to another.
- Formatting the type, size, and color of the font used to show the content of a cell, or to add a border around the cell.
- Aligning the content of a cell (e.g. to be justified at the left, middle, or right).
- Setting the ways that a numerical value should be displayed (e.g. number of decimal points, or as a percentage, and so on)
- Using Conditional Formatting, so that the value of a cell determines the way it is formatted (e.g. to show negative values in red, or to suppress the display of zeroes).

Note also that there are additional tabs available in Excel, but which are generally hidden by default and can be exposed if they are needed. The other core tabs (and any extra ones that may be needed) are discussed later (within context as they are used).

3.3 CALCULATIONS USING ARITHMETIC

The arithmetic operators +, −, *, /, and ^, can be used to create calculations within a cell (+ for addition, − for subtraction, * for multiplication, / for division, and ^ for raising to a power). The operator & is a simple way to join two text strings. These are generally self-explanatory (however, an example can be seen in the earlier Figure 1.2 (using the * operator), and many other examples are shown later.

3.4 FUNCTION BASICS

Functions perform pre-built sets of calculations based on input values that the user has specified. Their role is:

- To evaluate operations that cannot generally be done with direct arithmetic (such as the IF function).
- To create more flexibility in the working environment, even where the operations could typically be performed with arithmetic (such as the SUM function).

Figure 3.3 **The Formulas Tab (left-hand-side only)**

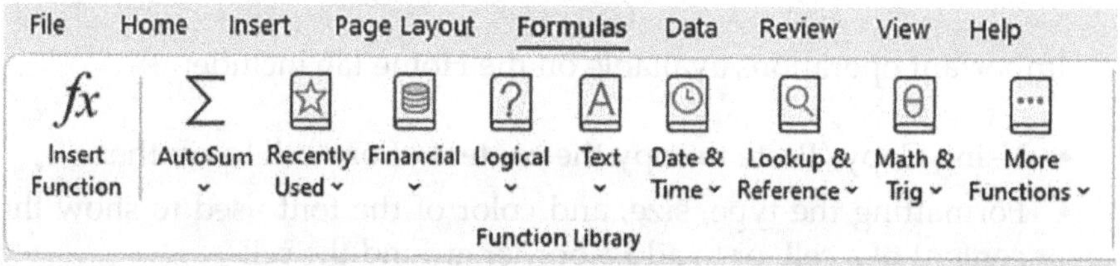

Figure 3.3 shows the left-side of the Formulas tab. This can be used to access most functions, each of which is assigned to a category that has a drop-down menu. For example, using the drop-down for the Math&Trig category one would see several functions, including SUM (this step is not shown in the Figure).

Figure 3.4 shows a simple model about the operations of a single-car taxi (or cab) service. The inputs and calculations for the model are in column C (whilst column E shows the formulas used). The model calculates revenues, costs, and profits for the business (using inputs such as price, number of trips per day, days per year, and so on). The SUM function is used in cell C14 to add up the items in the two-cell range C12:C13, in order to calculate the total Fixed Cost.

Also note that:

- The function can be used to add the value in only two cells. For example, in cell C16 the function could have been used in the form SUM(C10, C14). Note that in this case, the input cells need to be delimited with a comma. If a colon were used, i.e. SUM(C10:C14), then all cells in the range would be included in the calculation (i.e. C10, C11, C12, C13, and C14).

Figure 3.4 **Example of the SUM Function**

	A	B	C	D	E
1					
2					Formulas
3		Price Per Trip ($)	25		
4		Trips Per Day	20		
5		Days Per Year	300		
6		Trips (p.a.)	6000		C6=C4*C5
7		Revenue (p.a.)	150000		C7=C3*C6
8					
9		Fuel and Variable Costs per Trip	5		
10		Fuel and Variable Costs Total (p.a.)	30000		C10=C9*C6
11					
12		Salaries and Related Benefits	80000		
13		Other Fixed Operating Costs	20000		
14		Fixed Costs Total (p.a.)	100000		C14=SUM(C12:C13)
15					
16		Total Cost (p.a.)	130000		C16=C10+C14
17					
18		Profit (p.a.)	20000		C18=C7-C16

- The shading in some cells is used to highlight (to a user) those calculations which are assumed to be of most interest for reporting and decision-making purposes (i.e. the "output" cells).

Rather than using the menu on the Formulas tab, a function can be inserted using the Insert Function menu icon, which activates the menu from which one can choose a category and a function therein. Figure 3.5 shows this for the IF function.

Selecting OK (as in Figure 3.5) will activate the Function Arguments, as shown in Figure 3.6.

The IF function requires that the modeler defines a condition that the function will test, as well as the values to return when the condition is met or not. (If the user does not define the return values, then these are by default the logical items TRUE or FALSE, depending on the results of the test.)

Figure 3.5 **The Insert Function Menu**

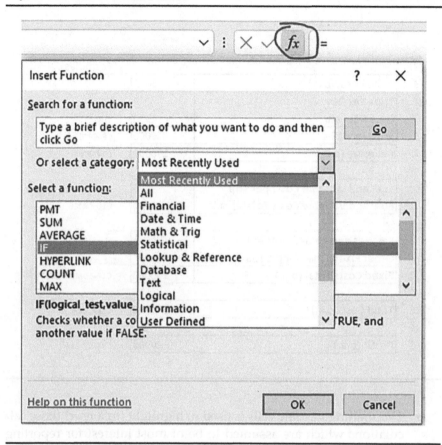

Figure 3.6 **The IF Function and Its Arguments**

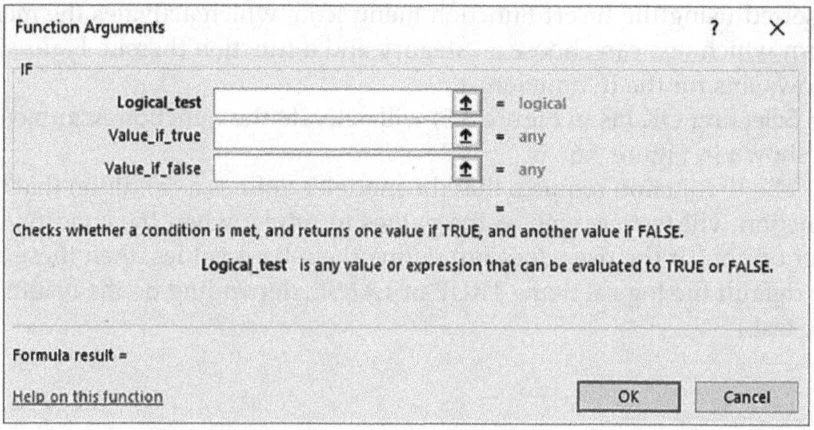

3.5 A CORE FUNCTION SET

The two functions SUM and IF are extremely useful: With these alone, one could build a surprisingly large range of models. Nevertheless, it is important to have good familiarity with a much larger set of functions. Some of these are needed for general calculations, to capture condition-ality and logic, to calculate specific items in finance and economics, to conduct data and statistical analysis, and so on.

This section lists the functions that are used or referred to later in the text (where details of individual functions are explained as required). This list may be considered as itemizing the core set of functions that are needed in common applications (including some that are required for frequent aspects of data manipulation and analysis).

Functions which perform general calculations, including compari-sons, conditionality, and aggregations include:

- SUM, MIN, MAX, COUNT, COUNTA, AVERAGE, ABS, PRODUCT, POWER, SUMPRODUCT.
- IF, IFS, SUMIFS (SUMIF), MINIFS, MAXIFS, COUNTIFS, AVER-AGEIFS.

In both general financial modeling and data analysis, the following functions are indispensable:

- CHOOSE, XMATCH, INDEX, and XLOOKUP form the "core set" of lookup and reference functions that are useful in many common applications.
- INDIRECT, ADDRESS, and CELL are used in more advanced applications, including relating to data analysis and data-driven model structures.
- MATCH and LOOKUP are legacy functions that are no longer needed *per se* but were widely used and important in earlier ver-sions of Excel.
- HLOOKUP and VLOOKUP are functions that are used by some modelers, but their use provides no benefit compared to alterna-tives, and we do not recommend using them.

In calculations relating to growth or to interest rates one often needs:

- EXP and LN are mathematical functions that calculate the exponential and the natural logarithm, and required for calculations relating to continuously compounded processes, for example.
- EFFECT, NOMINAL, and FVSCHEDULE are useful in general growth-related calculations, including those that relate to interest rates.

In quantitative financial analysis, data analysis, statistics, and probability, important functions are:

- AGGREGATE is a "wrapper" function that embeds the capabilities of several statistical functions. SUBTOTAL is similar, but with less features.
- MODE.SNGL, SMALL, LARGE, RANK, STDDEV, PERCENTILE, CORREL, PEARSON, and COVARIANCE are useful for statistical analysis. (There are several variations of some of these functions which are not listed here.)
- DSUM, DMAX, DAVERAGE, DCOUNT, DCOUNTA, and DGET are some of the main database functions.
- LINEST, as well as SLOPE and INTERCEPT, can be used in regression analysis.
- MMULT and MINVERSE are needed in matrix calculations (which are needed in optimization modeling, credit analysis, and other areas).
- FREQUENCY can be used to count the number of items in each bin of a defined set (as can COUNTIFS).

In economic analysis, important functions include:

- NPV and IRR (as well as XNPV and XIRR) are used for general investment- and returns-analysis.
- PMT, RATE, NPER, FV, and PV (as well as IPMT, PPMT, CUMIPMT, and CUMPRINC) are used in relation to the repayment of loans, such as mortgages.

Functions that can assist in general data cleaning and manipulation include:

- CLEAN and TRIM are useful to clean up data that is imported from another system, for example that may contain excess blank spaces or non-visible characters.
- FIND and SEARCH find a text field within (a larger) one.
- REPLACE and SUBSTITUTE replace some text with an alternative.
- LEFT, RIGHT, and MID return the associated part of a larger text field (e.g. left-hand side).
- LEN determines the length (number of characters) of a text item.
- TEXT can be used to convert a number into a numerical-looking text field, such as to link the labels of charts to cells in Excel.
- REPT can be used to repeat something several times.
- TEXTJOIN is a flexible way to join several text fields (rather than using the & symbol or the CONCATENATE function).
- UNIQUE, SORT, SORTBY, FILTER, and TRANSPOSE are useful in general modeling as well as data analysis.

Finally, some functions that are useful in areas such as error-management, model auditing and documentation, data analysis, and other applications are:

- TRUE and FALSE. These are logical items that are returned after a condition is checked. They are also functions that have no parameters. The NOT function reverses the results of a condition that has been checked.
- AND and OR return the logical items TRUE or FALSE after checking several conditions simultaneously.
- ISBLANK, ISLOGICAL, ISTEXT, ISNUMBER, and ISERROR return the logical items TRUE or FALSE depending on the content of the cell to which they are applied. Their (implied) categories represent a set of exhaustive and exclusive possibilities for the content of an Excel cell (e.g. blank, logical, etc.)
- IFNA and IFERROR allow one to replace error values with alternative values.
- FORMULATEXT can be used to display the formula that is used in another cell. This can be useful for documentation and presentation purposes and is used extensively in the screen clips in this book.

3.6 FURTHER PROPERTIES AND USES OF FUNCTIONS

Functions are designed to be robust and to take as wide a variety of inputs as possible. In some cases, a function may not return the values that one may initially expect, due to the way that "unusual" inputs are treated. For example, when logical items (FALSE and TRUE) are used as inputs the results would be:

- For arithmetic operations, the items are treated as if they were 0 or 1. Thus, the formula =TRUE+TRUE+FALSE, will return two.
- For the SUM function (and for many other functions) logical items are ignored. Thus, the formula =SUM(TRUE, TRUE, FALSE) would return zero.

Whilst most functions are entered into a single cell and create results only in the same single cell, there are cases where the output range of a function requires multiple cells. Examples include:

- TRANSPOSE. This is entered into a single cell but returns a multi-cell range which contains the transposed value of the input range (i.e. with rows and columns switched). The size of the output range is the same as the size of the input range but does not depend on the values within the input range.
- UNIQUE. This provides a list of the unique values that are present within the input range. The size of the output range depends only on these values (not on the size of the input range).

This property that the return range of Excel functions adjusts to the required size is sometimes referred to by saying that functions have a "dynamic output range."

Figure 3.7 shows an example of the UNIQUE function being entered (into cell D2), using the inputs from the range of cells B2:B17.

Figure 3.8 shows the result (i.e. a range) which contains the list of those items in the input range that are unique.

Note that:

- The #SPILL error message would be shown (in cell D2) if there were already content in the cells below D2 that would need to be overwritten when the dynamic output range is populated.

Figure 3.7 **Entering the UNIQUE Function in a Single Cell**

	A	B	C	D	E
1					
2		USA		=unique(B2:B17)	
3		USA			
4		Canada			
5		Italy			
6		Itly			
7		USA			
8		US			
9		France			
10		Italie			
11		France			
12		Germany			
13		Spain			
14		USA			
15		UK			
16		UK			
17		Germany			
18					

- The # symbol can be used to refer to all the cells of a dynamic output range. For example, Figure 3.9 shows the use of the symbol within the COUNTA function (in cell F2) to count the number of cells that contain content within the dynamic range that starts at cell D2.

3.7 CALCULATION SETTINGS AND OPTIONS

It is important to be aware that Excel is typically (by default) set on its "Automatic" calculation mode. This is one of the three core modes (or options), which are:

- Automatic.
- Automatic except for Data Tables.
- Manual.

These can be seen in the Calculation area of the Formulas tab (see Figure 3.10).

Figure 3.8 **The Dynamic Output Range of the UNIQUE Function**

	A	B	C	D	E	F	G
				D2 =UNIQUE(B2:B17)			
1							
2		USA		USA			
3		USA		Canada			
4		Canada		Italy			
5		Italy		Itly			
6		Itly		US			
7		USA		France			
8		US		Italie			
9		France		Germany			
10		Italie		Spain			
11		France		UK			
12		Germany					
13		Spain					
14		USA					
15		UK					
16		UK					
17		Germany					
18							

(Excel also contains calculation options relating to how to perform iterative calculations in the case that circularities are present in a model, but this is beyond the scope of the text.)

Under the Automatic setting, the Excel workbook recalculates (by its own initiative i.e. automatically) whenever it may be required (for example, as soon as the value of an input is changed or a new formula is created or copied). There is no need to "run" the model as such (in the sense used in computer science, where a program needs to be initiated explicitly for it to perform the calculations).

If the Manual option is chosen, changes to input values will have no immediate effect. For example, if the setting is switched to Manual, and the input values are changed to all be zero, then the model's calculations do not update (i.e. they are not zero, but remain at the existing values), as shown in Figure 3.11.

Figure 3.9 **Using # To Refer to a Dynamic Output Range**

	A	B	C	D	E	F	G	H
						=COUNTA(D2#)		
1								
2		USA		USA		10		
3		USA		Canada				
4		Canada		Italy				
5		Italy		Itly				
6		Itly		US				
7		USA		France				
8		US		Italie				
9		France		Germany				
10		Italie		Spain				
11		France		UK				
12		Germany						
13		Spain						
14		USA						
15		UK						
16		UK						
17		Germany						
18								

F2 cell selected.

Figure 3.10 **The Calculation Options on the Formulas Tab**

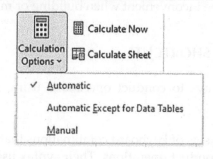

Figure 3.11 **Effect of Changes to Input Values in Manual Setting**

	A	B	C	D	E
1					
2					Formulas
3		Price Per Trip ($)	0		
4		Trips Per Day	0		
5		Days Per Year	0		
6		Trips (p.a.)	6000		C6=C4*C5
7		Revenue (p.a.)	150000		C7=C3*C6
8					

The values of the calculated cell will update either if the Calculate Now option (see Figure 3.10) is used or if the shortcut key (F9 key) is pressed. The main benefit of working in the Manual setting is if one has a large workbook whose recalculation is slow: When making several changes to it (adapting it structurally or adding functionality, etc.), it may be more efficient to allow oneself to implement several sets of changes before performing each recalculation. In general, however, the use of the Manual setting can lead to confusion or potential incorrect conclusions, so that when using the model for day-to-day purposes (rather than building it or making structural changes), it is typically better to use the Automatic setting. For similar reasons (about the speed of recalculation), the option Automatic Except for Data Tables is useful in models which also contain several Data Tables. These are used in sensitivity analysis (see Chapter 4), but their presence requires the model to recalculate, which slows down workings that can be inconvenient when building or modifying a model.

3.8 KEYTIPS AND SHORTCUTS

Excel has many ways to conduct operations using shortcuts, as well as KeyTips:

- Shortcuts are sets of keyboard combinations that define an alternative way to conduct operations. Their syntax uses the + symbol to denote the keys are to be used simultaneously (i.e. selecting all at the same time).

Figure 3.12 **Accessing the Menu Using KeyTips**

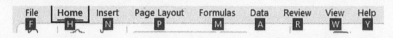

- KeyTips provide an alternative way to replicate the actual steps involved in accessing the Excel menu. Their syntax uses the – symbol to denote the operations are conducted one after the other.

The KeyTip menu is activated by pressing the Alt key. Figure 3.12 shows the result of doing so, from which one can also see that the subsequent pressing of the M key would active the Formulas tab (and within that, other letters would be shown that can be used to activate the operations).

The following provides a brief overview of some of the most important shortcuts and KeyTips. As it is a large subject, readers may wish to conduct further research and experimentation in this area, after mastering the basic ones discussed here. (The accessibility and definitions may also vary according to one's computing environment.)

Shortcuts and KeyTips are most relevant to replace the direct menu operations that would need to be conducted frequently when building or using models. These typically relate to:

- Copying or reusing formulas.
- Formatting cells and ranges.
- Auditing and tracing the logic.

The copying of a formula involves four underlying steps:

- Selecting the range to be copied.
- Activating the Copy menu.
- Selecting the range to be pasted.
- Activating the Paste (or Paste Special) menu.

For example, Figure 3.13 shows that the range of calculations can be selected using the mouse.

Figure 3.13 **Selecting a Range to be Copied**

	A	B	C
1			
2			
3	Price Per Trip ($)		25
4	Trips Per Day		20
5	Days Per Year		300
6	Trips (p.a.)		6000
7	Revenue (p.a.)		150000
8			
9	Fuel and Variable Costs per Trip		5
10	Fuel and Variable Costs Total (p.a.)		30000
11			
12	Salaries and Related Benefits		80000
13	Other Fixed Operating Costs		20000
14	Fixed Costs Total (p.a.)		100000
15			
16	Total Cost (p.a.)		130000
17			
18	Profit (p.a.)		20000
19			

This range could be copied and pasted into the next column. Figure 3.14 shows the result (columns F and G are added for convenience of reference, and of course would not be part of this process).

The shortcuts that can be used in this case (i.e. to copy and paste the ranges) are:

- Ctrl+C to activate the copy.
- Ctrl+V to perform the paste.

Note also that Ctrl+Z undoes the last operation performed.

Finally, the model could be adapted to make clear that it concerns a business consisting of two cabs (whose items should be added, for example using the SUM function), and where the input values for each can be set or modified independently. Figure 3.15 shows an example (the inputs for the second cab use different numbers to reflect that the second cab is intended to be used for longer trips than the first).

Figure 3.14 **Results After Pasting**

	A	B	C	D	E	F	G
1							
2						Formulas	
3		Price Per Trip ($)	25	25			
4		Trips Per Day	20	20			
5		Days Per Year	300	300			
6		Trips (p.a.)	6000	6000		C6=C4*C5	D6=D4*D5
7		Revenue (p.a.)	150000	150000		C7=C3*C6	D7=D3*D6
8							
9		Fuel and Variable Costs per Trip	5	5			
10		Fuel and Variable Costs Total (p.a.)	30000	30000		C10=C9*C6	D10=D9*D6
11							
12		Salaries and Related Benefits	80000	80000			
13		Other Fixed Operating Costs	20000	20000			
14		Fixed Costs Total (p.a.)	100000	100000		C14=SUM(C1: D14=SUM(D12:D13)	
15							
16		Total Cost (p.a.)	130000	130000		C16=C10+C1 D16=D10+D14	
17							
18		Profit (p.a.)	20000	20000		C18=C7-C16 D18=D7-D16	

Figure 3.15 **The Adjusted and Completed Model**

	A	B	C	D	E	F	G	H
1								
2			Cab 1	Cab 2		Total		Formulas
3		Price Per Trip ($)	25	75				
4		Trips Per Day	20	5				
5		Days Per Year	300	320				
6		Trips (p.a.)	6000	1600				
7		Revenue (p.a.)	150000	120000		270000		F7=SUM(C7:D7)
8								
9		Fuel and Variable Costs per Trip	5	15				
10		Fuel and Variable Costs Total (p.a.)	30000	24000		54000		
11								
12		Salaries and Related Benefits	80000	75000				
13		Other Fixed Operating Costs	20000	15000				
14		Fixed Costs Total (p.a.)	100000	90000		190000		
15								
16		Total Cost (p.a.)	130000	114000		244000		F16=SUM(C16:D16)
17								
18		Profit (p.a.)	20000	6000		26000		F18=SUM(C18:D18)

As noted earlier, a "copy/paste" activity really has four steps, the first and third of which involve selecting ranges. If a range of contiguous cells is to be selected, some useful shortcuts are:

- Ctrl+Shift+Arrow (e.g. right arrow) Starting from the first cell in the range to be selected, one is automatically taken to the end of the range in the direction of the arrow key used.
- Ctrl+Shift+*. This selects the set of cells (in all directions) that are contiguous with the current cell.

Note that by default a Paste operation will copy all formulas and formats. The Paste Special menu provides more richness or options as to what should be pasted (into the second range), as shown in Figure 3.16.

Figure 3.16 **The Paste Special Menu**

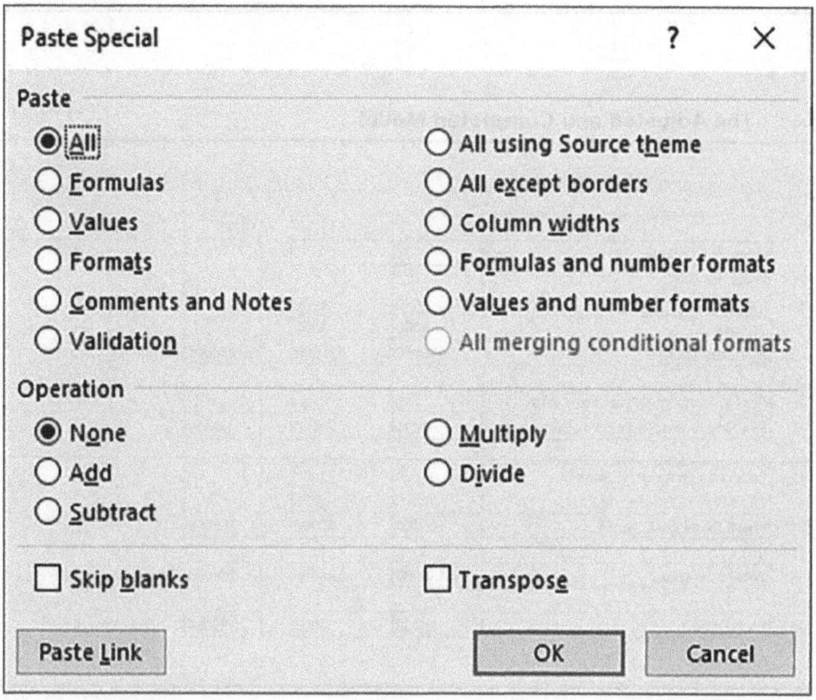

The Paste Special menu can itself be accessed with shortcuts or KeyTips:

- Alt-E-S if choosing to use a KeyTip.
- Ctrl+Alt+V if choosing to use a shortcut.

The options within this can be selected either with the mouse or by using the appropriate shortcut or letter in the KeyTip sequence. For the KeyTips, the relevant letters are those which are underlined in Figure 3.16, so that:

- Alt-E-S-F accesses Paste Formulas (i.e. where cell formatting is not altered in the destination cell).
- Alt-E-S-V accesses Paste Values (i.e. where the value is pasted, not the formula, nor the formatting).
- Alt-E-S-T accesses Paste Formats (i.e. where only the format is pasted).
- Alt-E-S-R accesses Paste Formulas and Number Formats.

For the shortcuts, after pressing Ctrl+Alt+V (at the same time), the keys must be released, at which point the Paste Special menus is invoked, and the last letter of the sequence can be used by itself:

- Ctrl+Alt+V – F to access Paste Formulas (i.e. where cell formatting is not altered in the destination cell).
- Ctrl+Alt+V – V to access Paste Values (i.e. where the value is pasted, not the formula, nor the formatting).
- Ctrl+Alt+V – T to access Paste Formats (i.e. where only the format is pasted).
- Ctrl+Alt+V – R to access Paste Formulas and Number Formats.

Note also that many Excel operations can be accessed quickly by using right-click to activate the context sensitive menu. For example, selecting a row or column and using right-click would invoke several possibilities, including to insert or delete the row or column.

3.9 ABSOLUTE AND RELATIVE REFERENCING

When copying a formula from one cell to another, Excel's default method uses "relative" referencing. That is, the copied formula refers to input cells that have the same position relative to it as the original formula has to its inputs. This is visible in the earlier Figure 3.14, where column F shows the formulas contained in column C, and column G shows the formulas in column D that resulted from the copy/paste process applied to column C.

For the copied formula to refer to the same input cells that were used in the original formula, one needs to use "absolute" referencing. This can be achieved by using the $ symbol within the formula to be copied. As a formula can be copied horizontally, vertically, or both, the $ symbol can be placed before the column references and/or the row numbers within the formula to be copied, as needed. It can be applied to some or all row and column references, or to none. It can be inserted manually into the formula, or the F4 key can be used to cycle through the possibilities. In other words, when used in a formula, the $ symbol means that the column letter or row number that immediately follows the $ will be treated as a fixed reference if the formula were to be copied. (The $ has no effect on the value displayed by a formula.)

For example, in a model like that shown earlier for the business with two cabs, let us suppose that there are some additional fixed central operating costs that are not directly caused by either cab, but which are to be allocated to each in proportion to the number of trips that each made per year. Figure 3.17 shows the result of this (cell G6 calculates the total trips made, which is used to calculate the percentages in row 7, and which are then multiplied by the operating cost shown in C9, to give, in cells D9 and E9, the amount allocated to each cab).

Figure 3.17 **Central Costs Allocated According to Trips**

	A	B	C	D	E	F	G	H
1								
2				Cab 1	Cab 2		Total	
3		Price Per Trip ($)		25	75			
4		Trips Per Day		20	5			
5		Days Per Year		300	320			
6		Trips (p.a.)		6000	1600		7600	
7		% of Total		79%	21%		100%	
8								
9		Central Operating Costs (p.a.)	2500	1974	526		2500	

Figure 3.18 **Formulas Used to Allocate Central Cost**

D6=D4*D5	E6=E4*E5	G6=SUM(D6:E6)
D7=D6/$G6	E7=E6/$G6	G7=SUM(D7:E7)
D9=$C9*D7	E9=$C9*E7	G9=SUM(D9:E9)

Note the percentages in cell D7 and E7 are calculated using the same single figure (that in G6) for the denominator. Similarly, the allocated amounts in D9 and E9 use the same single figure (that in cell C9) for the numerator. However, rather than the formulas being constructed separately in each individual cell, they can be created only in cells D7 and D9 (using the $ symbol within each). The formula in D7 is then copied to cells E7, and that in D9 is copied to E9. Figure 3.18 shows the result.

This use of $ is extremely important in practice and is visible in many of the examples that are shown later.

3.10 AUDITING AND LOGIC TRACING

This section summarizes the most important ways to track the flow of calculations or logic in a model (i.e. to trace the precedents and dependents of a formula). Figure 3.19 shows the Formula Auditing menu (which is on the Formulas tab of Excel), and on which many of the important items can be found.

The Show Formulas icon (or its shortcut Ctrl+`) is a toggle that switches between the normal view and the formula view (i.e. it can be used a second time to switch back to normal view). When switching back and forth between views, one may have to adjust the column widths of

Figure 3.19 **The Formulas/Formula Auditing Menu**

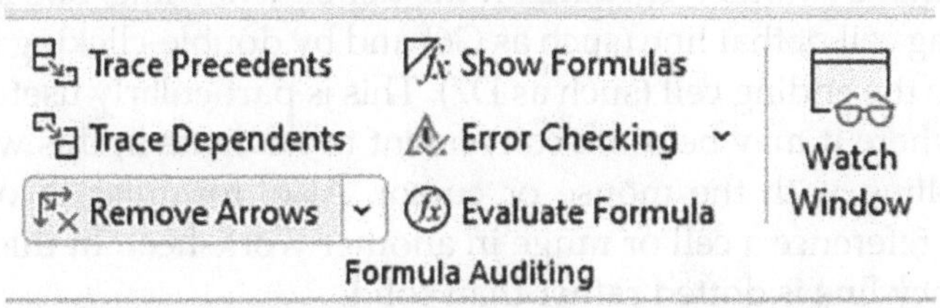

⊟ Trace Precedents	☑ Show Formulas	
⊟ Trace Dependents	⚠ Error Checking ⌄	Watch
⊮ Remove Arrows ⌄	⨍ Evaluate Formula	Window
	Formula Auditing	

Figure 3.20 **The Formula View**

	A	B	C	D	E	F	G
1							
2				Cab 1	Cab 2		Total
3		Price Per Trip ($)		25	75		
4		Trips Per Day		20	5		
5		Days Per Year		300	320		
6		Trips (p.a.)		=D4*D5	=E4*E5		=SUM(D6:E6)
7		% of Total		=D6/$G6	=E6/$G6		=SUM(D7:E7)
8							
9		Central Operating Costs (p.a.)	2500	=$C9*D7	=$C9*E7		=SUM(D9:E9)
10							

Excel for convenience of viewing. Figure 3.20 shows the formulas view of the model used earlier (i.e. that in Figure 3.17).

When using the Show Formulas view, one would typically ask questions such as:

- What is the general nature of the calculations?
- Are the formulas along each row or down a column consistent?
- What specific functions are being used?
- Which cells or range have $ signs and are therefore used several times?
- Where there are gaps or blanks?
- Are there any unusual items?

Returning to the normal view, the Trace Precedents and Trace Dependents icons (see the top-left of Figure 3.19) can be used to track the direction of logic starting from a single cell. For example, in Figure 3.21, the Trace Dependents has been used from cell C9 (showing that D9 and E9 are directly dependent), whereas Trace Precedents has been used from cell D7 (showing that C6 and G6 are the precedent cells).

Note that by double-clicking on the dependency line, one is taken to the starting cell of that line (such as G6) and by double-clicking again one is taken to the ending cell (such as D7). This is particularly useful in large models where it may be more convenient to navigate in this way rather than scrolling with the mouse or cursor. Also, formulas in one worksheet can reference a cell or range in another worksheet. In this case, the dependency line is dotted rather than solid.

Figure 3.21 **Using Trace Dependents and Trace Precedents**

	A	B	C	D	E	F	G	H
1								
2				Cab 1	Cab 2		Total	
3	Price Per Trip ($)			25	75			
4	Trips Per Day			20	5			
5	Days Per Year			300	320			
6	Trips (p.a.)			6000	1600		7600	
7	% of Total			79%	21%		100%	
8								
9	Central Operating Costs (p.a.)		2500	1974	526		2500	

Figure 3.22 **Inspecting a Formula Using the F2 Key**

	A	B	C	D	E	F	G	H
1								
2				Cab 1	Cab 2		Total	
3	Price Per Trip ($)			25	75			
4	Trips Per Day			20	5			
5	Days Per Year			300	320			
6	Trips (p.a.)			6000	1600		7600	
7	% of Total			=D6/$G6	21%		100%	
8								
9	Central Operating Costs (p.a.)		2500	1974	526		2500	

The Trace Precedents menu can also be accessed using shortcuts:

- Ctrl+[will select the direct precedents that are on the same worksheet.
- Ctrl+{ or Ctrl+Shift+[will select all precedents that are on the same worksheet (direct and indirect).

For Trace Dependents, the shortcuts are:

- Ctrl+] will select the direct dependents that are on the same worksheet.
- Ctrl+} or Ctrl+Shift+] will select all dependents that are on the same worksheet (direct and indirect).

Another way to see precedents of a formula on the same worksheet is to use the F2 key. (However, for visual reasons, this is only useful when the precedents cells are close to the original cell.) Figure 3.22 shows an

Figure 3.23 **The Watch Window**

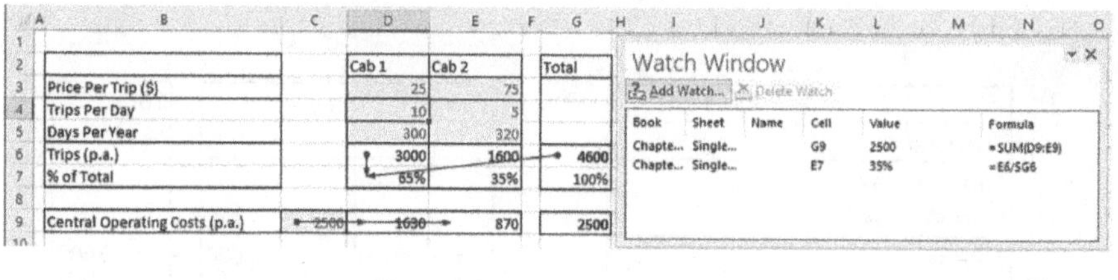

illustration of this being used from within cell D7 to highlight the precedent cells D6 and G6.

Finally, the Evaluate Formulas and the Watch Window (see the earlier Figure 3.19) can be useful to diagnose more complex forms of errors or unusual behaviors (if one is unable to do so from simpler inspection of the formulas and tracing). By using Evaluate Formulas, one will see the step-by-step evaluation of a calculation. For example, if an IF function is not returning the value that one expects, then this icon can be used to see the evaluation steps. It is also useful to diagnose errors or check complex calculations in which the steps are embedded in a larger formula.

The Watch Window can be used to track the values of several items (cells) that one specifies (using the Add Watch icon). It is especially useful when the items whose value one wishes to track are situated far apart or in other worksheets of a large model. Figure 3.23 shows an example. The value of cell D4 has been changed compared to the earlier model (from 20 to 10), and the Watch Window shows the value of cell G9 (which is unchanged) and that of cell E7 (which alters from 21% to 35%).

3.11 NAMED RANGES

Individual cells and ranges can be given user-defined (or "friendly") names that can be used to refer to them instead of using cell references. For example, Figure 3.24 shows the use of the Name Manager (situated on the Formulas tab) to give a name to each model input.

If the model is built in this way, then the formulas used would be as shown in column E of Figure 3.25.

Named ranges can also be used to navigate around a model. Figure 3.26 shows that names will be shown in the NameBox, and selecting these will take one to that cell or range.

Figure 3.24 **Using the Name Manager**

Figure 3.25 **Simple Model with Named Inputs**

	A	B	C	D	E
1					
2					Formulas
3	Price Per Trip ($)		25		
4	Trips Per Day		20		
5	Days Per Year		300		
6	Trips (p.a.)		6000		C6=Trips_per_day*Days_per_year
7	Revenue (p.a.)		150000		C7=Price_Per_Trip*C6

Figure 3.26 **The Name Box**

Figure 3.27 **Accessing the Go To (F5) Functionality**

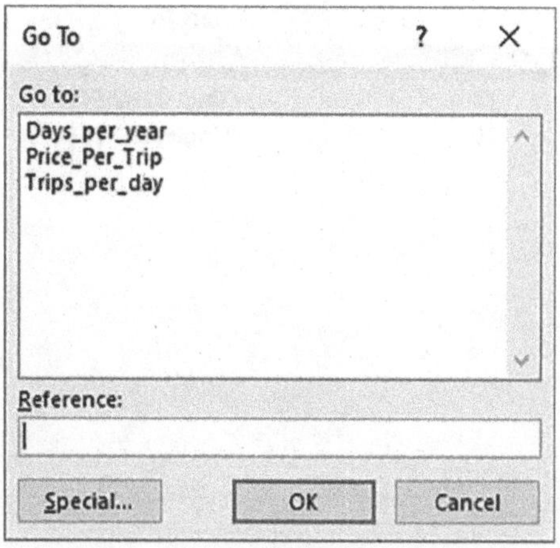

The Go To menu (or its shortcut F5) also allows one to navigate around the model by selecting one of the named ranges (see Figure 3.27):

The author's view is that the selective use of named ranges can help to navigate around large models, and also that their use is indispensable when writing macros (or VBA code). However, the author does not, in general, recommend building models using named ranges in the formulas and calculations (but rather, simply using the row-column syntax). Whilst they are appealing when viewed in the context of individual calculations, when used in large models, the set of names can become overwhelming and complex to manage and maintain. For example, the model shown in Figure 3.25 is that for a business with a single cab. If the business were expanded to include a second cab (as shown earlier in Figure 3.15), then the set of named ranges would need to be adapted, creating extra work and potential complexity. Similarly, as the number of items increases, then the number of names could become very large. On the other hand, the cell references are already well-defined and follow a standardized naming convention (i.e. row-column references) and are easy to locate. Nevertheless, some modelers do have a strong preference for named ranges. Therefore, it is important to be familiar with them to some extent. (A detailed discussion of their uses, including the advantages and disadvantages, can be found in the author's *PFM*.)

3.12 BEST PRACTICES: OVERVIEW

The term "best practices" refers to a set of principles whose overall objective is to make a model easy to understand and use (i.e. transparent), flexible to adapt, as simple as possible, and accurate. The need for such principles arises because the values of calculations in Excel do not (generally) depend on how the model is laid out (i.e. where the input cells are placed in relation to the calculations). Nor (in general) do the values depend on the format or coloring of the cell content, nor on the labels used to describe the variables. So, for example, a model that is well-built and well-structured could easily and quickly be "destroyed" (from a transparency perspective) by moving many cells to other places in the model, so that the structure is much poorer whilst the results are identical. Therefore, it is useful to try to standardize some things and reduce complexity, especially where such complexity does not add any genuine value.

There are several core elements to good practices (that are largely accepted by most modelers as such):

- Ensuring a clear distinction between input values and formulas. The distinction should be made at a structural, as well as at a visual level: Structurally, the values of input assumptions should be held in self-contained cells or ranges (to which formulas refer), and not embedded within the formulas. Visually, input cells should have color-coded fonts and/or shading (or some other format that is different from cells containing calculations and labels). It can be also useful to color-code the core outputs (so that inputs, calculations, and output cells use different colors to each other). Thus, it should be clear for another user how the model should be used (such as which cell are the inputs, so that the value of these can be altered if desired), as well as which cells are outputs (and therefore are considered as important for decision-making). All items in the model should use labels that are as clear as possible.

- Having an easy-to-follow logic. This means trying to establish a "left-to-right" and "top-to-bottom" flow (so that one can "read" the model in a natural order) and minimizing the total length of audit paths (e.g. the total length of the precedent lines that would result of one traced back from the outputs to the inputs). This generally favors keeping items that are related to each other close together. For example, calculations and their inputs should be placed as close together as possible. Similarly, formulas should be built so that each step is simple and the overall logic is built step-by-step. As long as there is a clear overall structure, a model which is larger (more rows or columns) but which is made up of simple steps, is much easier to understand than one which is smaller but where the steps are combined together.

- Building "modular" structures, so that the overall model consists of the linking of these together. Visually, these blocks can be distinguished by formatting their borders. This increases transparency as well as flexibility (since it is easier to replace or relink a module than it is to rebuild many more formulas or the whole model).

Given the wide variety of ways that a model can be built in Excel, some topics are more widely accepted as best practices than others. For example, the author believes that named ranges should not be used, or only to a limited extent (see earlier comments), whereas some modelers are avid users of them. Similarly, the author believes that circular references within Excel should be avoided completely (VBA macros can be used to resolve such issues when they are unavoidable); see *PFM* for more. When trying to implement best practices, there are sometimes trade-offs to be made. However, the core principles are to focus on complexity reduction and on transparency, whilst retaining the core functionality. The following sections explore some issues related to best practices in more detail.

3.13 BEST PRACTICES: FLOW

As an example of issues relating to the direction of the flow of logic, it is often better to avoid diagonal dependency paths and rather to create only horizontal and vertical paths (especially in large models). For example, Figure 3.28 shows the case where the input cell C3 is used in several calculations that are displaced from it physically, creating diagonal dependencies.

Figure 3.28 **Diagonal Dependency Paths**

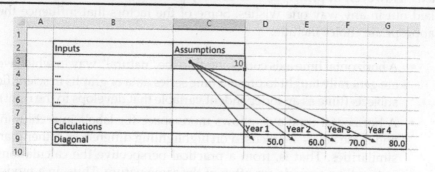

Figure 3.29 **Horizontal and Vertical Dependency Paths**

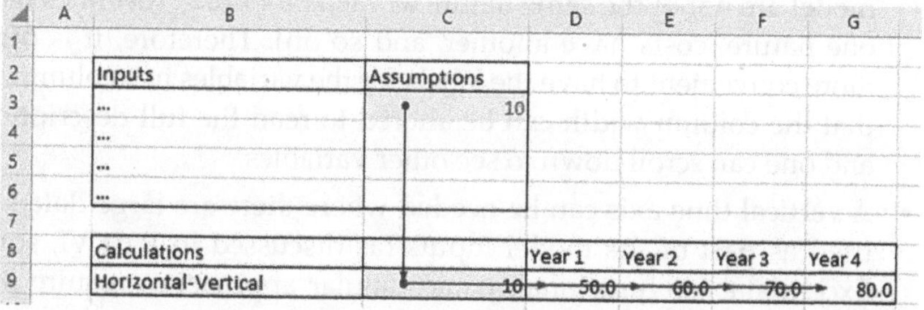

Figure 3.29 shows that by using an additional reference cell to pass the input value (C9), one can create a horizontal-vertical flow. In fact, with this approach, the total length of all of the audit paths is less than it is in Figure 3.28 (since the path from C3 to C9 is used only once). Note also that this approach also creates a very simple form of "modular" structure, in the sense that it could be copied and reused elsewhere in the model by changing only the value referred to in cell C9 (whereas the structure in row 9 of Figure 3.28 could not be copied as easily because of relative referencing).

3.14 BEST PRACTICES: TIME AXIS

The flow of a model is also closely linked to its overall layout. One issue is whether the time axis of a model should be in the horizontal or vertical direction of Excel. Many traditional Excel models use a horizontal time axis. However, in principle, it is usually possible for most models to be laid out in any way one wishes. Some of the factors that influence the appropriate choice include:

- A horizontal time axis corresponds to the "natural" way in which we are generally taught to present time series data or graphs in scientific subjects (time as an independent variable that develops to the right).
- A horizontal time axis allows more space for labels in a column, and these labels are focused on highlighting differences rather than similarities. That is, from a practical perspective the calculations in two time periods are often of the same nature. Thus, in a model with many periods, there is often little need to inspect the formulas or values in each individual period (summary information being more important in general). On the other hand, the variables in the model are not of the same nature as each other (e.g. revenues have one nature, costs have another, and so on). Therefore, it is often more convenient to have the labels for the variables in a column, so that the column width can be altered to read the full description, and one can scroll down to see other variables.
- A vertical time axis can be needed where there are large data sets used as part of the model inputs (as discussed in Part VI, some Excel database functionality and tabular approaches require that data sets have a columnar structure).

In some cases, the time axis may need to have both a vertical and a horizontal axis (see the discussion about triangular structures in Chapter 10).

3.15 BEST PRACTICES: MULTIPLE WORKSHEETS

There can be a temptation to use many worksheets. However, whilst doing so can create the appearance of a modular structure, it is also typically associated with complex audit paths that run across worksheets and which are also typically diagonal. In general, it is better to aim to build models in as few worksheets as possible. Valid reasons to use multiple worksheets include when several worksheets contain links to external data sources, or where independent data sets are contained in each sheet, or where the analysis in a particular sheet is structurally different to that of the main model. Nevertheless, if multiple worksheets are used, then the number of direct references between them should be minimized. For example, rather than having a formula such as =SUM(FirstSheet!B2:B12) created in a second sheet of the model, the calculation should be done in a cell of the first worksheet (as =SUM(B2:B12)), with the second worksheet then using a simple cell reference to access this result. Thus, in principle all (or as many as possible) calculations should be done on the same worksheet as the data used in those calculations. Cross-sheet transfer of information should be done by simple cell references. (In more advanced uses, the INDIRECT function can be used; see *PFM* for more.)

3.16 BEST PRACTICES: FORMATTING

The formatting of cells and ranges using colors for the fonts and borders around key areas is important for several reasons:

- Coloring can be used to make the role of each item clear (inputs, calculations, outputs), and hence aid a user's understanding.
- Borders can be placed around key modules or areas which contain items that are closely related. This reinforces the understanding of the model by breaking it visually into components. Note that it is often preferable to use bold borders around a large or main range and lighter borders around sub-ranges contained within it.

The Home tab (see the earlier Figure 3.2) contains many of the required menu items to format effectively and quickly. The operations are largely self-explanatory. Some shortcuts are also useful:

- The Format Painter ("paintbrush icon"; see Figure 3.2) can be used to copy the format of one cell or range to another. Double-clicking on the icon will keep it active, so that it can be applied to multiple ranges in sequence (until it is deactivated by a single click or by using the ESC key).
- The shortcut Ctrl+1 can be used to display the Format Cells menu, which can be an alternative to working on the Home tab.

Note also that the formatting of numbers is important to aid transparency and understanding. For example, an item that is known to be a percentage (such as a growth rate, or a proportion) should be formatted as such. Also, only significant figures should be displayed (such as 5.3%, rather than 5% or 5.29528762%).

Some shortcuts to select ranges quickly can also be useful when one desires to apply the same format to all cells in the range, or to place a border around the whole range. For example, to rapidly place a border around a range of (non-empty) cells, one can select any cell in the range and then:

- Use Ctrl+* (or Ctrl+Shift+Space) to select the Current Region of the cell (i.e. all cells which are contiguous to some other cell).
- Use Ctrl+& to place borders around this range (on some keyboards, Shift may be required to access the & symbol, i.e. the actual keystrokes could be Ctrl+Shift+7, where Shift+7 accesses the & symbol).
- Use Ctrl+(Shift)_ to remove all borders from a selected range or cell.

3.17 MODEL TESTING, CHECKING, AND ERROR MANAGEMENT

It is often said that every model contains errors. In fact, the term "error" can refer to a wide variety of issues, including:

- "Model error." This is the gap between the real-life situation and what is captured by the model. That is, models are simplifications, so even if implemented exactly as intended, there are very likely to be aspects of the situation that are not captured. The methods discussed in Chapter 2 are relevant to formulating the model and understanding at what point a model (as an approximation or simplification) is acceptable or not. In some situations, one will be able to observe the real-life outcome and then adapt the model appropriately for subsequent application (such as if a model is used repeatedly to make the same form of decision on a regular basis).
- "Implementation error." This is where there is an unequivocal mistake. For example, one uses the + operator to add two items (such as price and volume) that should have been multiplied. Similarly, one may have created a formula that omits or includes a cell that it should not (such as if the SUM function is used but refers to an incorrect input range).
- "Scenario error." The model may calculate correctly in many situations, but there are exceptions or rarer scenarios where the calculations do not work. For example, if the denominator of an item is a calculated quantity, then an error will arise if it evaluates to zero

(which may occur only in rare cases). Similarly, the process to look up an item in a data set may fail if the item is not present (which, once again, may not be the common or default case, perhaps arising if a user searches for "US" rather than "USA," for example).

Implementation errors can be reduced or eliminated by testing the model robustly before using it. Key principles involved include:

- Build the model using best practice principles to ensure that it has a clear flow, is as transparent and as simple as possible.
- Perform the calculations in individual steps, rather than using large, embedded formulas. For example, when using an IF function where the return values in each case are themselves calculated items, then is it generally best to calculate the two values separately, with the function using simple cell references to link to these calculations.
- When building formulas or using functions, think about in what circumstances the calculation may fail or produce an error: Try to understand the conditions where the formulas would fail or "break" (such as causing a denominator to become zero).
- Test the model by using very simple values for all the inputs (such as 0 or 1) and observing the effect on the outputs.
- Test the model using a range of more realistic values (a sort of simple sensitivity analysis), and check that the results are sensible and as expected.
- Test the formulas with extreme values, or values at which they might fail (which typically are items such as very large positive and negative values, as well as zero and $+/-1$).

Some techniques that are available to manage "scenario errors" include:

- Documenting the validity of the model and the assumptions used. (This can be done in a separate worksheet within the model, in an external document, and/or using specific in-cell Comments and Notes with the main model area.)
- Using functions (such as IFNA and IFERROR) to return alternative values when some forms of errors arise.
- Using the Data/Validation menu to restrict the values that can be entered into cells. An example is shown in Chapter 4 (see Figure 4.9 and the associated discussion).

3.18 GRAPHS AND CHARTS

Graphs and charts can be used to show key model output, as appropriate. When using charts, it is important to choose the type of chart carefully. Before creating a chart, one should ideally:

- Identify clearly, explicitly, and concisely what message is to be conveyed.
- Consider the best way to convey this message (which may not be with a chart at all).
- If a chart (or graph) is to be used, decide which chart is most suitable.

Generally, the most useful and important charts are:

- Line graphs.
- X-Y scatter plots.
- Bar charts (row form).
- Waterfall charts.

Pie charts should almost always be avoided: They rarely (if ever) display a clear comparison of items or of trends and can be replaced with better displays.

The Charts menu on the Insert tab can be used to create the relevant chart and is largely self-explanatory at a basic level. It is worth noting that once a chart has been created, clicking on it will result in extra menu tabs appearing that relate to chart operations (such as Chart Design and Format).

4

Sensitivity and Scenario Analysis

4.1 INTRODUCTION

In Chapter 2, we discussed the concept of sensitivity analysis as the exploration of the changes that occur to the value of a calculated item when one or more of the input values are changed. We noted its importance not only for decision support after a model is complete, but also during the design and planning, building, and testing phases of a model. This chapter focuses on the practical aspects of implementing sensitivity analysis in completed models. It also covers the related topic of scenario analysis and variations analysis and discusses Excel's GoalSeek feature. The Further Topics section briefly covers some fundamental aspects of the related topics of optimization, risk and uncertainty assessment, and simulation.

4.2 BASIC OR MANUAL SENSITIVITY ANALYSIS

At the simplest level, sensitivity analysis can be performed by simply directly (or "manually") changing the values of an input and observing the effect on the calculations. This is useful when building and testing a model, for example to perform a basic check that the calculations are working as intended (especially for more complex formulas or chains of logic).

4.3 AUTOMATING SENSITIVITY ANALYSIS: AN INTRODUCTION

In principle, the aim of the manual approach discussed above is to observe the effect, rather than to record the results for decision-making purposes. To record the results, one could copy and paste the values of the inputs and of the calculated fields into a summary area. However, it is almost always more efficient and preferable for the analysis to be "automated": That is, one pre-defines a set of input values to use for the sensitivity results and uses the features of Excel to automatically calculate the value(s) of the output(s) for each input value. This can be done with Excel's DataTables, which are discussed in the next section.

4.4 USING DataTables

The DataTable feature is accessible as one of the drop-down items under the Data/What-If Analysis menu. Figure 4.1 shows the input box that appears when the menu is selected.

Figure 4.1 shows that the DataTable menu requires that the input cell(s) that are to be varied are entered as cell references in the dialog box. Therefore, before starting the process to use a DataTable one should in fact first consider the answers to the following questions:

- Which is the output item(s) that we wish to conduct the sensitivity analysis on?
- Which inputs should be varied?

Figure 4.1 **Accessing a DataTable Using Data/What-If Analysis**

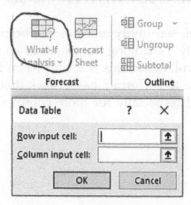

- How many inputs are to be varied simultaneously: One, two, or more?
- What are the specific values to use for the inputs that are to be varied?

In addition, before using the DataTable menu, one should set up the appropriate tabular structure in Excel. This consists of:

- A row and/or column range that defines the values to use for the input(s) that is (are) to be varied.
- A cell reference link to the output, and which is placed in the appropriate "diagonally offset" position.

In order to demonstrate this, we can use the earlier model for the profitability of a single cab (taxi) business. For convenience, Figure 4.2 shows the model again.

To conduct a sensitivity analysis of Revenues (cell C7) one could set up any of the structures shown in Figure 4.3 (which are shown in the

Figure 4.2 **Recap of Cab (Taxi) Business Profit Model**

	A	B	C	D
1	MODEL			
2				
3		Price Per Trip ($)	25	
4		Trips Per Day	20	
5		Days Per Year	300	
6		Trips (p.a.)	6000	
7		Revenue (p.a.)	150000	
8				
9		Fuel and Variable Costs per Trip	5	
10		Fuel and Variable Costs Total (p.a.)	30000	
11				
12		Salaries and Related Benefits	80000	
13		Other Fixed Operating Costs	20000	
14		Fixed Costs Total (p.a.)	100000	
15				
16		Total Cost (p.a.)	130000	
17				
18		Profit (p.a.)	20000	
19				

Figure 4.3 **Three Raw DataTable Structures**

	E	F	G	H
	SENSITIVITY ANALYSIS			
		20	25	30
	=C7			
		=C7		
	20			
	25			
	30			
	=C7	20	25	30
	250			
	300			
	350			

Formulas/Show Formulas view, and are formatted with borders and cell shading for clarity).

Note that, in each case, only a single model output (cell C7 or Revenues) is being analyzed. However, it is not yet specified which input cell(s) is (are) to be varied. For example, in numerical terms, the base case Price Per Trip is 25, and the base case Trips Per Day is 20, so it is still undefined whether the set {20, 25, 30} used in the top row or left column of the first two tables (in Figure 4.3) corresponds to Price or to Trips per Day: It is the role of the DataTable menu (see Figure 4.1) to require that the user specifies which model input is intended to be represented by such items. That is:

- Where the values to use are in the top row (as in the first table in Figure 4.3), one must specify the model input cell which corresponds to the "Row input cell."

- Where the values to use are in the left column row (as in the second table in Figure 4.3), one must specify the model input cell which corresponds to the "Column input cell."

- Where there are values in both the top row and left column row (as in the third table in Figure 4.3), one must specify the model input cells in the same way as described for each item separately.

Figure 4.4 **Completing a Two-Way DataTable**

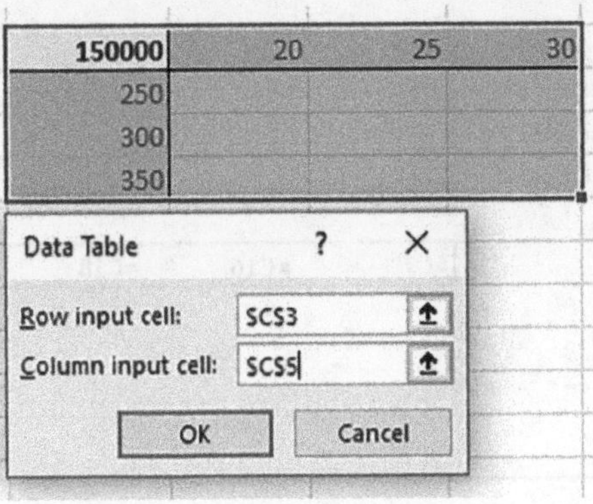

To complete each table, one must select the full range of the table, and use the Data Table menu, to specify the corresponding inputs. For example, in the case of the third table, one would complete it as shown in Figure 4.4 (assuming the top row represents Price, and the left column represents Days Per Year).

Figure 4.5 **The Completed Two-Way DataTable**

150000	20	25	30
250	100000	125000	150000
300	120000	150000	180000
350	140000	175000	210000

(If there is only a row or column input cell, the other is simply left blank.)

The result for this two-way table would be as shown in Figure 4.5.

Note that if only one input is to be varied, then the table has space on the other axis that could be used analyze additional model outputs. Once again, either a row-form or a column-form table could be used. For example, Figure 4.6 shows the raw structures (in the Formulas/Show Formulas view) for a row-form and column-form table to analyze the Revenue (cell C7), the Total Cost (cell C16), and the Profit (cell C18). The intention is that the first table is used to conduct the sensitivity analysis according

Figure 4.6 **The Raw DataTable Structures for DataTables with Multiple Outputs**

	20	25	30
=C7			
=C16			
=C18			

	=C7	=C16	=C18
250			
300			
350			

to the Price (cell C3), while the second is intended to be the sensitivity of the same items to the Days Per Year (cell C5).

(Once again, to complete this, one would use a process like that shown in Figure 4.4.)

4.5 CHECKING THE RESULTS, LIMITATIONS, AND TIPS

After creating a DataTable, one should check that the results are correct. For example, one can ask questions such as:

- Can I see the model's base case value within the DataTable?
- Do the results look directionality correct?
- Is the behavior (e.g. increases or decreases in value) along a row or down a column in line with what we should expect? A value that is constant along a row or column can be a sign of an error, since the model output is in that case not sensitive to the input that is being varied.

If a DataTable does not show the expected results, there are several possibilities. The main ones are:

- One has incorrectly specified the identity of the row and column inputs. It is quite easy (especially for new users) to define what should be a row input as a column input (or vice versa). Similarly, it is possible to mix up which input is which, especially in a two-way DataTable where each input has a similar order of magnitude (such as Price Per Trip and Trips Per Day in the above example).

- The Excel Calculation options are set to "Automatic Except for Data Tables," so that the Data Tables do not show the updated (recalculated) values: Either press F9, or switch to Automatic calculation (to avoid having to press F9 or Calculate Now each time.

- There is a mistake in the model. For example, the formula that should calculate Revenues may not reference the Price or has accidentally been hard-coded or overwritten (i.e. within the model's formulas, the input does not affect the output in the way that it should). The formulas should be checked for accuracy, which may also involve using the auditing or dependency tracing tools described in Chapter 3.

DataTables also have some features that limit their use or may also cause inadvertent errors. Some of the most important being:

- They can be cut and pasted (or moved), but not copied. If copied, the values shown in the interior are not calculated, but are simply the pasted values from the original DataTable, and as such are no longer linked to the model. The reason to want to copy a table could be to conduct the analysis on a different model output. In this case, the copying process can be used to create the structure and format to be used for a new DataTable, but the linking of the output and the inputs would need to be redone.

- Once built, the range of a DataTable can extended by adding to the rows or columns as appropriate and then relinking the inputs. However, it cannot be reduced in size: The interior section must first be cleared (using Excel's Home/Clear/Clear Contents), or the original one entirely deleted, and a new DataTable created which has the correct dimensions.

- The model input cells that are defined as the row or column inputs within the DataTable dialog must be within the same worksheet as the DataTable. This is only a minor restriction: For example, it would be possible to place all DataTables in a separate worksheet by initially – within this worksheet – creating a duplicate set of those model inputs that are to be varied and then overwriting the original model input cells (that are in another worksheet) with cell references to the new inputs.

4.6 CREATING FLEXIBILITY IN THE OUTPUTS THAT ARE ANALYZED

Where a model which has several outputs and one wishes to create two-way DataTables to analyze these (as the same set of input values is used), one can either:

- Create a DataTable for each output, or
- Re-use a single DataTable and switch the output that is being referred to. This can be done manually or with a Lookup function (and best implemented using the Automatic calculation option).

As an example of the second point, one could first set up a summary area which points to the various outputs of interest (the top table area in Figure 4.7). The user can then choose which of the outputs to sensitize (see the shaded cell E9), with the cell F9 using the XMATCH function to find the relative position of this item within the list of outputs (i.e. Profit is the third of these).

Figure 4.7 **Summary Area with Selection Menu**

E	F	G	H	I	J
SENSITIVITY ANALYSIS					
Output Summary	Value				
Revenue	150000				F4=C7
Cost	130000				F5=C16
Profit	20000				F6=C18
Output for Sensitivity	Position				
Profit	3				F9=XMATCH(E9,$E$4:$E$6,0)

The DataTable then replaces a direct cell reference to the output with an appropriate Lookup function. For example, in Figure 4.8 the CHOOSE function is used in cell E11 (see column J for the formulas used). Note also that the INDEX function could have been used instead to create a similar functionality.

One of the advantages of this approach is that the number of DataTables is reduced, so that the model is smaller and recalculates more quickly than if more DataTables are present (since each interior cell requires a separate recalculation of the model).

Figure 4.8 **DataTable with Choice of Outputs to Analyze**

E	F	G	H	I	J
SENSITIVITY ANALYSIS					
Output Summary	Value				
Revenue	150000			F4=C7	
Cost	130000			F5=C16	
Profit	20000			F6=C18	
Output for Sensitivity	Position				
Profit	3			F9=XMATCH(E9,SE$4:SE$6,0)	
20000	20	25	30	E11=CHOOSE(F9,F4,F5,F6)	
250	-25000	0	25000		
300	-10000	20000	50000		
350	5000	40000	75000		

Note that to make the choice process of the items in cell E9 more robust, one could use Excel's Data/Data Validation menu. This can be used to ensure that only an item from the Output Summary table can be chosen by the user, as shown in Figure 4.9.

Figure 4.9 **Using Data Validation to Restrict a User's Choices to Valid Items**

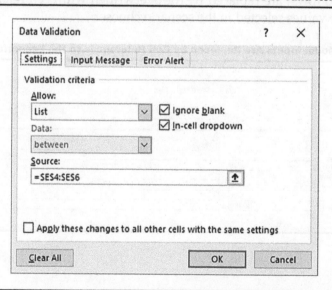

4.7 SCENARIO ANALYSIS

Scenario analysis is a general term to analyze the effect on an output when several input values are changed simultaneously. A DataTable is a special case in which only one or two items are varied. To be able to change more than two, one can first create numbered (or named) scenarios which specify the input combinations that are to be used. Then, a DataTable can be used in which one runs a one-way sensitivity analysis, where it is the scenario name or number that is varied.

As an example, Figure 4.10 shows essentially the same model as above, but with the following modifications:

- Two rows are added towards the top to create some extra space that is needed.

- A "scenario-chooser" module is set up in columns E to J. There are five possible scenarios, and the user chooses which one should be shown (using cell E4, which is set to the value of four).

- The INDEX function is used in cells E5 and E7 to pick out (select) the value that is to be used for that input in that scenario (cell E5 shows the value for Price Per Trip, and E7 that for Days Per Year). Note that the CHOOSE function could have been used instead.

- The original model input cells (C5 and C7, after the addition of the two rows) are replaced by (or overwritten with) cell references to the values selected in the scenario chooser.

Figure 4.10 **Model Inputs Are Replaced by Cell References to the Scenario Chooser**

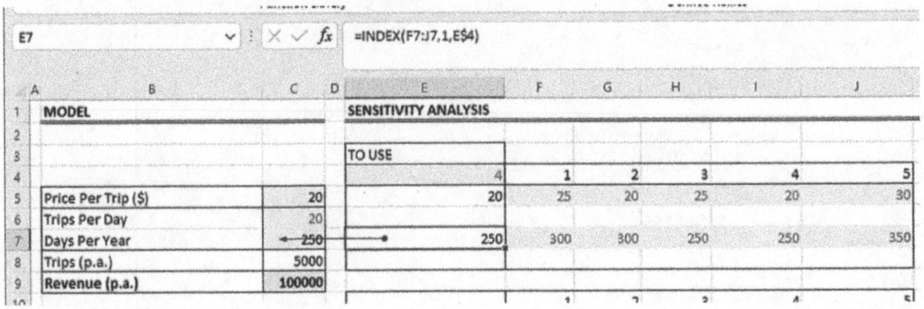

| | | | | E7 | | | | =INDEX(F7:J7,1,E$4) | |

Figure 4.11 **Implementing the Scenario Results Using a DataTable**

E	F	G	H	I	J
SENSITIVITY ANALYSIS					
TO USE					
4	1	2	3	4	5
20	25	20	25	20	30
250	300	300	250	250	350
	1	2	3	4	5
100000	150000	120000	125000	100000	210000

Data Table   ?   ✕

Row input cell: SES4   ⬆

Column input cell: ⬆

OK   Cancel

Then, one creates a DataTable where the input cell is the scenario number. For example, Figure 4.11 shows the raw structure (as well as the completed results, for convenience) of a row-form DataTable.

Finally, it is worth noting that the "scenario chooser" area (i.e. the functionality in the cells E3:J8) is another example of "modularization" (as also discussed in Chapter 3 within the topics of best practices): It is a self-contained area whose results (cells E5 and E7) are used in order to link to the main model. (The main model also has some modularization in its structure, such as separate areas for calculations of revenues and costs.)

4.8 VARIATIONS ANALYSIS

When several model inputs are changed simultaneously from their initial value to their final value, each output also has an initial and final value. "Variations analysis" is where one seeks to break down the total change into that caused by each input. This analysis can be done by creating

Figure 4.12 **Simple Example of Variance Analysis**

	E	F	G	H
SENSITIVITY ANALYSIS				
TO USE				
	1	1	2	3
	25	25	20	20
	300	300	300	250
		1	2	3
	150000	150000	120000	100000

scenarios that are defined by changing the value of one item at a time and retaining that change in all subsequent scenarios. Figure 4.12 shows the step-by-step effect of changing one item at a time in this way.

(The results for the intermediate stages may depend on the order in which changes are made; if – in scenario 2 – the Trips Per Day was changed instead of the Price Per Trip, then the results would be different. This is due to interactions between the items within the model's logic and is analyzed in more detail in Chapter 19.)

4.9 USING GoalSeek

Excel's GoalSeek feature allows one to find the value of a model input so that an output also has a specific (desired or target) value. It is sometimes thought of as a "reverse" sensitivity analysis. For practical reasons, it is often better to:

- Adjust the model by including a cell containing the target value of the output that one wishes to achieve.
- Calculate in Excel the difference between this target and the actual model output.
- Use GoalSeek to find the input value that leads to this being zero.

For example, Figure 4.13 shows that two rows have been added at the end of the original model: Cell C20 contains a hard-coded value for the desired level of the Profit, while C21 calculates the difference between this and the current model output. The GoalSeek feature (also under the Data/What-If Analysis drop-down) is then set to search for the value of Price Per Trip (cell C3) that will result in this difference being zero (so that the target will have been achieved).

When the OK button is pressed, the value in cell C3 will change to 30, and the cell C18 (i.e. the Profit) will recalculate to the desired figure of 5000.

Figure 4.13 **Example of Using GoalSeek**

	A	B	C	D	E	F	G
1		MODEL					
2							
3		Price Per Trip ($)	25				
4		Trips Per Day	20				
5		Days Per Year	300				
6		Trips (p.a.)	6000				
7		Revenue (p.a.)	150000				
8							
9		Fuel and Variable Costs per Trip	5				
10		Fuel and Variable Costs Total (p.a.)	30000				
11							
12		Salaries and Related Benefits	80000				
13		Other Fixed Operating Costs	20000		Goal Seek	?	X
14		Fixed Costs Total (p.a.)	100000				
15					Set cell:	$C$21	
16		Total Cost (p.a.)	130000		To value:	0	
17					By changing cell:	$C$3	
18		Profit (p.a.)	20000				
19						OK	Cancel
20		Target for Profit	50000				
21		Difference (for GS)	30000	C21=C20-C18			

4.10 FURTHER TOPICS: OPTIMIZATION, RISK, UNCERTAINTY, AND SIMULATION

Sensitivity and scenario analysis are powerful tools to support general-purpose decision-making. However, when conducting them, one need not have explicitly considered the nature of the variations that are used for the input values. There are some related methods that are generally used in more advanced modeling and for specific situations, and which make the distinction of causality more explicit:

- Optimization is associated with the situation where the underlying process that causes variation is due to processes that one can control (i.e. a decision situation).

- Risk (and uncertainty) analysis is associated with the situation where the underlying process that causes variation is not under one's control (and is therefore likely to have an uncertain, random, or probabilistic behavior).

Examples of optimization situations are:

- A company may be able to work with a partner firm to invest in a mix of projects (with each partner taking a specific stake in each project), with the proportion to invest in each project being an optimization situation. The objective may be to maximize the long-term value creation (or short-term profits, or some medium range targets). There could be one or more constraints, such as keeping the total capital expenditure to below some threshold amount or restricting the level of cash outflows in any period.

- A fund manager may have a fixed amount of money to invest in a set of stocks (or other assets) and wishes to find the best amount (or weighting) to allocate to each. One important common application is known as Markowitz (portfolio) optimization. Here, each asset has an assumed return and risk (defined by its standard deviation), and the asset returns may also be correlated with each other (or to co-vary). The aim is to find – for any given return target – the portfolio which achieves this by minimizing the risk (i.e. the standard deviation of the portfolio). Alternatively, one can fix the amount of risk and find the portfolio which maximizes the return. This problem can be expressed in mathematical terms (and using the corresponding Excel functions): Given a portfolio (called X) composed of assets, each with a corresponding weighting:

$$X = w_1Y_1 + \cdots + w_nY_n$$

The variance of the portfolio is given by:

$$V(X) = \sum_{i=1}^{n}\sum_{j=1}^{n} w_i w_j CovMatrix(Y_i, Y_j)$$

(where *CovMatrix* is the matrix of the covariance of returns, whose individual elements may be as calculated using the COVARIANCE.S function; see Chapter 20 for more).

In Excel, if the weights are contained in a column range (called Weights), the variance can be calculated using the matrix multiplication function MMULT (as well as TRANSPOSE):

$V = $ MMULT (TRANSPOSE (Weights), MMULT (CovMatrix, Weights))

This optimization problem is then to find the matrix of weights to meet the objectives (i.e. minimize risk for a given return or maximize return for a given risk). If there are no constraints imposed (such as on the weights needing to be positive), then there is a mathematical solution to this problem (that requires matrix inversion using the MINVERSE function). However, in general, constraints need to be imposed. For example, one may wish to have only positive weights (i.e. no short selling), or to allocate a minimal amount (such as 5%) to each asset or asset class, and so on. In these (constrained) cases, one generally needs to use numerical methods, such as are contained within Excel's Solver add-in. The methods embedded within it "search algorithms" to find the optimal values (weights) subject to some constraints. The add-in can also be used with VBA macros. (The author's *PFM* provides more details of doing so.)

Examples of risk and uncertainty analysis include:

- Assessing the range of outcomes for the cost of a project, given that some events may happen that create delays or result in cost overruns.
- Assessing the range of possible values that a portfolio of stocks could have in one week's time. There are many possible values, even as some are more likely than others. For example, one may be interested in what may happen in the worst 5% of cases.

One of the tools to conduct risk analysis is simulation (Monte Carlo Simulation). This generates many scenarios randomly. The "random" generation is in fact done in a way so that the frequency of individual outcomes corresponds to (or represents) the frequency with which one would expect to observe the cases in the real-life situation. The result is that the output has many possible values that follows a probability distribution (corresponding to the statistical frequency that one would expect to see in the real-life situation). For example, if one were to create 1,000 representative scenarios for the possible value in one month's time of an investment portfolio, then the 5% percentile of these represents the (highest) value that the portfolio could have in the worst 5% of cases.

To create random scenarios in Excel, one can begin with the RAND() function. This generates a random number that is between 0 and 1, and which is uniformly distributed (i.e. any number in the range is as likely as any other). This can be converted into a sample of another statistical distribution by inversion. For example, the NORM.INV function takes a probability value as its input (as well as the mean and standard deviation) and finds the corresponding x-value for a variable that is normally distributed. This process generates a random sample that is representative of the distribution (i.e. if many samples were drawn, the totality of these would converge to set data points that occur with the same frequency as for the pure theoretical distribution). For example, the embedded combination of functions:

$$NORM \cdot INV \left(RAND(), 10\%, 5\%\right)$$

would generate a random sample from a normally distributed process whose mean is 10% and standard deviation is 5%. Several inverse functions exist in Excel, and some others can be calculated directly. When there are several inputs that one wishes to treat in this way, it is also possible to correlate the random samples.

In a simulation model, the random samples are used in place of some of the fixed input values (i.e. rather like in a scenario analysis, but where the scenarios are generated automatically). The RAND() function (and hence formulas dependent on it) will recalculate (resample) every time the worksheet is recalculated (or F9 is pressed). In general, the process to run many scenarios and to store the results is best handled with a VBA macro (the macro(s) involved are relatively simple, since they only need to consist of a repetitive loop, where each run forces a recalculation of the workbook and writes the results into an array). However, in simple models, the results can also be generated by using a DataTable.

Simulation has many practical uses in general business modeling and in finance. For example, it can be used to assess the risk in capital investment projects, budgets, and cash flow forecasts. It can be used to calculate the value of some types of options and derivatives, to simulate credit portfolios and losses, and so on. The subject of risk assessment is a major area for advanced financial modeling as well as for general business risk. The interested reader may wish to note that the author has also written a book in this area: *Business Risk and Simulation Modelling in Practice: Using Excel, VBA and @RISK.*

Part Three

General Calculations and Structures

5

Growth Calculations for Forecasting

5.1 INTRODUCTION

The models used so far in this text had only a single time period. In practice, most models need to have multiple periods: First, the values of items change over time (for reasons such as business growth, inflation, management decisions, as well as investments occurring earlier and paybacks happening later). Second, many economic criteria are evaluated by taking the time value of money into account (i.e. that receiving a dollar in the future is worth less than receiving one today).

This chapter covers growth-based forecasting methods. It focuses on the use of the effective growth rate approach. The Further Topics section discusses the use of logarithmic methods for growth forecasting. These methods are often combined with ratio-based forecasting methods, which are covered in Chapter 7.

5.2 GROWTH MEASUREMENT AND FORECASTING

The application of a growth rate to an item means that its value increases in proportion to the rate. For example, if the initial amount is $100, and the periodic growth rate is 10%, then the increase in value is 10% of $100 (i.e. $10), so that next period's value is $110.

That is, using general terminology:

$$V_1 = V_0 + V_0 \cdot g_1$$

Which can also be written as:

$$V_1 = V_0 \cdot (1 + g_1)$$

(where V_0 is the value in the initial period, g_1 is the periodic growth rate, and V_1 is the resulting value for the next period).

Figure 5.1 shows an example of this type of calculation in Excel. Cell C5 contains the value in the initial period, cell D5 contains the assumption for the growth rate, and cell E5 contains the forecasted value.

Figure 5.1 **Basic Growth Forecast**

E5				$\times \checkmark fx$	=C5*(1+D5)	
	A	B	C	D	E	F
1						
2			STARTING DATA	FORECAST	FORECAST	
3						
4			Year 0	Growth Year 0 to 1	Year 1	
5		Sales Revenue	100	10.0%	110	
6						

Note that when the term "growth rate" is used without further qualification, the period is generally implicitly assumed to be annual. Growth rates for non-annual periods (such as quarterly, or the length of a particular model period) can be converted to annual figures using simple compounding and decompounding formulas that are described later.

In reverse, if the value in the current period (period 1) is $110, whereas the value in the prior period (period 0) was $100, then the growth rate can be calculated as 10%. That is, given the values for the item in two consecutive periods, the growth rate is simply:

$$g_1 = \frac{(V_1 - V_0)}{V_0} = \frac{V_1}{V_0} - 1$$

(i.e. it is the change (increase) in value as a proportion of the initial amount).

This definition of the growth rate is known as the "effective" growth rate. This term essentially means that the rate is "directly observable" in the data (or at least by using simple arithmetic). It is the most common method used in financial modeling applications (especially those that

Figure 5.2 **Historical Information and Growth Forecasting**

	A	B	C	D	E	F	G
1							
2			HISTORICAL DATA			FORECAST	
3							
4			Year -1	Year 0	Growth Year -1 to 0	Growth Year 0 to 1	Year 1
5		Sales Revenue	95	100	5.3%	8.0%	108
6					E5=(D5/C5)-1		G5=D5*(1+F5)

relate to corporate finance, and to other cases where the focus of the modeling is related to discrete periods of time). It is also sometimes known as the "classical" or "geometric" method. (The Further Topics section covers the alternative methodology, which is based on logarithms.)

In general, when building a forecasting model, one is likely to have some historical information. This could be used to inform the assumptions about the future growth rate, as well as giving an initial value to use as a forecasting base. For example, Figure 5.2 shows the case where there is historical data on Sales Revenue for two prior years (cells C5 and D5) and this is used to calculate the historical growth rate (cell E5), in this case 5.3% per annum (p.a.). The forecast assumption (cell F5) is for growth to be slightly higher (i.e. 8.0% p.a.) than the historical value, and this is used (cell G5) to calculate the forecast Sales Revenue in Year 1.

5.3 LOGIC REVERSALS

When a model contains a forecast and a historical component, there is often a "reversal" of logic as one transitions from the historical period to the forecasting period. For example, with reference to Figure 5.2.

- For the historical part, the growth rate is calculated (in cell E5) from the actual values of the item (Sales Revenue).
- For the forecasting part, the value of the item (cell G5) is calculated from the growth rate assumptions. (The historical figure(s) is used only as a reference for the forecasting assumptions.)

This "reversal of logic" property is not specific to the use of growth rates as a forecasting method; it occurs quite generally when historical data and forecasting logic are both contained in a model (which is common). For this reason, it is important to make it clear to a user which area of the model is which. Doing so helps to avoid the potential errors of a user overwriting forecasting formulas with new data as it becomes available in the future. To make the distinction between the areas clearer, one can use borders, formatting, and labels (one could even password-protect cells so their content cannot be changed).

5.4 FORECASTING STRUCTURES IN PRACTICE

In fact, the structure used in Figure 5.2 has a clear "left-to-right" logic (or flow). That is, the information required in each calculation is in the cells which are to the left of that calculation. However, the layout has a significant disadvantage if it is used in a model with more time periods: The column structure in the forecast period alternates between showing growth rates and values of the Sales Revenue.

It is usually much more readable to have a single row containing the Sales Revenue and another row for the growth rates. This shown in Figure 5.3. This also shows the dependency arrows to highlight that the flow of logic is still left-to-right. However, due to the "logic reversal," the historical part uses a top-to-bottom flow. While this does not strictly correspond to best practices, the overall logic is generally quite clear and transparent since the range used is small and is essentially self-contained.

When extended to include a longer forecasting period (such as five periods), the model could look like that in Figure 5.4 (which selectively shows some of the dependency paths).

Figure 5.3 **Common Layout of Growth Forecasting**

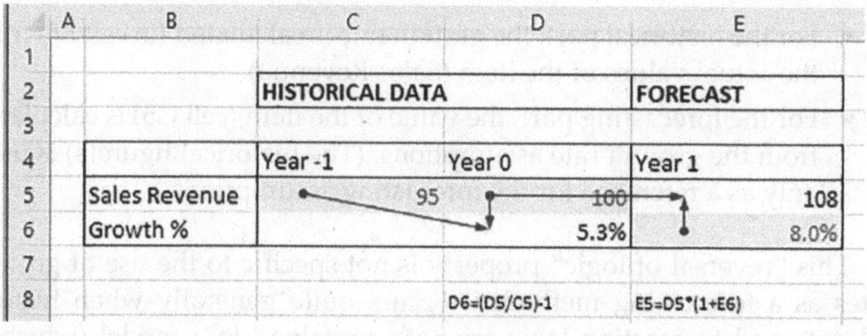

	A	B	C	D	E
1					
2			HISTORICAL DATA		FORECAST
3					
4			Year -1	Year 0	Year 1
5		Sales Revenue	95	100	108
6		Growth %		5.3%	8.0%
7					
8				D6=(D5/C5)-1	E5=D5*(1+E6)

Figure 5.4 **Multi-period Forecast Using the Common Layout**

	A	B	C	D	E	F	G	H	I
1									
2			HISTORICAL DATA		FORECAST				
3									
4			Year -1	Year 0	Year 1	Year 2	Year 3	Year 4	Year 5
5		Sales Revenue	95	100	108.0	116.6	122.5	128.6	135.0
6		Growth %		5.3%	8.0%	8.0%	5.0%	5.0%	5.0%
7									
8				D6=(D5/C5)-1	E5=D5*(1+E6)	F5=E5*(1+F6)	G5=F5*(1+G6)	H5=G5*(1+H6)	I5=H5*(1+I6)

5.5 SIMPLIFYING THE SENSITIVITY ANALYSIS AND REDUCING THE NUMBER OF PARAMETERS

Where a model has a significant number of time periods, it can be useful to "reuse" a growth rate assumption, so that there is a smaller number of underlying input values. This allows for sensitivity analysis to be conducted more simply.

For example, the model shown in Figure 5.4 has five separate growth rate (input) assumptions (cells E6, F6, G6, H6, and I6), although there are only two different values within them (i.e. 8.0% p.a. in Year 1 and Year 2 and 5.0% p.a. in Year 3, Year 4, and Year 5). The model could be adapted so that the two values are contained in separate input cells and the remaining three cells of the five linked to the appropriate input. In the first instance, this could be done as shown in Figure 5.5. That is, the two inputs are placed in cells E6 and G6, with F6 linking to E6, and H6 and I6 linking to G6.

Figure 5.5 **Reducing the Number of Separate Input Assumptions**

	A	B	C	D	E	F	G	H	I
1									
2			HISTORICAL DATA		FORECAST				
3									
4			Year -1	Year 0	Year 1	Year 2	Year 3	Year 4	Year 5
5		Sales Revenue	95	100	108.0	116.6	122.5	128.6	135.0
6		Growth %		5.3%	8.0%	8.0%	5.0%	5.0%	5.0%
7									
8				D6=(D5/C5)-1	E5=D5*(1+E6)	F5=E5*(1+F6)	G5=F5*(1+G6)	H5=G5*(1+H6)	I5=H5*(1+I6)
9						F6=E6		H6=G6	I6=H6

However, it would often be clearer to structure the model so that the two inputs are in a separate area than the formulas. Figure 5.6 shows this approach: Two columns have been inserted (the new E and F), and the growth rates for the five cells then linked to these.

Figure 5.6 **Full Separation of Inputs from Calculations**

A	B	C	D	E	F	G	H	I	J	K
1										
2		HISTORICAL DATA		FORECAST Assumptions		FORECAST Calculations				
3										
4		Year -1	Year 0	Year 1-2	Year 3+	Year 1	Year 2	Year 3	Year 4	Year 5
5	Sales Revenue	95	100			108.0	116.6	122.5	128.6	135.0
6	Growth %		5.3%	8.0%	5.0%	8.0%	8.0%	5.0%	5.0%	5.0%
7										
8			D6=(D5/C5)-1			G5=D5*(1+G6)	H5=G5*(1+H6)	I5=H5*(1+I6)	J5=I5*(1+J6)	K5=J5*(1+K6)
9						G6=$E$6	H6=$E$6	I6=$F$6	J6=$F$6	K6=$F$6

Once this is done, the running of a sensitivity analysis using a DataTable becomes simple and transparent. Figure 5.7 shows a two-way DataTable of the Sales Revenue in Year 5 for various combinations of the two assumptions, and in which the base case is indicated for reference.

Figure 5.7 **DataTable of Year 5 Revenues to Two Growth Assumptions**

		Year 3+			
	135.0	0.0%	2.0%	5.0%	8.0%
Year 1-2	0.0%	100.0	106.1	115.8	126.0
	4.0%	108.2	114.8	125.2	136.3
	8.0%	116.6	123.8	135.0	146.9
	12.0%	125.4	133.1	145.2	158.0

In models with yet more time periods (such as in long-term project forecasting and some valuation models), one could have more assumption columns (such as three), so that different rates could be used for various time horizons. For example, one could use:

- A rate for Year 1 only ("short-term"). This may be able to be estimated with more accuracy than the growth rate in subsequent years.
- A rate for Year 2 and Year 3 ("short- to medium-term").
- A rate that applies from Year 4 onwards ("long-term").

5.6 DEALING WITH INFLATION

Therefore, the items calculated within a model should also generally be in nominal terms. This means that the values are those that would observe (or the "sticker" prices that one would pay). This is distinct from "real terms" measures, where inflation is stripped out. For example, with an inflation rate of 4.0% p.a., a change in nominal price of an item by 3.0% in one year would mean that prices have changed (decreased) in real terms of –1.0% over the year.

The benefits of nominal terms are several:

- Most day-to-day and other economic variables (e.g. house prices, financial market variables, stock prices, interest rates, bond yields) are observed in these terms. Therefore, is it easier to compare model values (including input assumptions or estimates) with real data.

- Second, a pure real-terms model can lead to mistakes in economic analysis. For example, since depreciation costs are non-inflationary, a real-terms model that contains depreciation would generally overstate it in relative terms, with consequences for profit, taxation, cash flow, etc.

In some cases, it can make sense to calculate some model items in real terms, with this being used as an intermediate calculation step to which an inflation adjustment is then made before the items are fully integrated into the model's final calculations. For example, a contract clause may specify the growth rate in costs that a supplier is allowed to apply to some products. Similarly, a leasing contract for some office space could specify that annual leasing costs are to increase with inflation, so that the "growth rate" applied to calculate the leasing costs would simply be the assumed or forecast inflation rate. More generally, by treating inflation separately, one can isolate (or emphasize) the effect of changes that are due to inflation and those due to other factors. For example, the cost of salaries for administrative staff could be split into a component for inflation-link salary increases (that may be contractually driven) and a component that reduces aggregate costs due to productivity improvements. More generally, there are cases when a model may need to have several inflation factors. For example, prices may inflate at a different rate to some cost items or categories, and so on.

In principle, the inclusion of inflation rates as an assumption is like the use of growth rates as assumptions. However, whereas growth rates

Figure 5.8 **Using Inflation as a Separate Item**

	HISTORICAL DATA		FORECAST Assumptions		FORECAST Calculations					
INFLATION	Year -1	Year 0	Year 1-2	Year 3+	Year 1	Year 2	Year 3	Year 4	Year 5	
Inflation Factor		1.00			1.04	1.08	1.10	1.13	1.15	
Growth %			4.0%	2.0%	4.0%	4.0%	2.0%	2.0%	2.0%	
REAL TERMS	Year -1	Year 0	Year 1-2	Year 3+	Year 1	Year 2	Year 3	Year 4	Year 5	
Sales Revenue	97	100			104.0	108.2	111.4	114.7	118.2	
Growth %		3.1%	4.0%	3.0%	4.0%	4.0%	3.0%	3.0%	3.0%	
NOMINAL TERMS	Year -1	Year 0	Year 1-2	Year 3+	Year 1	Year 2	Year 3	Year 4	Year 5	
Sales Revenue		100.0			108.2	117.0	122.9	129.1	135.7	
Growth %					8.2%	8.2%	5.1%	5.1%	5.1%	

G13=G5*G9   H13=H5*H9   I13=I5*I9   J13=J5*J9   K13=K5*K9
G14=G13/D13-1   H14=H13/G13-1   I14=I13/H13-1   J14=J13/I13-1   K14=K13/J13-1

are usually applied to individual items, inflation is typically applied to several items (that are each initially forecast in real terms). Therefore, for inflation, it can be useful to have this first calculated in a separate area which is then linked into all items where it is needed. Figure 5.8 shows an example that is similar to that used earlier. Row 6 contains the inflation assumptions, which are used in row 5 to calculate an inflation index (based on a starting value of 1.00). This factor is used to multiply variables that need to be inflated. In this case, Sales Revenue is initially calculated in real terms (row 8–10) before its inflated value is calculated (row 13). Row 14 calculates the aggregate growth rate that results from the combined effect of real terms growth and inflation.

Note that most of the models in this text include inflation implicitly. That is, all values are assumed to be directly in nominal terms. This not only makes the models smaller and easier to build, understand, and use, but also has some theoretical advantages, as noted earlier.

5.7 CONVERSIONS FOR MODEL PERIODS

Although growth rates are typically measured on an annual basis, it is quite possible (and frequent) that the time axis of the Excel model is of another length (such as quarterly). In such cases, the periodic growth rate would be needed either as a direct model input parameter, or as a calculated item. This section describes an example of such a conversion. The process is straightforward, so that the reader should be able to generalize this to other situations.

For example, the effective growth rate that applies during a quarter can be derived from an annual rate by solving the equation

$$\left(1 + g_{quarterly}\right)^4 = 1 + g_{annual}$$

i.e.

$$g_{quarterly} = \left(1 + g_{annual}\right)^{\frac{1}{4}} - 1$$

If the annual rate is 10% p.a., then the quarterly rate is approximately 2.4% per quarter. Similarly, a quarterly growth rate of 3.0% would translate into an annual rate of around 12.55% p.a.

While fairly simple, it is important to note that these formulas apply because there is an implicit assumption that growth process are continually compounding. This contrasts with time-period conversions for interest rates, which is discussed in detail in Chapter 12 (and where, in general, the formulas to convert between time periods depend on assumptions about the compounding frequency).

5.8 FURTHER TOPICS: LOGARITHMIC AND EXPONENTIAL GROWTH

This chapter has focused on the use of effective growth rates, or the classical or geometric method, which is the method most commonly used in many financial modeling applications (whose focus is typically on modeling the value of an item at (or within) discrete periods of time). In some applications (especially in quantitative finance, such as the valuation of derivatives), the focus is on processes that develop continuously in time.

Chapter 12 discusses compounding processes in detail. For the purposes here, we note that for continuous compounding, the effective growth rate is linked to a "stated" growth rate by the formula:

$$1 + g_{eff} = e^{g_s}$$

(where g_{eff} is the effective rate, g_s is the stated rate, and e is the exponential base number (2.718...)).

In reverse (for a continuously compounded process), the stated growth rate can be derived from the effective growth rate using:

$$g_s = LN\left(1 + g_{eff}\right)$$

(where LN is the natural logarithm).

Note from earlier that given the values in two periods the effective growth rate is:

$$g_{eff} = \frac{\left(V_1 - V_0\right)}{V_0} = \frac{V_1}{V_0} - 1$$

So that:

$$g_s = LN\left(1 + g_{eff}\right) = LN\left(\frac{V_1}{V_0}\right)$$

For example, if the initial amount is \$100, the next year is \$110, then the effective growth rate is 10% p.a., while the stated growth rate is 9.53% p.a. (continuously compounded). For this reason, this method of measuring growth is also known as the "logarithmic" method.

When a (continuously compounded) stated rate is to be used in forecasting, one would simply use a formula such as:

$$V_1 = V_0 \cdot e^{g_s}$$

For this reason, the method is sometimes also known as the "exponential" (forecasting) method.

Note that the forecasting models built with each method (classical/geometric and logarithmic/exponential) would produce the same results, as long as the information is used in a consistent manner (i.e. in accordance with the formulas above).

Figure 5.9 demonstrates the equivalence of the methods if the same historical data is used in a consistent way. In cell D6, the effective growth rate is calculated as 5.3% p.a. while (in cell D11) the stated growth rate is calculated as 5.1% p.a. Similarly, for the forecast part, the values for the assumptions (cell E6 and E11) are slightly different, since these are used in different forecasting formulas (i.e. those in E5 and E10).

The additional complexity that may seem to arise from using the exponential (continuous compounding) approach does bring with it some advantages: Most important is that the total (stated) growth over

Figure 5.9 **Comparison of Measurement and Forecasting Results**

	A	B	C	D	E	F
1						
2			HISTORICAL DATA		FORECAST	
3						
4		CLASSICAL	Year -1	Year 0	Year 1	
5		Sales Revenue	95	100	108.0	E5=D5*(1+E6)
6		Growth %		5.3%	8.0%	
7				D6=(D5/C5)-1		
8						
9		LOGARITHMIC	Year -1	Year 0	Year 1	
10		Sales Revenue	95	100	108.0	E10=D10*EXP(E11)
11		Growth %		5.1%	7.7%	
12				D11=LN(D10/C10)		

several time periods is simply the total of the (stated) growth rates in each period (and therefore the average growth rate is also the average of the periodic rates). This is because exponents can be added (or the "logarithm of the product is equal to the sum of the logarithms"). For example, for a model with three periods, one would have:

$$V_1 = V_0 \cdot e^{g_{s,1}}$$

$$V_2 = V_1 \cdot e^{g_{s,2}}$$

$$V_3 = V_2 \cdot e^{g_{s,3}}$$

So that:

$$V_3 = V_0 \cdot e^{g_{s,1}} \cdot e^{g_{s,2}} \cdot e^{g_{s,3}}$$

Or:

$$V_3 = V_0 \cdot e^{(g_{s,1}+g_{s,2}+g_{s,3})}$$

Thus, the total growth over the three periods is the sum of the three growth rates, and the average growth per period is the average of these (i.e. the sum of them divided by three):

$$g_{s,avg} = \frac{g_{s,1} + g_{s,2} + g_{s,3}}{3}$$

In other words, if one applied this average growth rate to each period of the forecast, the value at the end would be the same, since:

$$V_3 = V_0 \cdot e^{3 \cdot g_{s,avg}}$$

Of course, in Excel, the total and average rates could be calculated by applying the SUM and AVERAGE functions to the range containing the three rates. If an additional period were added, the input range to the function could very quickly and simply be extended.

On the other hand, when using the classical geometric approach, the equivalent formulas would be:

$$V_3 = V_0 \cdot \left(1 + g_{eff,1}\right) \cdot \left(1 + g_{eff,2}\right) \cdot \left(1 + g_{eff,3}\right)$$

so that the average growth rate would be:

$$g_{eff,avg} = \left(\left(1 + g_{eff,1}\right) \cdot \left(1 + g_{eff,2}\right) \cdot \left(1 + g_{eff,3}\right)\right)^{\frac{1}{3}} - 1$$

The adaption of these formulas if another period were added would require quite much more work. Fortunately, the process can be made easier and flexible by using the FVSCHEDULE function for the compounding part (i.e. for the first of the two equations immediately above). The average rate can be calculated from the compounded amount using the ^ operator (or the POWER function).

Figure 5.10 demonstrates the growth rates that would be calculated for each method (of some non-specified process, so that they would be consistent. The range C3:G3 contains logarithmic rates, and the range C4:G4 contains the effective rates. Row 8 shows that the two rates within each period are consistent with each other, as per the above description.

Figure 5.11 shows the use of this data to calculate the total growth (change) over the five years, as well as the annual average, for each method. For the logarithmic based, the SUM and AVERAGE functions (in cells I3, J3), are applied to the historic data. The average rate calculated in cell J3 is then used

Figure 5.10 **Raw Data on Growth Rates Measured by Each Method**

	A	B	C	D	E	F	G	
1								
2			Year 0	Year 1	Year 2	Year 3	Year 4	
3		Stated Rate	5.13%	7.70%	3.64%	2.64%	4.26%	
4		Effective Rate	5.26%	8.00%	3.70%	2.68%	4.35%	
5								
6								
7								
8		Consistency check	0.000000	0.000000	0.000000	0.000000	0.000000	
9			C8=C3-LN(1+C4)	D8=D3-LN(1+D4)	E8=E3-LN(1+E4)	F8=F3-LN(1+F4)	G8=G3-LN(1+G4)	

Figure 5.11 **Calculation of Total and Average Growth Using Each Method**

	A	B	H	I	J	K
1						
2				Total Change	Average	Final Value Based on $100 start
3		Stated Rate		23.4%	4.7%	126.3
4		Effective Rate		26.3%	4.8%	126.3
5				I3=SUM(C3:G3)	J3=AVERAGE(C3:G3)	K3=100*EXP(J3*5)
6				I4=FVSCHEDULE(1,C4:G4)-1	J4=FVSCHEDULE(1,C4:G4)^(1/5)-1	K4=100*(1+J4)^5
7						
8		Consistency check		0.000000	0.000000	0.000000
9				I8=I3-LN(1+I4)	J8=J3-LN(1+J4)	K8=K2-K4

(in cell K3) as an input to the EXP function. It is based on an assumed $100 starting value, giving $126.3 as the final value after five years of growth. The analogous calculations are done in row 4 with respect to the effective growth method. The total change is calculated using the FVSCHEDULE function (cell I4), and the ^ operator used (cell J4) to total calculate the average (i.e. as the fifth root). This average is applied (in cell K4) to give ending value. The values in cells K3 and K4 are the same, indicating that the methods provide the same results if each is used consistently (including how the historical growth rates are calculated).

6

Modular Structures and Summary Reports

6.1 INTRODUCTION

This chapter covers some enhancements to the structures and calculations that are often useful to enhance the transparency and flexibility of a model. It covers:

- The use of summary areas within modular structures.
- Examples of typical calculations that are frequently useful to include in these areas.
- Further comments on formatting and sensitivity analysis.
- The use of initialization areas.

6.2 MOTIVATION FOR SUMMARY AREAS AND THEIR PLACEMENT

In models with many time periods, it is not generally practical to visualize all the forecast columns at the same time. Figure 6.1 shows a model that is conceptually similar to that used earlier but which has quarterly time periods (rather than annual) for five years, so that the forecast contains 20 columns (extending to column Z, which is not shown in the image).

(Note that this model is not intended to be fully consistent with the one from Chapter 5, since the periodic value of Sales Revenue in each model is similar, even as one model is annual and the other is quarterly.)

In general, in a model with many time periods, the logic in most (or all) of the forecast columns are the same from one period to the next

Figure 6.1 **An Initial Five-Year Model with Quarterly Periods**

	A	B	C	D	E	F	G	H	I	J	K	L	M	N	O	P	Q	R	S
1																			
2			HISTORICAL DATA		FORECAST Assumptions		FORECAST Calculations												
3																			
4			Prior 1	Prior 0	Year 1-2	Year 3+	Year 1	Year 1	Year 1	Year 1	Year 2	Year 2	Year 2	Year 2	Year 3	Year 3	Year 3	Year 3	Year 4
5							Q1	Q2	Q3	Q4	Q1	Q2	Q3	Q4	Q1	Q2	Q3	Q4	Q1
6																			
7		Sales Revenue	98	100			102.0	104.0	106.1	108.2	109.3	110.4	111.5	112.6	113.8	114.9	116.1	117.2	118.4
8		Growth %		2.0%	2.0%	1.0%	2.0%	2.0%	2.0%	2.0%	2.0%	2.0%	2.0%	2.0%	1.0%	1.0%	1.0%	1.0%	1.0%
9																			
10							G7=D7*(1+G8)								O7=N7*(1+O8)				
11							G8=$E8								O8=$F8				

(there may sometimes be changes to the structure or values in the earlier periods). In principle, there is in general no real need to have all of them constantly visible.

On the other hand, there are typically some individual pieces of information or aggregate values that may be of interest such as:

- What is the total revenue in the first five years?
- What is the revenue in any particular year (e.g. Year 3)?
- At what point do the revenues first reach or exceed a target figure (e.g. exceed $120 per quarter)?

(Of course, many other forms of analysis could be of interest, including the average growth rate between two specified time periods, or the net present value (NPV) or for the internal rate of return (IRR) of the cash flows, which are measures discussed in detail in Part IV.)

It can often make sense to build the answers to these questions in a new area that is on the left-hand side of the calculations. In that way, these core metrics are easy to see (something which may need to be done frequently), while the forecast calculations on the right-hand-side are simply present for reference when needed. This approach is a continuation of the "modular" approach that is already used in Figure 6.1. That is, it is a stand-alone structure that contains all its required input assumptions and the calculations. By including summary reports on the left, the concept of modularity is retained (i.e. the module contains all of its inputs, calculations, and outputs). Note that in addition to modularity per se this approach has other advantages:

- The important (summary) items are immediately visible to a user (without having to scroll or search for them).

- The risk of errors is reduced. For example, if summaries were placed on the right-hand-side of the calculations (i.e. twenty columns to the right) then not only would these be less readable and accessible, but also there would be a risk that the summary formulas could be overwritten by accident (such as if one copies a formula from the left to all cells on the right using the shortcut Ctrl+Shift+Right Arrow).

The left-to-right flow used in this approach is not standard best practice from a layout perspective. However, since the structure is modular, the flow is in fact quite clear, so that the overall logic is very transparent (which – along with complexity reduction – is arguably the most important principle).

6.3 EXAMPLE I: SUMMARIES AND CONDITIONAL SUMMARIES

To build a summary value which contains the total revenue over five years, one can use the SUM function, applied to the full five-year range of quarterly data. The total for a specific year can be calculated in a similar way, but using the SUMIFS functions, in which the identity of the specific year is used to check a condition within the range containing the dates.

Figure 6.2 shows an example of the summary calculations. Note that before building these formulas, some adaptations of the model were made:

- Additional columns were inserted toward the left (columns C to E).

- A row was inserted (row 6) to create additional ways of referring to the dates. Notably, by using the & operator to join text fields, the period Q1 of Year 1 can be referred to as "Year 1_Q1.."

Figure 6.2 **Summary of Five-Year and Specified Year**

					HISTORICAL DATA		FORECAST Assumption		FORECAST Calculations		
		SUMMARIES AND REPORTS									
					Prior 1	Prior 0	Year 1-2	Year 3+	Year 1	Year 1	Year 1
									Q1	Q2	Q3
									Year 1_Q1	Year 1_Q2	Year 1_Q3
		Five Year Total	Selected Year	Total							
	Sales Revenue	2294.8	Year 3	461.9	98	100			102.0	104.0	106.1
	Growth %					2.0%	2.0%	1.0%	2.0%	2.0%	2.0%
		C9=SUM(J9:AC9)		E9=SUMIFS(J9:AC9,$J$4:$AC$4,D9)							

The SUM function is used in cell C9, with its input range being J9:AC9. The SUMIFS function is used in cell E9, with the specified year for its analysis having been defined in cell D9. (This approach allows one to quickly change the annual period that one wishes to analyze, such as to be able to perform sensitivity analysis on it.)

6.4 EXAMPLE II: TARGETS, FLAGS, AND MATCHING

To find when a revenue target is met for the first time, one could create a new row which contains a "flag" field. A flag field is simply an indicator that uses the IF function to check whether the condition is met. Note that while an IF function will by default return either TRUE or FALSE (which are logical items), it is often more robust to build the function to return 1 and 0 instead. (This is generally recommended, so that the items can be more easily worked with numerically – such as added up – since many Excel functions ignore logical items, as discussed in Chapter 3.)

Figure 6.3 shows an adapted model in which a new row (row 12) is used for this purpose.

The following are the main points to note:

- The target value for the revenues that is to be checked is defined as an input, in cell D12.

- The IF function is used (from column J, rightwards) to return the values 1 or 0 according to whether the revenue in that period is greater or equal to the target value.

- The XLOOKUP function is used (cell E12) to find the date in which the target is first met. The XLOOKUP function implicitly contains two steps: The first finds the relative position in the range J12:AC12

Figure 6.3 **Using Flag Fields to Find When a Target is Met**

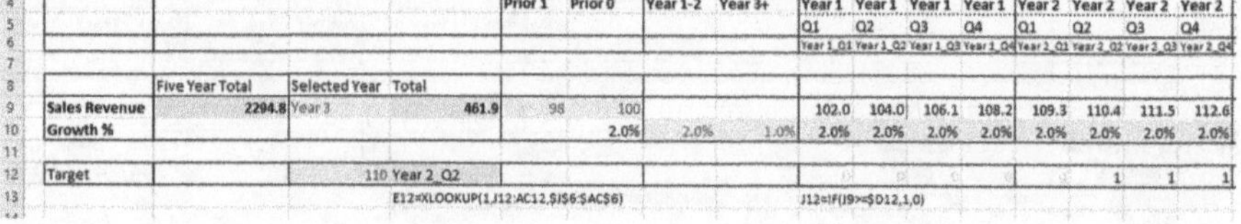

at which the value 1 (i.e. the result of the flag) occurs for the first time. The second looks up the item in this position within the range containing the dates (in this case the range J6:AC6). In fact, these steps could be broken out individually, if it were desired: The first is equivalent to using the XMATCH function (which would return the value 6 for the relative position). The second could be conducted by using the INDEX function to look up the relevant date in the range J6:AC6 (i.e. the date that is in the sixth position, as derived by the XMATCH function.)

6.5 SENSITIVITY ANALYSIS

Once the summary reporting structure is set up, one can use it to run sensitivity analysis. For example, Figure 6.4 shows a one-way DataTable which calculates – for different values of the target – the period in which the target is reached for the first time. That is, with reference to Figure 6.3, cell D12 is varied, and its effect on D13 is captured.

Figure 6.4 **Using a DataTable for Items in the Summary Report**

Target	Year 2_Q2
105	Year 1_Q3
108	Year 1_Q4
110	Year 2_Q2
112	Year 2_Q4
115	Year 3_Q3

6.6 COMMENTS ON FORMATTING

The model above also used Excel's Conditional Formatting feature (on the Home tab). This was applied to the range of flag cells (row 12), and used to set the font color to grey of those (flag) cells which are zero. Figure 6.5 shows one step in this process. To format the font, one would need to click the Format button, and use the menu that would appear.

Note that sometimes, rather than formatting only cells whose values are exactly zero, it can make sense to use the drop-down menu to format cells which are between a small negative and positive number, such

Figure 6.5 **Setting a Conditional Format Rule**

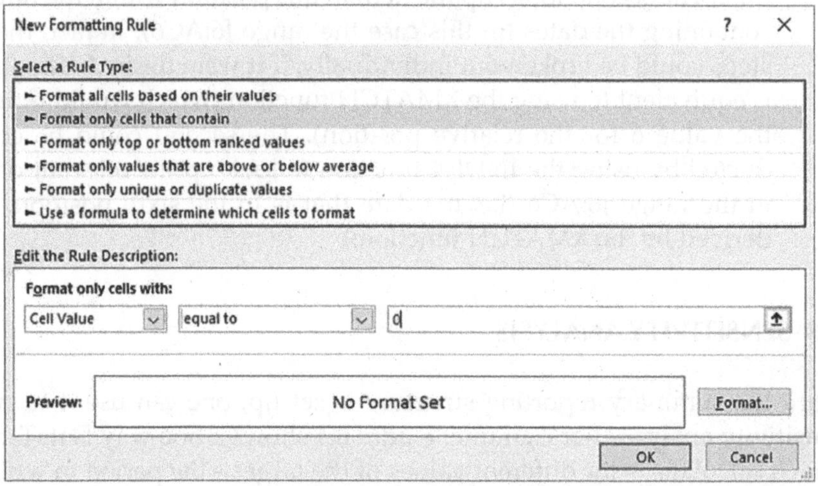

as –0.000001 and 0.000001. This deals with the case where there may be rounding errors in the Excel calculations.

6.7 INITIALIZATION AREAS

Figure 6.6 shows that in the model currently under discussion, the latest historical value for Sales Revenue is used directly to calculate the value in the first period. Due to the layout of the model, the formula in the first period only is different to that in all other periods, which use the values immediately to the left and below.

This type of inconsistency in formulas can lead to errors, since – without close inspection of the model – one would not be aware of them. For example, one could inadvertently copy the formula in cell J9 to the columns to the right. This would result in incorrect formulas, due to relative referencing when copying (i.e. since the formula in J9 refers to cell G9, if it were copied to K9, the new formula would refer to H9). To avoid this inconsistency, there are several options:

- To switch columns F and G with columns H and I. However, this would create new inconsistencies and poor logical flow.
- To add an "initialization" column which brings in the relevant base value to be contiguous with the forecast range. Thereafter, the

Figure 6.6 **Dependencies without Initialization Area**

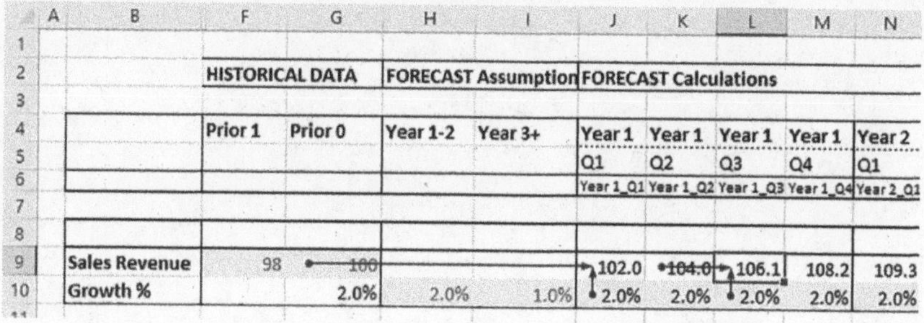

Figure 6.7 **Use of an Initialization Area to Be Able to Have Consistent Formulas in the Forecast**

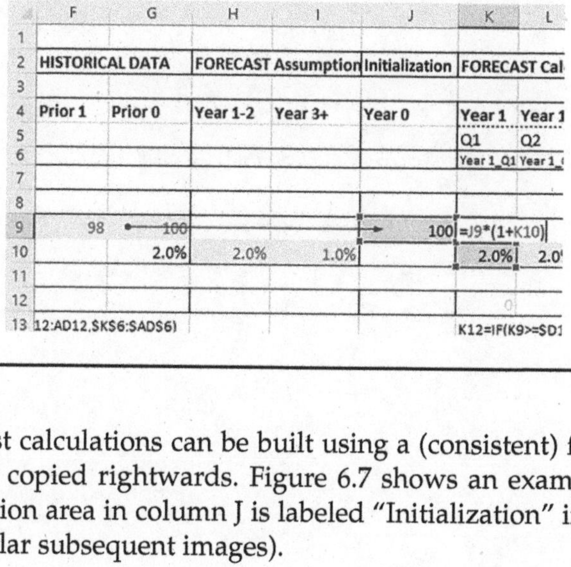

forecast calculations can be built using a (consistent) formula that can be copied rightwards. Figure 6.7 shows an example (the initialization area in column J is labeled "Initialization" in cell J2 and in similar subsequent images).

Another benefit of the initialization area is that one can use it to implement any adjustments that may be required. For example, the model is based on quarterly periods, and it is implicit that the historical data in columns F and G are quarterly figures. However, it is possible in other contexts that one may be given only annual historical data (such as say 390 for cell F9 and 400 for cell G9). In such cases, the initialization cell can be used to contain the adjusted amount (such as 400 divided by 4), so that this "base" value is used to derive the subsequent (quarterly) calculations.

7

Scaling and Ratio-driven Forecasts

7.1 INTRODUCTION

There are often situations where the value of an item in a model could reasonably be represented as a proportion of sales revenue. For example:

- The value of customer invoices outstanding. If customers typically settle their invoices one month after the goods are delivered, invoices outstanding and sales revenue should be closely related.
- Operating cost, such as postage and general supplies.
- Some marketing or promotional expenditure.
- General administrative expenditure. This could be split into a part which is fixed (and grows with inflation, for example), and a part that is variable in accordance with the sales revenue.
- Capital investment. The larger the business is (or is expected to be), the more investment would typically be required.
- Cost of some raw materials.

Of course, some operating costs items may be driven by factors other than sales revenue, and indeed a forecast in which everything scales to sales revenue may not be particularly useful nor insightful (see later in this chapter).

This chapter describes some typical uses and variations of this method. It covers practical considerations, such as the combined use of growth-based and ratio-based forecasting. It also highlights how to use the method most effectively, given that it may potentially be overused otherwise. The Further Topics Section describes some of the links between ratio-based forecasting and to general ratio analysis (which is itself discussed in detail in Chapter 19).

7.2 BASIC USES

In general, when applying this method, one would first forecast sales revenue (for example using the growth-based methods of Chapter 5), and then determine the other items from this using a scaling factor or proportion. Although the value of this proportion for the forecast period is an assumption, its historical values are equal to the values of the item divided by the sales revenues (i.e. to their ratio). Thus, the method is often described as ratio-based forecasting.

The method can be applied not only to "flow items" (i.e. those which occur over a period of time, such as cost) but also to "stock" items (i.e. those which are measured at a point in time, such as invoices outstanding, and finished goods inventory, the value of fixed assets and equipment)

Figure 7.1 shows an example. The Sales Revenue (row 6) has been forecast using the growth-based method. Then, the ratio approach is used to forecast General Supplies and Postage (in row 9) by applying the scaling factor (or ratio). The historical ratio is calculated in cell C10 (showing 2.0%), and this is used to inform the forecast assumptions for the scaling factors in cells E10 and F10 (the latter assumption of 1.5% could have been made due to an expectation that costs will fall for reasons not described here, for example).

(For convenience of presentation, the models in this Chapter do not contain a reporting or summary area on the left and are based on annual time-periods.)

Figure 7.1 **Historical Calibration and Ratio-Based Forecast for a Flow Item**

Figure 7.2 **Historical Calibration and Ratio-Based Forecast for a Stock Item**

		HISTORICAL DATA		FORECAST Assumptic		Initializati	FORECAST Calculations							
		Prior 1	Prior 0	Year 1-2	Year 3+	Year 0	Year 1	Year 2	Year 3	Year 4	Year 5			
Sales Revenue		95	100			100	108.0	116.6	122.5	128.6	135.0			H6=G6*(1+H7)
Growth %			5.3%	8.0%	5.0%		8.0%	8.0%	5.0%	5.0%	5.0%	D7=(D6/C6)-1		H7=$E7
General Supplies & Postage			2.0			2.0	2.2	2.3	1.8	1.9	2.0			H9=H6*H10
% of Sales			2.0%	2.0%	1.5%		2.0%	2.0%	1.5%	1.5%	1.5%	D10=D9/D6		H10=$E10
Invoices Outstanding			8.0			8.0	8.6	9.3	9.2	9.6	10.1			H12=H6*H13
% of Sales			8.0%	8.0%	7.5%		8.0%	8.0%	7.5%	7.5%	7.5%	D13=D12/D6		H9B=$E13

An identical set of calculations could be done for a stock item (such as Invoices Outstanding), once again using historical data to inform the future assumptions. Figure 7.2. shows an example.

7.3 LINKS TO LENGTH OF MODEL PERIODS

When using a ratio method for a stock item, it is important to note that the denominator for the scaling factor of the historical information (i.e. Sales Revenue) would be quite different according to the length of the model time period, whereas the numerator (value of stock item) is measured at a point in time (not dependent on the length of the period). On the other hand, for two flow items, each relates to the same time period. Therefore, care needs to be taken for stock items to ensure that the information is measured and used in a consistent way. For example, in the model under discussion, the periods are annual, so that (at any time point) the Invoices Outstanding are 8.0% of the periodic (annual) Sales Revenue (in Years 1 and 2, and then 7.5% of the same in Years 3+). However, if the model used quarterly periods, then the ratio would change to (approximately) 32% of the periodic (quarterly) Sales Revenue. (When a model is built from scratch, such adjustments are often taken care of automatically, since the forecast assumptions (cells E13 and F13) would typically have been directly calibrated with reference to the historical figures by the model builder.)

7.4 DAYS' EQUIVALENT APPROACHES

Instead of modeling directly with scaling factors or ratios, one can use a "days' equivalent" approach. For example, an item that could be calculated as 10% of annual Sales Revenue could instead be represented as being equivalent to 36.5 days of average daily Sales Revenue.

Figure 7.3 **Using the Days, Equivalent Method**

	Prior 1	Prior 0	Year 1-2	Year 3+	Year 0	Year 1	Year 2	Year 3	Year 4	Year 5		
	HISTORICAL DATA		FORECAST Assumptid		Initializat	FORECAST Calculations						
Sales Revenue	95	100			100	108.0	116.6	122.5	128.6	135.0		H6=G6*(1+H7)
Growth %		5.3%	8.0%	5.0%		8.0%	8.0%	5.0%	5.0%	5.0%	D7=(D6/C6)-1	H7=$E7
Invoices Outstanding		8.0			8.0	8.6	9.3	9.4	9.9	10.4		H15=H16*(H$6/365)
Days Sales		29.2	29.0	28.0		29.0	29.0	28.0	28.0	28.0	D16=D15/(D6/365)	H16=$E16

To implement this method, one first needs to calculate the average daily Sales Revenue in each period (for both the historical and forecast part), by dividing the annual figure by 365. This can be done either as an explicit line item (for maximum clarity), or be embedded in the calculations:

- For the historical part of the model, the days' equivalent value is calculated by dividing the value of the item by the average daily Sales Revenue.
- For the forecasting part, the value of the item is calculated by multiplying the days' equivalent assumption by the average daily Sales Revenue.

Figure 7.3 illustrates this approach to calculate Invoices Outstanding. Note that some rows (i.e. rows 9 to 14) have been hidden for convenience. The formulas use the "embedded" method for the average daily Sales Revenue, which is not broken out separately.

(Once again, if the model time periods were not annual, then the calculations would need to be adjusted accordingly. For example, in a quarterly model, the average daily Sales Revenue could be calculated by division by 365/4 or 92, and so on.)

7.5 EXAMPLE I: FORECASTING FROM REVENUES TO EBITDA

This Section provides a more comprehensive example to illustrate how some of the techniques discussed may be integrated in a larger model. The example is based on using the techniques relating to growth- and ratio-based forecasting, as well as summary areas. The model is still relatively simple and has the following line items:

Figure 7.4 **Price Forecast for the Example Model**

	A	B	C	D	E	F	G	H	I	J	K	L	M
1													
2			Method	HISTORICAL DATA		FORECAST Assumptions		Initialization	FORECAST Calculations				
3													
4				Prior 1	Prior 0	Year 1-2	Year 3+	Year 0	Year 1	Year 2	Year 3	Year 4	Year 5
5													
6	INCOME												
7													
8	Price Per Unit		Growth	10.0	10.2			10.2	10.4	10.6	10.6	10.6	10.6
9	Growth %				2.0%	2.0%	0.0%		2.0%	2.0%	0.0%	0.0%	0.0%

Figure 7.5 **Sales Revenue Calculation**

6	INCOME												
7													
8	Price Per Unit		Growth	10.0	10.2			10.2	10.4	10.6	10.6	10.6	10.6
9	Growth %				2.0%	2.0%	0.0%		2.0%	2.0%	0.0%	0.0%	0.0%
10													
11	Volume in Units		Growth	950	1000			1000	1080	1166	1225	1286	1350
12	Growth %				5.3%	8.0%	5.0%		8.0%	8.0%	5.0%	5.0%	5.0%
13													
14	Sales Revenue		Calculated	9500	10200			10200	11236	12378	12997	13647	14329
15	Growth %				7.4%				10.2%	10.2%	5.0%	5.0%	5.0%
16													

- Prices, forecast using a growth method.
- Volumes, forecast using a growth method.
- Sales Revenues, calculated from the above.
- Fixed cash operating costs, forecast using a growth method.
- Variable cash operating costs, forecast as a ratio.
- Total costs (excluding depreciation and amortization), calculated from the above.
- Earnings (profit) before interest, tax, depreciation, and amortization (EBITDA), calculated from the above.

Figure 7.4 shows the top part of a model in which the Price Per Unit is forecast using the growth-based method. This part therefore uses the methods described in Chapter 5 (with the differences being only the identity of the variable and the numerical values of the assumptions).

Figure 7.5 shows the same approach applied to Volume in Units, and the calculation of Sales Revenue as the product of Price Per Unit and Volume in Units. (Thus, the growth rates in Sales Revenue shown in row 15 are now items that are calculated from the Sales Revenue and are simply shown for clarity and reporting purposes.)

Figure 7.6 shows the calculation of Fixed Costs (rows 19–20). This is based on using a growth method (which here implicitly captures both the effect of inflation and of staff salary increases). It also shows the calculation of Variable Operating Costs (row 22–23), which are modeled as a ratio of the Sales Revenue.

Figure 7.6 **Calculation of Fixed and Variable Costs**

13											
14	Sales Revenue	Calculated	9500	10200			10200	11236	12378	12997	13647	14329
15	Growth %			7.4%				10.2%	10.2%	5.0%	5.0%	5.0%
16												
17	OPERATING COSTS (CASH ITEMS)											
18												
19	Fixed Costs	Growth	7000	7250			7250	7613	7993	8233	8480	8734
20	Growth %			3.6%	5.0%	3.0%		5.0%	5.0%	3.0%	3.0%	3.0%
21												
22	Variable Operating Costs	Ratio		3000				3259	3590	3639	3821	4012
23	% of Sales			29.4%	29.0%	28.0%		29.0%	29.0%	28.0%	28.0%	28.0%

Figure 7.7 shows the calculation of Total Operating Cost (the sum of Fixed and Variable Costs), and the calculation of EBITDA (i.e. the difference between Sales Revenue and Total Operating Costs; note the items in this model are all cash-related items, so that depreciation and amortization are excluded).

Figure 7.7 **Calculation of EBITDA in the Simple Model**

14	Sales Revenue	Calculated	9500	10200			10200	11236	12378	12997	13647	14329
15	Growth %			7.4%				10.2%	10.2%	5.0%	5.0%	5.0%
16												
17	OPERATING COSTS (CASH ITEMS)											
18												
19	Fixed Costs	Growth	7000	7250			7250	7613	7993	8233	8480	8734
20	Growth %			3.6%	5.0%	3.0%		5.0%	5.0%	3.0%	3.0%	3.0%
21												
22	Variable Operating Costs	Ratio		3000				3259	3590	3639	3821	4012
23	% of Sales			29.4%	29.0%	28.0%		29.0%	29.0%	28.0%	28.0%	28.0%
24												
25	Total Operating Cost	Calculated		10250			10250	10871	11583	11872	12301	12746
26	Growth %							6.1%	6.5%	2.5%	3.6%	3.6%
27												
28	EBITDA	Calculated		-50			-50	365	795	1125	1346	1583
29	As % Sales Revenue						-0.5%	3.3%	6.4%	8.7%	9.9%	11.0%
30												

7.6 USING RATIO-BASED FORECASTING EFFECTIVELY

The above example shows that the ratio-driven forecasting method is a useful one and is easy to implement. However, there is a risk that it can be overused or used in simplistic ways. For example, we can see that row 29 of Figure 7.7 shows that the EBITDA Margin (i.e. EBITDA as a percentage of Sales Revenue) is increasing. This is due to Fixed Costs growing less quickly than Sales Revenue. However, if the ratio-based method were used to determine Total Operating Cost directly (without the model having a Fixed Cost that is forecast using another method), then there would be a direct link between the ratio used for the forecasting assumption and the EBITDA margin: In fact, the EBITDA margin in any period would simply be 100% less the ratio assumed. Therefore, one would (almost) directly be assuming the level of the EBITDA margin. If the assumed forecast ratios are close to their historical values, then the forecast will simply reflect the past (scaled up by the Sales Revenues). This would often not provide a useful (nor realistic, insightful) forecast: Whereas the base case values may be reasonable as such, a sensitivity analysis would produce an unrealistically narrow range of variation.

Further, if one forecasts several line items using ratio-based methods for each, then it is quite easy to inadvertently create a situation whose result would be very similar (or identical) to that if all the items had been aggregated into one, and a ratio method applied to the aggregate. For example, if – in another modeling context – we wished to forecast the cost of materials as a ratio of the sales revenue, and calculated the amount owed to suppliers as a ratio of the cost of materials, then the amount owed to suppliers is implicitly also forecast as a percentage of sales revenues (i.e. the product of the two ratios). Similarly, one may initially forecast capital expenditures as a proportion of sales in the current year, but then decide to create a (seemingly better) forecast in which capital expenditure is derived from sales over the next three years (to reflect that the expenditure must be made ahead of time). However, these methods are very similar, and in fact the results are identical if the sales growth is constant in each period.

Thus, while the ratio-based method is often useful as part of an overall model, consideration should be given to its effect, especially if used for many items or for items that place a significant role in determining the output values of a model.

7.7 EXAMPLE II: RATIO-BASED FORECASTING OF CAPITAL ITEMS

This example illustrates a variation of the ratio-based method, where the item to be forecast is the Capital Investment (Capital Expenditure or CapEx), i.e. the investment in new physical property, plant, and equipment (PPE) or fixed assets (FA). On the assumption that PPE is required to produce the goods that are sold, it could be reasonable to derive the CapEx requirements from the Volume in Units (and hence to forecast increasing CapEx as more volume is sold in the future). However, when calculating the historical value of the ratio, one would be dividing a monetary amount (CapEx) by a unitary amount (Volume). The resulting figure represents a sort of "investment intensity" in the sense that it reflects the CapEx that was required per unit volume in the historical period. However, since Volume in Units is not a monetary amount (and therefore cannot be inflated), the use of such a ratio in the forecast period (i.e. multiplying the assumed ratio by the Volume in Units) will give a monetary figure for CapEx that is not inflated (in order words, that is expressed in the same terms as the historical amount). Therefore, if this method is used, one ideally also needs to add a general term for the inflation of capital goods. As noted in Chapter 5, such inflation can be captured either explicitly (as line items in the model) or implicitly (i.e. within the values assumed for the future ratios).

Figure 7.8 shows an example of the implementation of a volume-based ratio calculation so that it incorporates an inflation effect. In cell E34, the historical value of CapEx (cell E33) is divided by the corresponding Volume in Units (cell E11) to give a capital intensity ratio expressed in the monetary terms of Year 0. The forecast assumptions for capital intensity are also contained in row 34 (as for earlier structures). However, these are not yet inflated (and the assumption for Year 3 onwards is that investment intensity reduces so that the same amount of equipment could produce more). The inflation adjustment is made using the cumulative inflation factor (row 36). Finally, the CapEx is calculated by multiplying the forecast Volume in Units by the assumed value of capital intensity and by the cumulated inflation factor (row 33).

Figure 7.8 **Calculation of CapEx Using a Volume-Based Ratio and Inflation**

	A/B	C	D	E	F	G	H	I	J	K	L	M	N/O
1													
2		Method	HISTORICAL DATA		FORECAST Assumptions		Initialization	FORECAST Calculations					
3													
4			Prior 1	Prior 0	Year 1-2	Year 3+	Year 0	Year 1	Year 2	Year 3	Year 4	Year 5	
5													
11	Volume in Units	Growth	950	1000			1000	1080	1166	1225	1286	1350	
12	Growth %			5.3%	8.0%	5.0%		8.0%	8.0%	5.0%	5.0%	5.0%	
30													
31	PROPERTY, PLANT AND EQUIPMENT												
32													
33	Capital Investment (CapEx)	Ratio-Volume		100			100	110	121	104	111	119	I33=I$11*I34*I36
34	Capital Intensity ($/Volume)			0.100	0.100	0.080		0.100	0.100	0.080	0.080	0.080	
35	Capital Goods Inflation				2.0%	2.0%		2.0%	2.0%	2.0%	2.0%	2.0%	
36	Cumulative Inflation Factor						1.00	1.020	1.040	1.061	1.082	1.104	I36=H36*(1+I35)

7.8 FURTHER TOPICS: LINKS TO GENERAL RATIO ANALYSIS

Within a forecasting model (as well as a historical set of data) there are many ratios that could be calculated. However, the number of ratios that can be used as input assumptions is far more limited, since many ratios need to be consistent with each other. For example, the ratios of profit-to-sales, sales-to-assets, and profit-to-assets are related, since:

$$\frac{Profit}{Sales} \cdot \frac{Sales}{Assets} = \frac{Profit}{Assets}$$

In Chapter 19, we discuss the topic of ratio analysis in detail. Frequently calculated ratios for analysis purposes include:

- Profit/Sales (margin or return on sales).
- Profit/Assets (return on assets).
- Sales/Assets (asset turnover).
- Depreciation/sales.
- Capital investment/sales.
- Accounts receivable turnover (sales/accounts receivables).
- Working capital ratio (working capital/sales).
- Inventory turnover (cost of goods sold/inventory).
- Payables ratio (accounts payable/cost of goods sold).

Corkscrews and Reverse Corkscrews

8.1 INTRODUCTION

A "corkscrew" is a specific structure whose name is derived from the image formed when its dependency paths are traced. This chapter explains and provides examples of the two main variations:

- The "classical" corkscrew is where "flow" items are used to calculate "stock" items.
- "Implied" or "reverse" corkscrews is where "stock" items are used to calculate "flow" items.

8.2 CLASSICAL CORKSCREWS

In the classical structure, the value of a stock item is calculated over time by:

- Defining an initial value for an item at the end of the period immediately before the forecast begins.
- For each forecast period, setting the starting value of the item to be equal to its value at the end of the prior period (i.e. the value is "brought forward").
- Within each forecast period, using a line which shows the increase(s) in value due to activity in that period and another which shows the decrease(s.)

Figure 8.1 **Framework for a Corkscrew Structure**

Fixed Assets								
Starting								250
Increases (CapEx)								
Decreases (Depreciation)								
Ending							250	

Figure 8.2 **Linking of CapEx into the Corkscrew Structure**

	A	B	C	D	E	F	G	H	I	J	k
1											
2			Method	HISTORICAL DATA		FORECAST Assumptions		Initialization	FORECAST Calculations		
3											
4				Prior 1	Prior 0	Year 1-2	Year 3+	Year 0	Year 1	Year 2	Year
5											
11	Volume in Units		Growth	950	1000			1000	1080	1166	
12	Growth %				5.3%	8.0%	5.0%		8.0%	8.0%	
13											
31	PROPERTY, PLANT AND EQUIPMENT										
32											
33	Capital Investment (CapEx)		Ratio-Volume		100			100	110	121	
34	Capital Intensity ($/Volume)				0.100	0.100	0.080		0.100	0.100	
35	Capital Goods Inflation					2.0%	2.0%		2.0%	2.0%	
36	Cumulative Inflation Factor							1.00	1.020	1.040	1
37											
38	Fixed Assets										
39	Starting								250		
40	Increases (CapEx)								110		
41	Decreases (Depreciation)						20.0%				
42	Ending							250			

- For each forecast period, determining the value of the item at the end by adding the values for the starting, increases, and decreases. (The decreases are usually represented with a reversal of the sign of the natural amount in order that a pure addition can be performed; see later.)

Note also that the lines for the increases and decreases may often be simple references to cells elsewhere in the model that contain the results of detailed calculations that derive each. For example, the total increase in the value of equipment may result from the effect of several separate increases due to individual purchases of items of capital equipment.

Figure 8.1 shows the first stages in the creation of a corkscrew which is to be used to track the value of Fixed Assets (or property, plant, and equipment, or PPE).

Figure 8.2 shows the next step in the completion of the structure. That is, the line for the increase in value (row 40) is linked to the corresponding

Figure 8.3 **Linking of CapEx into the Corkscrew Structure**

38	Fixed Assets									
39	Starting								250	
40	Increases (CapEx)								110	
41	Decreases (Depreciation)					20.0%			-50	
42	Ending							250		

line in the model (row 33) that contains the detailed calculations of CapEx (capital expenditure, which is calculated as was done in Figure 7.8).

In large models, one may also have a separate area which contains the calculations for the decrease (i.e. due to depreciation), and which is used to link into the corkscrew. For the purposes of simplicity of presentation here, we calculate depreciation directly within the structure, using a percentage of the period's starting value. Figure 8.3 shows this, using an assumption that 20% of the starting value is depreciated in each period (and where the sign is reversed compared to its natural value).

The three items (in row 39, row 40, and row 41) can be added (using the SUM function or the + operator) to give the value at the end of the period. This is shown in Figure 8.4.

Figure 8.4 **Completion of Structure for the First Period**

Fixed Assets								
Starting								250
Increases (CapEx)								110
Decreases (Depreciation)					20.0%			-50
Ending							250	310

The formulas can then be copied rightwards to all other periods. The result is shown in Figure 8.5. This also shows the dependency paths (to highlight the corkscrew aspect)

Figure 8.5 **Completed Structure with Dependency Paths Shown**

38	Fixed Assets										
39	Starting							250	310	369	400	431
40	Increases (CapEx)							110	121	104	111	119
41	Decreases (Depreciation)					20.0%		-50	-62	-74	-80	-86
42	Ending						250	310	369	400	431	464
43												

8.3 BENEFITS AND FURTHER USES

Corkscrew structures are beneficial as they create transparency and flexibility due to:

- Time separation. The separation between values of stock items at the beginning of a period and those at the end makes for a clearer reading of the model. If a single line item were used, then it would not be as clear whether the value in a particular time-period refers to the value at the period start or at the end.

- Flow items separation. The flow items that cause increases and decreases may often have a different nature to each other and need to be treated separately. For example, in the case of the plant and machinery calculations, the capital expenditure is a cash flow item, whereas the depreciation is a non-cash item; the distinction between them is very important in economic modeling and investment evaluation.

- Integration of model parts. The structure facilitates that the flow items be brought together in a clear way, since these items are typically calculated in separate parts of the model that could be physically quite distant to each other.

The additional clarity caused by separation of period start and period end values also helps the creation of ratio calculations, which are often useful for analysis cross-checking purposes. Figure 8.6 shows the results of calculating the ratio of the value of the fixed assets to the sales within

Figure 8.6 **Basic Ratio Analysis of Assets to Sales**

A	B	I	J	K	L	M
1						
2		FORECAST Calculations				
3						
4		Year 1	Year 2	Year 3	Year 4	Year 5
5						
43						
44	Fixed Assets/Sales					
45	Asset Value [Starting]/Periodic Sales	2.2%	2.5%	2.8%	2.9%	3.0%
46	Asset Value [Ending]/Periodic Sales	2.8%	3.0%	3.1%	3.2%	3.2%
47	Asset Value [Average]/Periodic Sales	2.5%	2.7%	3.0%	3.0%	3.1%
48						

the period. When doing so, the asset base to use could be either the starting value, ending value, or the average of these.

Note that the value of each ratio changes over time: This is due to the forecasting method (i.e. which is based on Volume, and not on Sales Revenue) as well as to the specific values of the assumptions used. Clearly, if the forecasting method were changed to be based on Sales Revenue, then the ratios in Figure 8.6 would simply be a direct reflection (repetition) of the value of the assumptions used.

In addition to modeling fixed assets, the structure is used in practice for many stock-type items, such as:

- The value of finished goods inventory, which can be calculated from the initial value of inventory, the increase in inventory each period (due to production), and the reduction (due to sales of finished goods).
- The amount owed on a bank loan (or other financing arrangements), which can be from the initial loan amount, the periodic interest charges and the repayments made (in accordance with the loan terms). Examples of this are shown in Chapter 12 and Chapter 13.
- The amount of taxes owed, where current period profits increase taxes due, while some taxes may have been paid during the period, thus decreasing the taxes due.
- The value of retained profits (or equity) that a company has. This can be calculated by considering the increases each period (due to profits made by the company) and decreases (for example due to dividends paid to shareholders).

(These approaches are widely used in the modeling of financial statements; see Chapter 17.)

8.4 REVERSE CORKSCREWS

In the previous example (i.e. with a classical corkscrew structure), it was the flow items that are calculated within the model. Thus, as soon as the initial (stock) value is specified, the stock valued at period start and period end are fully determined (and calculated by the corkscrew). However, there are situations where one prefers to model the starting or ending values of the stock items (rather than having them determined by the corkscrew).

Figure 8.7 **Calculation of Net Flow Items**

36	Fixed Assets									
37	Starting			250	281	309	260	273		
38	Net Flow			31	29	-50	13	14		138=139-137
39	Ending		250	281	309	260	273	287		

For example, one may build a model where the ending value of fixed assets (or PPE) is derived as a ratio of Sales Revenue. In this case, the difference between starting and ending values in each period must equal the net flow for the period (i.e. the net effect of increases and decreases in flows). This is called a "reverse corkscrew" because – although the core structure is (at least initially, or in concept) the same – the calculations of flow items are not brought into the corkscrew from the model; rather the net flow amount is calculated within the corkscrew. Therefore, the net flow item may then feed back into other model calculations, rather than being derived from these.

Figure 8.7 shows an example of the calculations of the net flow item, given that the starting and ending values of Fixed Assets are calculated using another method (such as a sales ratio).

However, a "net flow" value (such as row 38 of Figure 8.7) is generally not sufficiently precise or useful. It is typically composed of items with different natures or roles. In this case, the net flow implicitly represents the value of capital investment (CapEx) less depreciation. One of these is a cash item (CapEx), whereas the other is not (depreciation). (More generally, typically one item needs to be linked to the Income Statement, and the other to the Cash Flow Statement; see Chapter 17).

The net flow can therefore be split into its components. However, this requires additional assumptions for one of the components (such as depreciation as a percentage of Fixed Assets). The other component is then fully determined from this (i.e. as a residual or balancing amount).

Figure 8.8 shows a partially completed example, in which there is a row for the increases (row 38) and one for the decreases (row 39). The Fixed Assets at period end are forecast using a sales ratio, leaving the flow items as not yet forecasted.

If we make an assumption regarding depreciation as a percentage of the starting value of Fixed Assets (and using a reversal of the natural sign) then the structure can start to be completed, as shown in Figure 8.9.

Figure 8.8 **Core Structure of a Reverse Corkscrew**

		Method	HISTORICAL DATA		FORECAST Assumptions		Initialization	FORECAST Calculations		
			Prior 1	Prior 0	Year 1-2	Year 3+	Year 0	Year 1	Year 2	Yea
Sales Revenue		Calculated	9500	10200			10200	11236	12378	
Growth %				7.4%				10.2%	10.2%	
PROPERTY, PLANT AND EQUIPMENT										
Fixed Assets		Ratio-Volume		250			250	281	309	
% of Sales				2.5%	2.5%	2.0%		2.5%	2.5%	
Fixed Assets										
Starting								250	281	
Increases (CapEx)										
Decreases (Depreciation)										
Ending							250	281	309	

Figure 8.9 **Inclusion of One Flow Item**

PROPERTY, PLANT AND EQUIPMENT											
Fixed Assets	Ratio-Volume		250			250	281	309	260	273	287
% of Sales			2.5%	2.5%	2.0%		2.5%	2.5%	2.0%	2.0%	2.0%
Fixed Assets											
Starting							250	281	309	260	273
Increases (CapEx)											
Decreases (Depreciation)					20.0%		-50	-56	-62	-52	-55
Ending						250	281	309	260	273	287

Figure 8.10 **Completion of Both Flow Items**

PROPERTY, PLANT AND EQUIPMENT											
Fixed Assets	Ratio-Volume		250			250	281	309	260	273	287
% of Sales			2.5%	2.5%	2.0%		2.5%	2.5%	2.0%	2.0%	2.0%
Fixed Assets											
Starting							250	281	309	260	273
Increases (CapEx)							81	85	12	65	68
Decreases (Depreciation)					20.0%		-50	-56	-62	-52	-55
Ending						250	281	309	260	273	287

Thereafter, CapEx can be determined as the residual balancing amount, as shown in Figure 8.10.

Of course, from this one can calculate related ratios (such as CapEx-to-Sales or CapEx-to-Volume) if these are of interest or useful for cross-checking purposes.

9

Waterfall Allocations

9.1 INTRODUCTION

There are many modeling situations where an item needs to be spread across several categories. An important case is known as a "waterfall." This term is to express the idea of a set of buckets that are placed under a waterfall, which are filled in order until the full amount has been allocated. The buckets each have a limited capacity, except for the last, which is a spill-over (river or lake) of essentially unlimited capacity that absorbs anything that has not been placed in the earlier buckets. (The analogy is not perfect, since it assumes that the total amount of water to be allocated is fixed and known.)

Examples of the uses are:

- Personal tax calculations. In many countries, one's income is split across bands which have different tax rates, so that the taxes due are calculated as the sum of the amount that is derived for each band.
- Incentive schemes. Often, a bonus will apply only if some target is reached. There may also be several targets or bands with the bonus amount or share being different in each.
- Profit sharing. In a basic profit share, profits may simply be split between two business partners (a proportion of total profit is paid to each). However, if the partners consider themselves to have different skills or to contribute different resources, the appropriate incentive system may be for profit share to depend on the level of profits. For example, a partner whose expertise is in growing the profitability of a business may be given a lower share of the initial profits, but a higher share of additional profits earned.

- Financing structures. Some debt financing structures have multiple tranches in which the interest rate that one pays varies according to the amount borrowed. Similarly, in corporate bankruptcy, the residual value is allocated to categories of claims in turn in their order of seniority, with the next category being considered only when claims in prior categories have been fully met.

- Insurance and reinsurance. An insured party may have to bear the first losses (or excess) with the insurance company being responsible for subsequent losses and a reinsurer responsible if losses exceed yet another threshold.

- Royalty and production share arrangements. In many areas, from book publishing to resource extraction, items are split between multiple parties in a banded way.

This chapter uses examples to demonstrate the calculations that are necessary for general waterfalls. It starts with a simple example of sharing cost between two parties and generalizes this to include more layers. It shows the applications of waterfalls in tax calculations and discusses options and variations for the layout and structure within Excel. The Further Topics section covers "capital return" (carried interest) waterfalls, which are commonly used in private equity contexts, and are slightly more complex.

9.2 EXAMPLE I: COST SHARING

The simplest case of a calculation is one in which there are only two buckets. For example, let us assume that a teenage girl would like a new computer that she has not yet selected. Her parents agree that she can choose any computer she wishes, but that she must pay the first $500 of the cost, with the parents picking up the rest. (If the teenager can find a suitable computer for $400, she can choose to buy that, and the parents would pay nothing.)

Figure 9.1 shows a possible way to implement this: The teenager pays the lower of the cost of the computer and the agreed limit for here contribution. This is captured in cell D5 (using the MIN function). The parents' contribution is calculated in cell D6 (i.e. they pay whatever is remaining after the teenager has contributed).

Figure 9.1 **General Split Using the MIN Function**

	A	B	C	D	E
1					
2	Cost of Computer			750	
3	Maximum Contribution of Teenager			500	
4					
5	Paid by Teenager			500	D5=MIN(D3,D2)
6	Paid by Parents			250	D6=D2-D5

Due to the relative simplicity of these calculations, one may not think of this as a waterfall. However, it helps to consider it as such to create a set of calculations that apply when there are more than two layers. To present the example more explicitly as a waterfall, it is first worth noting that the value \$500 – which defines the maximum contribution (or capacity) of the teenager's layer – in fact has several roles here: It represents all of:

- The capacity of the first layer.
- The upper limit of the first layer.
- The lower (starting) limit of the second layer.

Figure 9.2 shows the situation represented explicitly as a waterfall: Rows 2–5 show the features of the teenager's layer, and rows 6–9 show the allocation between the teenager and the parents.

Figure 9.2 **Two Category Waterfall Split – Vertical Layout**

	A	B	C	D	E
1					
2	Layer Features				
3	Starting			zero	
4	Capacity (Maximum Contribution)			500	
5	Ending			500	D5=D4
6	Allocation				
7	Cost of Computer			750	
8	Allocated to Teenager			500	D8=MIN(D7,D4)
9	Remaining for Parents			250	D9=D7-D8

Figure 9.3 **Two Category Waterfall Split – Horizontal Layout**

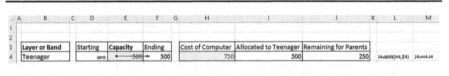

	A	B	C	D	E	F	G	H	I	J	K	L	M
1													
2													
3		Layer or Band		Starting	Capacity	Ending		Cost of Computer	Allocated to Teenager	Remaining for Parents			
4		Teenager		zero	500	500		750	500	250		I4=MIN(H4,E4)	J4=H4-I4

As for much of Excel modeling, there is a choice as to whether to structure the calculations vertically or horizontally. The vertical structure (as in Figure 9.2) can be useful if one intends to add a time-axis (in the horizontal direction). For example, column D could be used to represent the current year, with the columns E, F, G, and so on used for future years (and which may contain a copy of the calculations, perhaps with different input values for the capacity and expected cost). However, the horizontal layout can be used when there is no time axis and is also slightly easier to present when using screenshots and images. For these reasons, a horizontal structure is used the rest of this section. Figure 9.3 shows the same calculations when laid out horizontally.

This structure is easy to adapt to the case where there are three or more layers. For example, let us assume that the parents placed a cap of $1,000 on what they will contribute (which in the first instance would limit the total expenditure to $1,500). However, a favorite uncle agrees to contribute up to $750 to any costs above $1,500 (creating a new upper limit of $2,250), while a rich aunt agrees to pay any costs that exceed that limit. Thus, the last layer (i.e. that associated with the rich aunt) has an unlimited commitment (even as it may never be used, i.e. if the computer costs less than or equal to $2,250).

Figure 9.4 shows the information about the layers (or categories) for this situation:

Figure 9.4 **Capacities of the Multiple Layers**

Layers	Maximum Contribution
Teenager	500
Parents	1000
Uncle	750
Rich Aunt	*infinity*

Figure 9.5 **Completed Calculations of Multiple Layer Example**

	Layers	Starting	Capacity	Ending	Remaining: Start	Allocated to Band	Remaning: End			
	Teenager	zero	500	500	1800	500	1300	I3=MIN(H3,E3)	J3=H3-I3
	Parents	500	1000	1500	1300	1000	300	I4=MIN(H4,E4)	J4=H4-I4
	Uncle	1500	750	2250	300	300	0	I5=MIN(H5,E5)	J5=H5-I5
	Rich Aunt	2250	infinity	infinity	0	0	0	I6=MIN(H6,E6)	J6=H6-I6
	Total					1800		I8=SUM(I3:I6)

Figure 9.5 shows the completed set of calculations. Columns D, E, and F contain the information and calculations regarding each layer, i.e. the value at which it starts, its capacity (or maximum contribution), and the value at which it ends (which is the sum of the starting value and the capacity). It is a corkscrew structure in which the ending values of each layer are used as the starting value of the next. Similarly, columns H to J contain the calculations of the amount that is allocated to each layer. In the case shown, we use an assumed value for the computer purchase of $1,800 (instead of the earlier $750), meaning that the third layer becomes active (so the uncle will have to contribute $300, whereas the rich aunt will not need to contribute). Cell I8 is a cross-check calculation, which shows that the sum of the amounts allocated to each layer is the same as the initial amount for allocation.

It is important to note that the calculations in each row (of Figure 9.5) are essentially the same (as in the other rows): That is, the inputs are the starting value and capacity of each layer, and the starting value of the amount that is remaining to be allocated (i.e. columns D, E, and H). For the first layer, these values are input directly, whereas for the other layers, the two starting values are brought forward by the corkscrew structure. The fact that each line has the same logic means that each is a form of "module" (or model) which can be copied or reused to create a situation with any number of layers.

9.3 EXAMPLE II: TAX CALCULATIONS

In many practical applications, the amount in each layer (which we call "bands" in this section) may be needed in subsequent calculation steps. For example, in income tax calculations, each band could represent the amount of one's income in that band, and where each is subject to a different tax rate.

Figure 9.6 **Waterfall Structure for Tax Calculation**

	A	B	C	D	E	F	G	H	I	J	K	L	M	N
1														
2				Band Definitions				Remaining To Allocate						
3		Bands		Starting	Capacity	Ending		Start	Allocated	End		Rate	Amount	
4		Band 0		zero	15000	15000		45000	15000	30000		0%	0	M4=L4*I4
5		Band Starter		15000	25000	40000		30000	25000	5000		20%	5000	M5=L5*I5
6		Band Medium		40000	60000	100000		5000	5000	0		40%	2000	M6=L6*I6
7		Band High		100000	infinity	infinity		0	0	0		50%	0	M7=L7*I7
8														
9		Total							45000			Total	7000	
10												Rate (Avg)	15.6%	

Figure 9.6 shows an example where one's personal income (cell H4) is allocated to bands to which the tax rates (in column L) are applied, giving (in column M) the contribution of each band to the taxes due. The capacity of the bands is defined in column E, as earlier. Cell M9 adds the taxes for each layer to determine the total taxes due, and cell M10 shows this as a percentage of the personal income.

9.4 OPTIONS FOR LAYOUT AND STRUCTURE

The examples shown in the previous section used a horizontal layout. However, if the model has a time axis (in the horizontal direction), then a vertical layout of the waterfall may be preferable. In general, it is probably fair to say that a vertical structure is harder to read than the horizontal one, simply as it is less compact. However, the principles and calculations are the same.

A vertical waterfall structure can in principle be created in several ways:

- By item. In this case, the presentation is one in which for each item (band start, band capacity) the calculations for all the bands are kept together.
- By layer. This is where for each layer all the calculations are shown, which essentially means that each row in the above structure is transposed into a column.

The following briefly shows examples of each. Figure 9.7 shows the top part of a structure created using the "by item" approach. Note that

Figure 9.7 **Vertical Waterfall Structured by Item**

4	**Starting**		
5	Band 0	*zero*	
6	Band Starter	15000	D6=D17
7	Band Medium	40000	D7=D18
8	Band High	100000	D8=D19
9			
10	**Capacity**		
11	Band 0	15000	
12	Band Starter	25000	
13	Band Medium	60000	
14	Band High	*infinity*	
15			
16	**Ending**		
17	Band 0	15000	D17=D11
18	Band Starter	40000	D18=D6+D12
19	Band Medium	100000	D19=D7+D13
20	Band High	*infinity*	
21			
22	**Remaining: Start**		
23	Band 0	45000	D23=D2
24	Band Starter	30000	D24=D35

Figure 9.8 **Time Axis on a Vertical Waterfall Structured by Item**

	A	B	C	D	E	F	G
3							
4		**Starting**		Year 1	Year 2	Year 3	Year 4
5		Band 0		*zero*	*zero*	*zero*	*zero*
6		Band Starter		15000	16500	18150	19965
7		Band Medium		40000	44000	48400	53240
8		Band High		100000	110000	121000	133100
9							
10		**Capacity**		Year 1	Year 2	Year 3	Year 4
11		Band 0		15000	16500	18150	19965
12		Band Starter		25000	27500	30250	33275
13		Band Medium		60000	66000	72600	79860
14		Band High		*infinity*	*infinity*	*infinity*	*infinity*
15							
16		**Ending**		Year 1	Year 2	Year 3	Year 4
17		Band 0		15000	16500	18150	19965
18		Band Starter		40000	44000	48400	53240
19		Band Medium		100000	110000	121000	133100
20		Band High		*infinity*	*infinity*	*infinity*	*infinity*

the structure effectively is one in which the columns of the Figure 9.6 (from column D rightwards) are placed one under the other, while the labels (column B) are copied as required into each set of new rows.

Figure 9.8 shows the top part of the same structure in which a time axis has been added and in which the band capacity grows over time. For example, such growth may be expected to occur due to general inflation or specific tax policies by the fiscal authorities.

In contrast, when the "by band" approach is used, each row of Figure 9.6 is transposed in turn. Figure 9.9 shows the top part of a structure which uses this approach.

The by-band has the advantage of emphasizing that each band is essentially a separate model (even as the outputs of one are linked to the inputs of the next, i.e. through the corkscrew logic, which is also now less evident).

Figure 9.9 **Vertical Waterfall Structured by Band**

	A	B	C	D	E	F
3						
4		Band 0				
5		Starting		zero		
6		Capacity		15000		
7		Ending		15000		D7=D6
8		Remaining: Start		45000		D8=D2
9		Allocated to Band		15000		D9=MIN(D8,D6)
10		Remaining: End		30000		D10=D8-D9
11		Rate		0%		
12		Amount		0		D12=D11*D9
13						
14		Band Starter				
15		Starting		15000		D15=D7
16		Capacity		25000		
17		Ending		40000		D17=D15-D16
18		Remaining: Start		30000		D18=D10
19		Allocated to Band		25000		D19=MIN(D18,D16)
20		Remaining: End		5000		D20=D18-D19
21		Rate		20%		
22		Amount		5000		D22=D21*D19
23						
24		Band Medium				
25		Starting		40000		D25=D17
26		Capacity		60000		
27		Ending		100000		D27=D25-D26

This means that the "modular" structure of the logic is maintained. The creation of additional bands is easy, since one can in principle use copy/paste of one structure to create a new one.

9.5 FURTHER TOPICS: WATERFALLS FOR SHARING CAPITAL RETURNS OR CARRIED INTEREST

This section discusses the principles of a specific type of waterfall that is commonly in private equity contexts. Generically speaking, a deal will have a sponsor or General Partner ("GP") who will initiate, source, and arrange the deal, but will put in a relatively small proportion of the equity capital. The other parties (Limited Partners, or "LPs") provide most of the equity. Thus, the LPs will demand a larger share of the initial profits, whereas as the deal's profitability increases, a larger share will go to the GP.

Waterfalls are used to allocate any cash distributions between the GP and LPs. The core aspect of the calculations is that:

- The bands are defined using their upper limits (so that their capacity is determined by taking the difference between these).
- The upper band limits are determined from return-on-capital targets (i.e. are based on the capital invested and the return targets agreed by the parties). This point is the one that creates the most complexity in practice.

Figure 9.10 shows an example of the calculations for the first band. Row 3 shows that initial amount invested ($250 million in cell D3) and

Figure 9.10 **Capital Return Waterfall with Single Threshold**

	A	B	C	D	E	F	G	H	I	J	K	L
1												
2		Cash Flow			Initial Capital	Year 1	Year 2	Year 3	Year 4	Year 5	Year 6	
3		Cash Flow			-250	10.0	50.0	300.0	20.0	20.0	20.0	
4												
5		Injections (Period Start)				Year 1	Year 2	Year 3	Year 4	Year 5	Year 6	
6		Within period			250	0	0	0	0	0	0	E6=IF(E\$3<=0,-E\$3,0)
7												
8		First				Year 1	Year 2	Year 3	Year 4	Year 5	Year 6	
9		Starting				250	265	242	0	0	0	E9=D15
10		Return Expectation	10%			25	27	24				E10=E9*\$C10
11		Injections			250	0	0	0	0	0	0	E11=E\$6
12		Upper Band Limit (Based on Capital)				275	292	266	0	0	0	E12=E9+E10+E11
13		Total Distributions up to Upper Band Limit				10	50	266	0	0	0	E13=IF(E\$3>0,MIN(E\$3,E12),0)
14		Total Distributions above Upper Band Limit				0	0	34	20	20	20	E14=IF(E\$3>0,E\$3-E13,0)
15		Ending			250	265	242	0	0	0	0	E15=E12-E13

Figure 9.11 **Capital Return Waterfall with Alternative Value**

	A	B	C	D	E	F	G	H	I	J	K	L
1												
2		Cash Flow		Initial Capital	Year 1	Year 2	Year 3	Year 4	Year 5	Year 6		
3		Cash Flow		-250	10.0	50.0	300.0	20.0	20.0	20.0		
4												
5		Injections (Period Start)			Year 1	Year 2	Year 3	Year 4	Year 5	Year 6		
6		Within period		250	0	0	0	0	0	0	E6=IF(E$3<=0,-E$3,0)	
7												
8		First			Year 1	Year 2	Year 3	Year 4	Year 5	Year 6		
9		Starting			250	278	269	9	0	0	E9=D15	
10		Return Expectation	15%		38	42	40	1			E10=E9*$C10	
11		Injections		250	0	0	0	0	0	0	E11=E$6	
12		Upper Band Limit (Based on Capital)			288	319	309	11	0	0	E12=E9+E10+E11	
13		Total Distributions up to Upper Band Limit			10	50	300	11			E13=IF(E$3>0,MIN(E$3,E12),0)	
14		Total Distributions above Upper Band Limit			0	0	0	9	20	20	E14=IF(E$3>0,E$3-E13,0)	
15		Ending		250	278	269	9	0	0	0	E15=E12-E13	
16												

the cash distributions (in the range E3:J3). For the first band, the return target is set at 10% p.a. (cell C10). This target is applied to the initial capital invested to calculate the band threshold (shown in row 12). Then, the cash distributions are split between those that are within this band (row 13) and those that are above this band (row 14). Distributions within the band are removed from the balance of invested capital, and this balance is used in the corkscrew structure for the starting amount in the next period (row 15 and row 9).

In the simplest case (i.e. with two bands, and a single band limit to define the threshold), the items in the first band (row 13) will be split between GP and LPs according to some percentage, and the items above the threshold (i.e. in the second band) will also be split according to a different percentage (with more going to the GP than for the first band). This latter calculation is a simple multiplication of the total by the percentage of the split for each party, so is not shown.

Figure 9.11 shows the same structure in which the return threshold (cell C10) has been changed from 10% p.a. to 15% p.a. Note that the threshold (band limit, in row 12) increases accordingly.

In practice, one may wish to have three or four bands. For example, with four, the upper limit of the first may be defined by a 10% p.a. return target, the next by a 15% p.a. target, the next by a 20% p.a. target (and the fourth being anything above that). To isolate the returns that are within each band (not below it and not above it), one would copy the structure the required number of times and calculate the difference between the corresponding values of the within-band returns. Thus, the returns in the up-to-10% band are as shown in row 13 of Figure 9.10, the returns in the 10%-to-15% band would be calculated as the difference of the

Figure 9.12 **Capital Return Waterfall with Alternative Value**

				Year 1	Year 2	Year 3	Year 4	Year 5	Year 6
26	Third			Year 1	Year 2	Year 3	Year 4	Year 5	Year 6
27	Starting			250	290	298	58	49	39
28	Return Expectation	20%		50	58	60	12	10	8
29	Injections		250	0	0	0	0	0	0
30	Upper Band Limit (Based on Capital)			300	348	358	69	59	47
31	Total Distributions up to Upper Band Limit			10	50	300	20	20	20
32	Total Distributions above Upper Band Limit			0	0	0	0	0	0
33	Ending		250	290	298	58	49	39	27
34									
35	Distributions in Band			Year 1	Year 2	Year 3	Year 4	Year 5	Year 6
36	First			10	50	266	0	0	0
37	Second			0	0	34	11	0	0
38	Third			0	0	0	9	20	20
39	Final			0	0	0	0	0	0
40									
41	Total Distributions			10	50	300	20	20	20

corresponding values (in row 13) of Figure 9.11 and Figure 9.10. The same calculation would be done using the 20% target, from which the values for the 15% target would be subtracted, to give the returns that are in the 15%-to-20% band. For the last band, the equivalent of row 14 would provide the returns that are within this.

Figure 9.12 shows the result for this example. The top part shows the calculations for the 10% return threshold. The amounts that are within each band are shown in rows 36 to 39. Thus, row 36 contains the values in row 13 of Figure 9.10, row 37 is the difference between these items when comparing Figure 9.11 and Figure 9.10, row 38 is the difference between the items in Figure 9.12 and Figure 9.11, and row 39 is the remainder, taken from row 32 of Figure 9.11.

Figure 9.? Capital Return Waterfall with Alternative Value

corresponding values (in row 13) of Figure 9.11 and row of 9.10. The same calculation would be done using the 20% target, from which the values for the 15% target would be subtracted, to give the returns that are in the 15%-to-20% band. For the last band, the equivalent of row 14 would provide the returns that are within this.

Figure 9.12 shows the result for this example. The top part shows the calculations for the 10% return threshold. The amounts that are within each band are shown in rows in rows 36 to 39. Thus, row 36 obtains the values in row 43 of Figure 9.10; row 37 is the difference between these items when comparing Figure 9.11 and Figure 9.10; row 38 is the difference between the items in Figure 9.12 and Figure 9.11, and row 39 is the remainder taken from row 32 of Figure 9.12.

Interpolations and Allocations

10.1 INTRODUCTION

The waterfall structures discussed in Chapter 9 are a specific case of the general topic of allocations. In waterfalls, an item is allocated to buckets in order. This chapter discusses other forms of allocations, notably, smoothing, tapering, interpolations, and percentage splits. It also covers the basic aspects of the use of triangle structures, while the Further Topics section also discusses some aspects of this.

10.2 EXAMPLE I: LINEAR SMOOTHING

Recall the model used in Chapter 6 in which there were two growth rate assumptions: One was used for the growth rate in each quarter of the first two years, and one for the growth rate in subsequent quarters. In general, the rates will be different so that there is a potentially abrupt change in growth rate at the single transition from the last quarter of Year 2 to the first quarter of Year 3. Often it can make sense for the growth rate (or other input assumption) to taper in a more gradual way over time.

Figure 10.1 shows an example. It is very similar to that in Chapter 6, but with some small differences and additions. First, cell E8 defines the growth rate that is to be used in the first quarter only (rather than for the whole of the first two years). The value in cell F8 is that to which the growth rate should gradually reduce to over the two years, and to settle at thereafter. To aid the calculations, a model period number has been added (row 7). Then, in row 11 (from cells H11 rightwards) a formula has been created which uses a tapered amount for the first eight model periods, and the Year 3+ rate (from cell F11) thereafter.

Figure 10.1 **Overview of Model with Interpolated Growth Rates**

	A	B	C	D	E	F	G	H	I	J	K	L	M	N	O	P	Q	R	S
1																			
2			HISTORICAL DATA		FORECAST Assumpt		Initialization	FORECAST Calculations											
3																			
4			Prior 1	Prior 0	Year 1_Q1	Year 3+	Year 0	Year 1	Year 1	Year 1	Year 1	Year 2	Year 2	Year 2	Year 2	Year 3	Year 3	Year 3	Year 3
5								Q1	Q2	Q3	Q4	Q1	Q2	Q3	Q4	Q1	Q2	Q3	Q4
6								Year 1_Q1	Year 1_Q2	Year 1_Q3	Year 1_Q4	Year 2_Q1	Year 2_Q2	Year 2_Q3	Year 2_Q4	Year 3_Q1	Year 3_Q2	Year 3_Q3	Year 3_Q4
7		Model Period Number					0	1	2	3	4	5	6	7	8	9	10	11	12
8																			
9																			
10		Sales Revenue	98	100			100	108.0	115.6	122.5	128.6	129.9	131.2	132.5	133.8	135.2	136.5	137.9	139.3
11		Growth %		2.0%	8.0%	1.0%	8.0%	8.0%	7.0%	6.0%	5.0%	4.0%	3.0%	2.0%	1.0%	1.0%	1.0%	1.0%	1.0%
12																			

Figure 10.2 **The Formula Used in Cell H11**

```
=IF(H7<=8,
        $G11-(($E11-$F11)/(8-1))*(H7-1),
                                   $F11)
```

Figure 10.2 shows the tapering formula that is used in cell H11 (as well as rightward from there). Within the taper period, the initial amount is reduced by 1.0% in each period. This value is calculated as the difference between the values in cells E11 and F11, divided by the number of periods between them (i.e. it is 7.0% divided by 7, or 1% per period).

(Note that the calculation is based with reference to the initial cell G11 and uses the model period number (cell H7) to reduce by the appropriate amount. The calculation could instead be built in a relative form by reducing from the rate in the previous period; then the model period would be used only in the first part of the IF function to check the condition, but not within the main calculation of the rate.)

10.3 EXAMPLE II: PROPORTIONAL SMOOTHING

In the example above, the tapering (or smoothing) was implemented using an absolute change (1.0%) in the value from one period to the next. This means that, in relative terms, the change was increasing over time. That is, in Quarter 2 of Year 1, the reduction was from 8.0% to 7.0% (or 12.5% in relative terms), whereas in Quarter 4 of Year 2 it was from 2.0% to 1.0% (or 50% in relative terms).

It can often be more appropriate or logical for the relative change to be constant. For example, a reduction over seven periods of a value of 8.0% to a value of 1.0% requires a per period reduction (r) given by:

$$8\% \cdot (1+r)^7 = 1\%$$

(Thus, the reduction is approximately -25% per model period.)

This is sometimes also known as proportional, geometric, or exponential smoothing. Figure 10.3 shows an example of the resulting growth rate profile (and the Sales Revenue is initialized to the value of 100 for simplicity). The example also includes an enhancement to the smoothing calculations: The user can define the start and end dates (using cells E8 and F8), which were implicitly fixed (as periods one and eight) in the earlier example. The process is therefore defined by four parameters i.e. the start and end times, and the starting and ending values (cells C8:F8). Since the smoothing period here is only of length four (i.e. the values in

Figure 10.3 **Proportional Smoothing with Flexible Period Start**

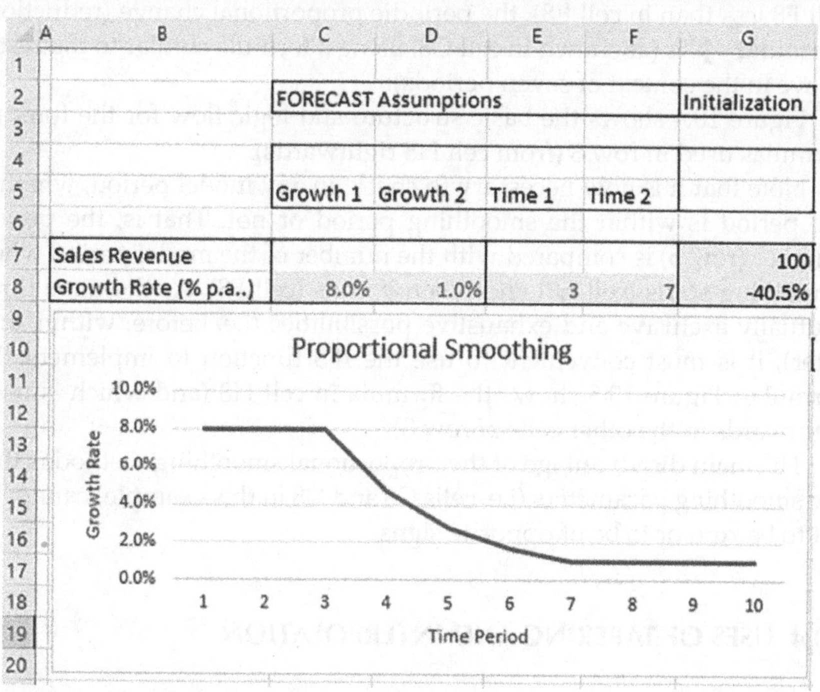

	A	B	C	D	E	F	G
1							
2			FORECAST Assumptions				Initialization
3							
4							
5			Growth 1	Growth 2	Time 1	Time 2	
6							
7		Sales Revenue					100
8		Growth Rate (% p.a..)	8.0%	1.0%	3	7	-40.5%

Figure 10.4 **Logic Flow for Each Forecast Formula**

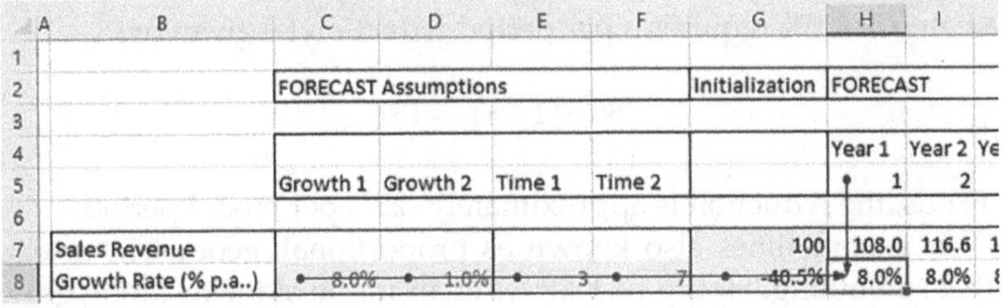

	A	B	C	D	E	F	G	H	I
1									
2			FORECAST Assumptions				Initialization	FORECAST	
3									
4								Year 1	Year 2 Ye
5			Growth 1	Growth 2	Time 1	Time 2		1	2
6									
7	Sales Revenue						100	108.0	116.6 1
8	Growth Rate (% p.a..)		8.0%	1.0%	3	7	-40.5%	8.0%	8.0% 8

Figure 10.5 **Formula Used in Cell H8**

$$=IFS(H5<=\$E\$8,\$C\$8,$$
$$H5>=\$F\$8,\$D\$8,$$
$$AND(H5>\$E8,H5<\$F8),\$C8*(1+\$G8)^{\wedge}(H5-\$E8))$$

cell F8 less than in cell E8), the periodic proportional change (reduction) is around –40% (as shown in cell G8, using a formula similar to that used above in the context of seven periods).

Figure 10.4 shows the basic structure and logic flow for the forecast formulas used in row 8 (from cell H8 rightwards).

Note that it is now necessary to check, in any model period, whether the period is within the smoothing period or not. That is, the period number (row 5) is compared with the number of the model period when smoothing starts (cell E8) and when it ends (cell F8). As there are three mutually exclusive and exhaustive possibilities (i.e. before, within, and after), it is most convenient to use the IFS function to implement the formulas. Figure 10.5 shows the formula in cell H8 (and which is used rightwards in the other cells of row 8).

The main disadvantage of the proportional smoothing method is that the smoothing parameters (i.e. cells C8 and D8 in this example) cannot be set to be zero or to be of opposite signs.

10.4 USES OF TAPERING AND INTERPOLATION

While the examples above showed downward tapering profiles, upward tapering is also possible. Indeed, the formulas used earlier automatically create upward profiles if the values of the input assumptions are set appropriately. There are many applications of upwards or downwards tapering, including to capture that:

- A current slow (rapid) rate in economic growth would increase (decrease) and revert to more normal levels.
- Interest rates or inflation would increase (decrease) from a low (high) level to a long-term average.
- The growth rate of a business (or the return-on-capital it generates) may use short-term assumptions that reflect bespoke aspects of the business but will revert to industry or general macroeconomic averages over time.

In some cases, it can make sense to have multiple tapering periods. That is, to taper from a short-term rate to a medium-term rate, and then from a medium-term rate to a long-term rate. The formulas used would be very similar in principle, but with the appropriate adjustment. For example, one could use the IFS function (in place of IF) to check which of the tapering periods a particular model period is in, and then apply the appropriate formula that determines the tapered growth rate.

It is also possible to use the tapering methodology for multiple variables, and these may interact. For example, due to some assumed productivity improvements that will happen shortly, unit costs may taper downwards in real terms and then start to flatten out. At the same time inflation may start low but taper upwards subsequently. In aggregate, nominal terms costs (as a calculated figure) may therefore initially decrease for several time periods (as the effect of the productivity improvements outweigh the effect of inflation), before increasing (as productivity improvements flatten, and inflation rises). Figure 10.6 shows an example of this.

10.5 TRIANGLES

Triangles are structures that are used to capture the effect of a set of projects that are launched at different points in time, but where each project has the same future generic profile from the time of its launch onwards. Examples of this type of situation include:

Figure 10.6 **Example of the Effect of a Combined Smoothing**

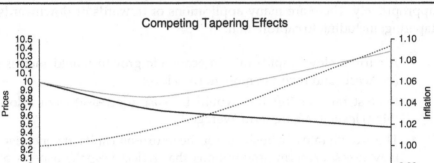

- For a set of items of equipment or machinery that is purchased over time, where each has the same future profile of depreciation. That is, for any piece of equipment, the percentage of the value that depreciates during a fixed time period after its purchase is the same as for any other piece of equipment. For example, every item could depreciate by 20% during the first year after its purchase (even though the items are bought at different times), and similarly each item could depreciate by 15% in the second year after its purchase.
- For a portfolio of insurance contracts, the time profile of claims made on each contract (as a percentage of the premium paid) could be the same (on average).
- For the business planning of a project-based company, the set of future projects that are likely to be available in the future may not yet have been identified specifically, even as their general nature and number is likely to be able to be estimated. Pharmaceutical, biotech, real estate, or natural resources industries are typical of this type of situation.

A triangle calculation has two core inputs:

- A time-specific profile containing the actual dates and amounts for each project.
- A time-generic profile containing the way in which each project develops over time.

Figure 10.7 **Triangle Inputs: Time-Specific Purchases and Generic Time Allocation**

A	B	C	D	E	F	G	H
1							
2	TIME-SPECIFIC PROFILE OF EQUIPMENT PURCHASES		2026	2027	2028	2029	2030
3	Purchases (Start of Year)		800	750	1000	500	800
4							
5	GENERIC DEPRECIATION SCHEDULE		1	2	3	4	5
6	Depreciation % of Initial Value	100%	35%	30%	20%	10%	5%

Figure 10.7 shows an example applied to the depreciation of equipment. That is, row 3 shows the time-specific profile of equipment purchases, and row 6 shows the generic profile of depreciation of equipment after its purchase. (Note that in general, the generic profile can contain any types of values. In this specific example, it is "coincidence" that it consists of percentages that add to 100%. That is, in this particular context, the full purchase value of the equipment, and no more, must depreciate over time.)

Figure 10.8 **Time-Specific Allocations (Step 1)**

		C					
5	GENERIC DEPRECIATION SCHEDULE		1	2	3	4	5
6	Depreciation % of Initial Value	100%	35%	30%	20%	10%	5%
7							
8	Specific Time Profile Triangle		2026	2027	2028	2029	2030
9	2026		35%	30%	20%	10%	5%
10	2027			35%	30%	20%	10%
11	2028				35%	30%	20%
12	2029					35%	30%
13	2030						35%

The first step in using this information is to map the generic profile onto the same axis as that of the specific time profile. Figure 10.8 shows how this can be structured. That is, a set of rows is created that corresponds to the number of specific time periods, and the generic development profile is mapped to that. For example, cell E6 contains the assumption that in the second year after purchase, 30% of any project depreciates, so that a project that is initiated in 2027 will depreciate by 30% in 2028.

Then, a similar structure can be used to form the total depreciation profile by multiplying the items in the (percentage) triangle of Figure 10.8 by the values of the projects launched on the specific dates. Figure 10.9 shows the result of doing that. Note that the values in cells C16:C20 are created by using the formula =TRANSPOSE(D3:H3) in cell C16.

Figure 10.9 **Time-Specific Allocations (Step 2)**

Specific Time Profile Triangle			2026	2027	2028	2029	2030
	2026		35%	30%	20%	10%	5%
	2027			35%	30%	20%	10%
	2028				35%	30%	20%
	2029					35%	30%
	2030						35%
Depreciation			2026	2027	2028	2029	2030
	2026	800	280	240	160	80	40
	2027	750		263	225	150	75
	2028	1000			350	300	200
	2029	500				175	150
	2030	800					280
Total Depreciation		3850	280	503	735	705	745

Figure 10.10 **Triangle Outputs Feeding a Corkscrew**

	A	B	C	D	E	F	G	H
1								
2		TIME-SPECIFIC PROFILE OF EQUIPMENT PURCHASES		2026	2027	2028	2029	2030
3		Purchases (Start of Year)		800	750	1000	500	800
4								
5		GENERIC DEPRECIATION SCHEDULE		1	2	3	4	5
6		Depreciation % of Initial Value	100%	35%	30%	20%	10%	5%
7 21								
22		Total Depreciation	3850	280	503	735	705	745
23								
24		Equipment $ 000		2026	2027	2028	2029	2030
25		Starting		0	520	768	1033	828
26		(+) Investment		800	750	1000	500	800
27		(-) Depreciation		-280	-503	-735	-705	-745
28		Ending	0	520	768	1033	828	883

The output of this could itself be used as the input to a corkscrew that calculates the total value of equipment at any point in time. Figure 10.10 shows an example of this.

Note that the column structure of the triangle could be extended further to the right than that shown above. For example, a project initiated in 2030 will have its final depreciation in 2034. So – while the number of rows in a triangle is equal to the number of specific time periods for the project launches – the number of columns could be larger (i.e. up to the sum of the number of specific periods for project launches plus the number of periods in the generic future development, less one). This is not done here for ease of simplicity of presentation.

10.6 FURTHER TOPICS: TRIANGLES

Finally, it is worth noting that it is possible – using more advanced modeling techniques – to avoid having to build a triangle at all. That is (with reference to Figure 10.10), the values in row 22 can be calculated from those in row 3 and row 6 in a (nearly) direct fashion. The details of this are beyond the scope of this text, but include the following main steps that the interested reader could follow:

- Using algebra to derive the formula for the value of any element in a triangle as a function of the input arrays (whose elements one would refer to with an indexation number for algebraic purposes).
- Using a lookup function (such as INDEX) to create an Excel range which contains the reversed elements of one of the arrays. The need for this reversal can be seen from the algebraic formulation.
- Using the OFFSET function to dynamically reference the relevant part of the original and the reversed array (once again, this becomes clear from the algebraic formula).
- Using the SUMPRODUCT function to multiply the dynamically referenced arrays (i.e. where the OFFSET functions are embedded within the SUMPRODUCT function).

The same calculations can also be created as a VBA user-defined function (see *PFM* for the core elements required).

Part Four

Economic Foundations and Evaluation

11

Breakeven and Payback Analysis

11.1 INTRODUCTION

As discussed in detail in Chapter 2, a core principle in designing a model is to ensure that it calculates the values of the decision criteria. This part of the book discusses the most common measures that are used to evaluate general economic decisions. It is therefore essential to be familiar with these. The chapters in this part are organized as follows:

- Chapter 11 covers breakeven analysis in a single-period context, as well as the time-to-breakeven and payback periods in models with several time periods. These are some of the simplest yet powerful tools for day-to-day business analysis.

- Chapter 12 covers core concepts relating to interest rates and compounding. These build off the growth formulas introduced in Chapter 5 and are fundamental for any form of time-based analysis of the time-value-of-money, discounting, and return on investment.

- Chapter 13 covers calculations concerning interest-only loans and the repayment of fixed-rate loans using constant payment amounts. These are relevant for many types of loans including residential mortgages, vehicle financing, and some consumer loans.

- Chapter 14 covers discounting, the cost of capital, the net present value (NPV), as well as annuity and perpetuity formulas.

- Chapter 15 focuses on the internal rate of return (IRR) as a measure of profitability for a project whose investment and return phases may each have several time-periods. It also discusses some core principles of using economic measures for decision making and provides a comparison of the properties and uses of NPV and IRR in investment decisions.

11.2 SINGLE-PERIOD BREAKEVEN ANALYSIS: PRICES AND VOLUMES

Breakeven analysis is used to understand how key metrics (sales, costs, profit) of a business vary as the price, volume, or other key inputs are altered. The analysis is used not only to generate a better understanding the general behavior, but also to answer specific questions as to what value of price or volume are required so that the business achieves breakeven (that is, to achieve a profit of zero). Such information is often a useful reference for decision-making.

Figure 11.1 shows an example of a simple model that is very similar to some of those used earlier: The assumptions about Price and Volume (cells D3 and D4) are used to calculate Sales Revenue (cell D5), and these are combined with assumptions about Fixed Costs and Variable Costs to calculate cash profit, which for simplicity is

Figure 11.1 **Model Used for Single-Period Analysis**

	A	B	C	D	E	F
1						
2		INCOME				
3		Price Per Unit ($)		10.0		
4		Volume in Units (k)		900		
5		Sales Revenue ($k)		9000		D5=D3*D4
6						
7		OPERATING COSTS (CASH ITEMS)				
8		Fixed Costs ($k)		7000		
9		Variable Operating Costs ($k)	25.0%	2250		D9=D5*C9
10		Total Operating Cost ($k)		9250		D10=D8+D9
11						
12		EBITDA ($k)		-250		D12=D5-D10

Figure 11.2 **Cost Structure as Volume is Varied**

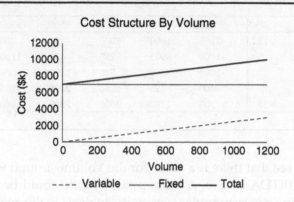

Figure 11.3 **Revenue, Cost, and Profit as Volume is Varied**

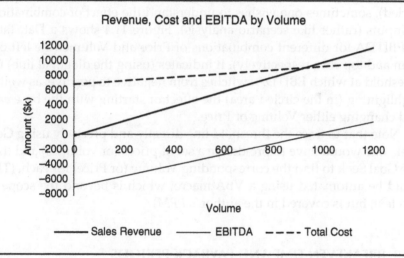

measured here by EBITDA (earnings before interest, tax, depreciation, and amortization).

A DataTable could be used to analyze the behavior of the cost structure (fixed, variable, and total) as either Volume or Price is varied. The results of doing so when Volume is varied are displayed in Figure 11.2.

Similarly, the Sales Revenue (cell D5), Total Cost (cell D10) and EBITDA (cell D12) could be calculated as Volume varies. This is shown in Figure 11.3.

Figure 11.4 **Thresholds and Combinations to Achieve Breakeven**

-250	800	900	1000	1100	1200
8.0	-2200	-1600	-1000	-400	200
9.0	-1600	-925	-250	425	1100
10.0	-1000	-250	500	1250	2000
11.0	-400	425	1250	2075	2900
12.0	200	1100	2000	2900	3800

One can see that there is a value for the Volume around 900 and 1000 for which EBITDA is zero. A more precise figure could be determined either by doing a very granular sensitivity analysis in this region or using Excel's Goal Seek feature. These would give a value for the breakeven volume of around 933.

Although Goal Seek can be useful in such contexts (where one input is varied), sometimes one wishes to understand the effect of combinations of inputs (rather like scenario analysis). Figure 11.4 shows a DataTable of EBITDA for different combinations of Price and Volume (the left column and top row, respectively). It indicates (using the diagonal line) the threshold at which EBITDA switches from negative to positive, as well as highlighting (in the circled area) the effect of starting with the base case and changing either Volume or Price.

Note that to trace the threshold line directly and precisely using Goal Seek, one would have to pre-define a set of prices (or volumes) and then use Goal Seek to find the corresponding Volume (or Price) for each. (This could be automated using a VBA macro, which is beyond the scope of this text, but is covered in the author's *PFM*).

11.3 BREAKEVEN TIME AND PAYBACK PERIODS

In a general forecasting model, there is likely to be a time component. If the project is of an investment-type, there will typically be an initial phase which is loss-making and/or requires capital investment, followed by a phase in which positive returns are made. If the project is at all economically viable, then there will eventually be a time when it achieves the breakeven point. One could measure the time-to-breakeven in different ways including:

Figure 11.5 **Time-Based Forecast from Sales to EBITDA**

	B	C	D	E	F	G	H	I	J	K	L
1											
2			REPORTING	FORECAST Assumptions		Initialization	FORECAST Calculations				
3				Year 1-2	Year 3+	Year 0	Year 1	Year 2	Year 3	Year 4	Year 5
4											
5	INCOME										
6	Price Per Unit					10.0	10.2	10.4	10.4	10.4	10.4
7	Growth %			2.0%	0.0%		2.0%	2.0%	0.0%	0.0%	0.0%
8	Volume in Units					900	972	1050	1102	1157	1215
9	Growth %			8.0%	5.0%		8.0%	8.0%	5.0%	5.0%	5.0%
10	Sales Revenue					9000	9914	10922	11468	12041	12643
11	Growth %						10.2%	10.2%	5.0%	5.0%	5.0%
12											
13	OPERATING COSTS (CASH ITEMS)										
14	Fixed Costs					7000	7350	7718	7949	8187	8433
15	Growth %			5.0%	3.0%		5.0%	5.0%	3.0%	3.0%	3.0%
16	Variable Operating Costs					2250	2479	2730	2867	3010	3161
17	% of Sales			25.0%	25.0%		25.0%	25.0%	25.0%	25.0%	25.0%
18	Total Operating Cost					9250	9829	10448	10816	11198	11594
19	Growth %						6.3%	6.3%	3.5%	3.5%	3.5%
20											
21	PROFIT MEASURES										
22	EBITDA					-250	86	474	652	843	1049
23	As % Sales Revenue					-2.8%	0.9%	4.3%	5.7%	7.0%	8.3%
24											

- (Breakeven time) The time that profit (or some other measure) reaches zero or a specific target.
- (Payback period) The time at which cumulated profits (or the cumulated value of another measure) reach zero or another target.
- (Discounted payback period) The time at which cumulated profits (or the cumulated value of another measure) reach zero or another target, after discounting the items to reflect that value realized in the future are worth less than the same value today.

Note that, in principle, the payback period would be longer than the breakeven time (on the assumption that the profit is negative in the early periods). Similarly, the discounted payback period would be longer than the payback period, since future positive values would be discounted to become smaller than if they were not discounted. This chapter provides examples of the breakeven time and of the payback period. The subject of discounting is treated in later chapters. (A reader with some existing knowledge may have noted that the discounted payback period is equivalent to the first time at which the net present value of cumulated future discounted profit becomes positive.)

Figure 11.5 shows a model with a forecast over time. The values in the initialization column (i.e. column F) are the same as those used in the previous Section (see Figure 11.1), while the forecast methods are the same as those used in earlier models (such as in Chapters 5–7).

Figure 11.6 **Completed Model with Forecast to Cash Flows**

	B	C	D	E	F	G	H	I	J	K	L	M
1			REPORTING	FORECAST Assumptions	Initialization	FORECAST Calculations						
2				Year 1-2	Year 3+	Year 0	Year 1	Year 2	Year 3	Year 4	Year 5	
3												
25	PROPERTY, PLANT AND EQUIPMENT											
26	Capital Investment (CapEx)						496	546	468	501	537	
27	Capital Intensity ($/Volume)			0.500	0.400		0.500	0.500	0.400	0.400	0.400	
28	Capital Goods Inflation			2.0%	2.0%		2.0%	2.0%	2.0%	2.0%	2.0%	
29	Cumulative Inflation Factor					1.00	1.020	1.040	1.061	1.082	1.104	
30												
31	CASH FLOW (Pre-Interest, Pre-Tax)											
32	EBITDA						86	474	652	843	1049	G32=G22
33	CapEX						-496	-546	-468	-501	-537	G33=-G26
34	Total						-410	-72	184	342	513	G34=G32+G33

Figure 11.6 shows the remainder of the model (with the rows 5–24 of Figure 11.5 hidden) and contains the forecast of investments in fixed PPE (similar to previous models). The cash flow is calculated (rows 31–34) by subtracting the CapEx from the EBITDA.

The time-to-breakeven for EBITDA is one year (as seen from cells F22 and G22 in Figure 11.5), while for the total cash flow it is three years (cell I34 in Figure 11.6).

Figure 11.7 **Completed Set of Calculations**

	B	C	F	G	H	I	J	K	L
1		REPORTING	Initialization	FORECAST Calculations					
2			Year 0	Year 1	Year 2	Year 3	Year 4	Year 5	
20									
21	PROFIT MEASURES								
22	EBITDA		-250	86	474	652	843	1049	
23	As % Sales Revenue		-2.8%	0.9%	4.3%	5.7%	7.0%	8.3%	
30									
31	CASH FLOW (Pre-Interest, Pre-Tax)								
32	EBITDA			86	474	652	843	1049	
33	CapEX			-496	-546	-468	-501	-537	
34	Total			-410	-72	184	342	513	
35	Cumulative Total		-250	-660	-732	-548	-206	307	
36									
37	EBITDA +ve?	1		1	1	1	1	1	
38	Total Cash Flow +ve?	3		0	0	1	1	1	
39	Cumulative Total Cash Flow +ve?	5		0	0	0	0	1	

Additional calculations are required to find the time-to-cumulative breakeven. These are shown in Figure 11.7 (once again, some rows and columns are hidden for convenience of presentation). The cumulative cash flow is calculated in row 35. Then the IF function is used to create

Figure 11.8 **The Formula View of the Completed Calculations**

A	B	C	F	G	H
1					
2		REPORTING	Initialization	FORECAST Calculations	
3			Year 0	Year 1	Year 2
20					
21	PROFIT MEASURES				
22	EBITDA		=F10-F18	=G10-G18	=H10-H18
23	As % Sales Revenue		=F22/F10	=G22/G10	=H22/H10
30					
31	CASH FLOW (Pre-Interest, Pre-Tax)				
32	EBITDA			=G22	=H22
33	CapEX			=-G26	=-H26
34	Total			=G32+G33	=H32+H33
35	Cumulative Total		=F22	=F35+G34	=G35+H34
36					
37	EBITDA +ve?	=XMATCH(1,G37:K37,0)		=IF(G22>=0,1,0)	=IF(H22>=0,1,0)
38	Total Cash Flow +ve?	=XMATCH(1,G38:K38,0)		=IF(G34>=0,1,0)	=IF(H34>=0,1,0)
39	Cumulative Total Cash Flow +ve?	=XMATCH(1,G39:K39,0)		=IF(G35>=0,1,0)	=IF(H35>=0,1,0)

flag indicator as to whether the EBITDA is positive (row 37), the cash flow is positive (row 38), or the cumulated cash flow is positive (row 39), with this latter field being the relevant one for the question at hand. The XMATCH function is used (in cells C37, C38, and C39) to find the relative position in each range where the condition is met for the first time, which is in position five for the cumulative cash flow (cell C39). (This result could be used as an input to an XLOOKUP function to find the actual year which corresponds to this relative position, which in this clearly is simply Year 5).

Figure 11.8 shows these calculations in the Show Formulas view, for reference.

12

Interest Rates and Compounding

12.1 INTRODUCTION

Interest rates are a fundamental measure of the cost of borrowing funds (or the return to lending them). As such, their consideration is a crucial part of being able to evaluate the viability of most investment projects and to value financial instruments, companies, and contracts.

This chapter covers the basic definitions and properties of interest rates and their meaning and interpretation. It starts with the use of stated rates and compounding frequencies to determine effective interest rates and then discusses average effective rates. It also describes the core concepts behind implied rates and the bootstrapping method to derive these.

12.2 STATED RATES AND CALCULATIONS WITHOUT COMPOUNDING

Interest calculations are – in principle – based on the use of a "stated" rate, such as 10% p.a. The rate is applied to a borrowed amount to calculate the interest charged during a period. The interest amount (I) accrues in a linear (or proportional) way in accordance with borrowed amount (B), the stated annual rate (r), and the time in years since the loan was initiated (t):

$$I = Brt$$

For example, for an initial borrowing of $100, with an interest rate of 6% p.a., after three months, the interest earned is $1.50 (i.e. 100 times 6% times 3/12). Note that the interest amount scales directly with the loan size, so that one can assume a nominal loan value of $1 for many purposes. However, for presentation purposes it is sometimes more convenient to use larger loan sizes, such as $100.

(In fact, in practice the "stated rate" may never be stated at all, but rather be implicit in other interest rate information that is given. This is discussed in detail later.)

12.3 COMPOUNDING TYPES AND EFFECTIVE RATES

Of course, since interest is accruing constantly, it is not generally practical for the borrower to pay the interest to the lender as soon as an interest charge arises. For example, the lender and borrower could mutually agree that at certain time points (such as at the end of each month), the charges accrued to that point are paid. The balance of the loan outstanding would then – at the very end of each month, after the interest payment has been made – be the same as at the start. On the other hand, it could be agreed that the accrued amounts are added to the loan balance at certain points, rather than being paid. In this case, the balance changes, so that subsequent interest calculations are based on a new balance. Implicitly, future interest is charged on the original balance as well as on cumulated interest charges. This is known as compounding.

The compounding of interest is essentially driven by the frequency or time points at which interest is added to the loan balance. There are various possibilities:

- Simple interest or no compounding. This means that no compounding time points are defined, so that interest charges accrue linearly (indefinitely) as per the formula above.

- Discrete compounding. This means that a finite set of compounding time points is defined (per year). For example, the frequency of compounding could be annual, semi-annual, quarterly, monthly, daily, hourly, and so on. At each of these points, interest earned is added to the loan balance. Thereafter, future interest charges are applied to this new loan balance and hence also to the accrued interest, and so on.

- Continuous compounding. This is the case where compounding is regarded as taking place on a continuous basis. It is the theoretical limiting case as compounding becomes very frequent and increases towards infinity.

Figure 12.1 shows an example. The stated rate is 12.0% p.a. which is compounded quarterly. Therefore, since interest accrues linearly prior to any compounding, in each quarter the interest charge is 3.0% (i.e. 12%/4) of the borrowings at the start of the quarter. The calculations use a corkscrew structure to bring forward loan balances compounded at the end of each quarter, and these are used as the starting values for the subsequent quarter. Therefore, for $100 initially borrowed (cell C7), the interest charge in the first period is $3.00 (D7), and the loan balance after compounding at the end of the first period is $103 (E7), which is then brought forward as the starting balance for the second quarter. The interest charges in the second quarter are 3.0% of the brought forward amount (i.e. $3.09 in cell D8), and so on. The final balance at the end of the four quarters is $112.55 (cell E10). This means that total interest charges are $12.55, so that the "effective" (or observed) interest rate is 12.55% p.a.

It is therefore important to make a distinction between a stated rate and the effective rate. Indeed, without further qualification, a statement such as "the interest rate is 12% p.a." does not define clearly how much interest would be paid (and it would be insufficient to be able to perform calculations or build a model). In fact, many Excel models (that are built with fixed and discrete time periods) directly use the effective rate (rather

Figure 12.1 **Example of Compounded Interest Calculations**

⊿ A	B	C	D	E
1				
2	Stated rate (% p.a)	12.0%		
3	Compounding p.a.	4		
4	Periodic rate (% per period)	3.0%		
5				
6	Period	Loan Start	Interest	Loan End
7	1	100	3.0	103.0
8	2	103.0	3.09	106.09
9	3	106.09	3.1827	109.27
10	4	109.27	3.278	112.55

than the stated rate) as their input assumption, even though this is often not made explicit.

To convert a stated rate to an effective rate (or vice versa) one needs to know the compounding frequency. For discrete compounding, the relationship between the stated annual rate and the effective annual rate is given by:

$$1+r_{eff} = \left(1+\frac{r_s}{m}\right)^m$$

(Where m is the number of compounding periods per year, and the subscripts refer to the respective rates in a way that is self-explanatory.)

With this formula (or by rearranging it), it is simple to convert a stated rate to an effective rate or vice versa. These conversions can also be done using the Excel functions EFFECT (i.e. from stated rate to effective rate) and NOMINAL (from effective rate to stated rate).

Figure 12.2 shows the direct calculation as well as the use of the EFFECT function to convert from a stated rate to an effective rate.

In the case of continuous compounding, one would have:

$$1+r_{eff} = e^{r_s}$$

(Where e is the exponent of natural logarithms, 2.7818. . .).

To use this latter formula to convert between the rates, one would need to use the EXP and LN functions. For example, to work out the stated (continuously compounded) rate from the effective rate, one would use:

$$r_s = LN\left(1+r_{eff}\right)$$

Figure 12.2 **Example of the EFFECT Function**

A	B	C	D	E
1				
2	Stated rate (% p.a)	12.0%		
3	Compounding p.a.	4		
4				
5	Effective Rate (Calculated)	12.55%		C5=((1+C2/C3)^C3)-1
6	Effective Rate (EFFECT)	12.55%		C6=EFFECT(C2,C3)

It is important to note that the above conversion formulas assume that the situation involves pure compounding. That is, the formulas do not apply if any payment of interest or repayment of the loan is made during the period at which compounding takes place. This is discussed in detail in the next chapter.

12.4 CONVERSION OF EFFECTIVE RATES FOR PERIODS OF DIFFERENT LENGTHS

It is often required that one converts an effective rate given for a period of a specific length to that for a period of a different length. For example, one may wish to convert a quarterly rate to an annual rate or vice versa. To convert a rate per quarter into an annual rate one may consider using a formula based on the "power" method:

$$r_{annual} = \left(1 + r_{quarterly}\right)^4 - 1$$

However, this formula would be correct only if the process compounds each quarter (or a multiple of that frequency, such as monthly or continuously). In theory, one could be given an effective rate for a quarter, but which only compounds annually, so that the correct approach would be to use the "linear" method:

$$r_{annual} = 4 \cdot r_{quarterly}$$

Thus, to convert between periods of different lengths requires knowledge of (or an assumption about) the compounding process. Generally, to be able to convert between two periods using the "power" method requires assuming that the compounding time points are co-incident with the ends of the two periods, and that the compounding period length must be a divisor of each of the period lengths. For example, to convert a four-monthly-rate to a six-monthly rate using the power method, requires that compounding is at least bi-monthly (or a multiple of that frequency, such as monthly or weekly). However, if compounding is continuous, then this issue is implicitly dealt with.

In practice, many modelers seem to ignore these implicit assumptions, and conduct periodic conversions using the "power" method without further consideration of the underlying compounding method. (However, for such conversions to be able to be done generally without

Figure 12.3 **Effective Periodic Rates for Different Compounding Frequencies**

	A	B	C	D	E	F	G
1							
2		Effective Rate per Quarter (%)	3.00%	3.00%	3.00%	3.00%	3.00%
3							
4					COMPOUNDING PERIOD		
5		Implied Effective Rates	None - Simple Interest	Annual	Semi-annual	Quarterly	Monthly
6		Monthly	1.00%	1.00%	1.00%	1.00%	0.990%
7		Quarterly	3.0%	3.0%	3.0%	3.0%	3.0%
8		Semi-Annual	6.0%	6.0%	6.0%	6.09%	6.09%
9		Annual	12.0%	12.0%	12.36%	12.55%	12.55%
10		Biannual	24.0%	25.44%	26.25%	26.68%	26.68%

any restriction or specifications requires an implicit assumption that compounding is continuous.)

Figure 12.3 shows numerical examples of these issues. It assumes that we are given an effective quarterly rate of 3.0% and that we wish to convert it into an effective periodic rate for periods of different lengths, depending on the assumption about the underlying compounding frequency. Column C shows the result of there being no compounding (i.e. of simple interest). The effective rate over a two-year period is then 24.0% (i.e. 8 times 3%). However, if compounding were annual (column D), then the effective rate over two years is 25.4% (the 12% annual rate having compounded twice). The diagonal form of shading highlights the main differences that results as one reads across the columns. In cell G6, we see that the effective rate for monthly compounding would be around 0.99% (which – when compounded three times – gives 3%).

12.5 AVERAGE EFFECTIVE RATES

The discussion so far has assumed that the interest rate is constant over time. When this is not the case, it is still easy to calculate total interest charges. For example, given a stated rate of 8.0% p.a. in the first year, and 12.0% p.a. in the second year, if each rate compounds quarterly, the stated rate per quarter is 2.0% (in the first year) and 3.0% (in the second year). Thus, over the two-year period (without any repayments) a loan balance of $1 would grow to approximately 1.2183, since:

$$(1+2\%)^4 (1+3\%)^4 \approx 1.2183$$

Figure 12.4 **Use of FVSCHEDULE Function**

A	B	C	D	E
1				
2	1	2.0%		
3	2	2.0%		
4	3	2.0%		
5	4	2.0%		
6	5	3.0%		
7	6	3.0%		
8	7	3.0%		
9	8	3.0%		
10		1.2183		C10=FVSCHEDULE(1,C2:C9)
11				
12		2.499%		C12=C10^(1/8)-1
13		10.38%		C13=C10^(1/2)-1

The average effective annual rate over the two-year period, would be given by the value (r) which satisfies:

$$(1+r)^2 = (1+2\%)^4 (1+3\%)^4$$

(Therefore, the average effective rate is approximately 10.38% p.a.)

Given the time profile of effective interest rates, the ending loan balance can also be calculated using the FVSCHEDULE function in Excel. Figure 12.4 shows an example. The function is used in cell C10 and is applied to the profile of interest rates in the range C2:C9 (i.e. which represent the quarterly stated rates that are compounded each quarter, as above). The first argument of the function is the starting loan balance, which is set to the notional value of $1. Cells C12 and C13 use this result to calculate the average effective rate expressed on quarterly and an annual basis, respectively.

12.6 IMPLIED RATES AND BOOTSTRAPPING

Bootstrapping is a technique to find the average effective rate within a single sub-period of a longer period, given that the total rate and the rates for all the other sub-periods are known. For example, let us assume that we wish to find the effective rate in the third year of a four-year period given that:

- The effective rate in each of the first two years is 8.0% p.a.
- The effective rate in the fourth year is 12.0% p.a.
- The average effective rate over four years is 10.0% p.a.

This can be done by writing out the compounding formula, using a placeholder for the unknown rate. That is, rate in the third year (r) must satisfy the equation:

$$(1+8\%)^2 (1+r)(1+12\%)=(1+10\%)^4$$

Thus, the rate is approximately 10.6% p.a.

The technique can be used in sequence. For example, Figure 12.5 shows a simplified form of the type of information that one may initially have about yields on zero-coupon government bonds of different maturities. That is, starting from today's date, in the second column, one knows the average effective rate for a one-year period, for a two-year period, a three-year period, and so on. The third column is for information only and shows the implied value of maturity of a $1 loan, given the effective rates in the second column. For example, given an average annual rate of 3.0% compounded over five years, the loan value would be 1.159, as shown in the last row. However, for the fourth column, one does not know the average rate within any year (apart from that for year one, which is simply the average rate, as it is only a one-year period).

Applying the bootstrapping technique, the average rate in the second year must satisfy:

Figure 12.5 **Yield Curve Bootstrapping Assumptions and Context**

Maturity (Years)	Effective Rate (Yield)	Value At Maturity	Implied 1-Year Rate
1	1.00%	1.010	1.00%
2	2.00%	1.040	?
3	2.50%	1.077	?
4	2.80%	1.117	?
5	3.00%	1.159	?

Figure 12.6 **Yield Curve Bootstrapping Results**

Maturity (Years)	Effective Rate (Yield)	Value At Maturity	Implied 1-Year Rate	
1	1.00%	1.010	1.00%	E3=D3-1
2	2.00%	1.040	3.01%	E4=D4/D3-1
3	2.50%	1.077	3.51%	E5=D5/D4-1
4	2.80%	1.117	3.71%	E6=D6/D5-1
5	3.00%	1.159	3.80%	E7=D7/D6-1

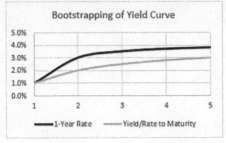

$$(1+1\%)(1+r)=(1+2\%)^2$$

(So that the rate is approximately 3.01% p.a.)
Similarly, the rate in the third year must satisfy:

$$(1+2\%)^2(1+r)=(1+2.5\%)^3$$

(So that the rate is approximately 3.51% p.a.)

The same process can be used in the fourth and fifth years. Figure 12.6 shows the results of this. The right-hand column shows the implied one-year rate within each one-year period, and the graph underneath this shows the time profile of that rates (as per the second and fourth column).

The graph within Figure 12.6 also shows that (in this case) the implied periodic one-year rates are greater than the long-term effective rates to maturity (or yield). This is because the effective rates are increasing but apply over the full period to maturity for each. Therefore, the rate within each single period needs to be higher to compensate for this. For example, since the rate in the first year is only 1.0% p.a., to achieve an average rate over two years of 2.0% p.a., the rate in the second year needs to be 3.01% p.a. (i.e. more than 2.0% p.a.).

13

Loan Repayment Calculations

13.1 INTRODUCTION

The compounding formulas used in Chapter 12 applied only to situations of pure compounding. That is, the assumption was that neither the interest nor the capital on the loan was repaid (prior to the end of the loan term). That is, interest charges (for non-simple interest) were added to the loan balance. In practice, during the life of a loan, payments may be made by the borrower to the lender. This chapter deals with two quite common situations:

- At regular intervals (after one or more periods), the accumulated compounded interest is paid off in full. This resets the outstanding loan balance to the original value, and the compounding process also restarts. The formulas used in Chapter 12 do not apply directly, but more general formulas can be developed to cover this situation (see later in this chapter).

- In each period, a constant payment is made that is sufficient to pay the interest charge in that period, as well as contributing to the gradual repayment of the loan balance. These types of loans are common for residential mortgages, vehicle leasing, and some consumer loans. Since the payment is constant, in the early periods most of the payment is used to cover the interest charges, but as the loan outstanding gradually reduces, the proportion used to pay interest also reduces, and more is used to repay the loan balance. In Excel, there are several functions that deal with situations where the periodic payments and the interest rate are constant over time.

Of course, there are many other possibilities for how interest or loan capital may be repaid. In the more complex cases, the payments could be defined by bespoke agreement between the lender and borrower, and the calculations could require a full set of modeling techniques to reflect the specific aspects of the situation.

13.2 EFFECTIVE RATES FOR INTEREST-ONLY REPAYMENTS

In the case that the cumulated interest on a loan is paid at regular intervals (after one or more compounding periods), then the loan balance resets on each such payment. The compounding process then resets, so that the formulas used in the last chapter are valid only up to that point. For example, if the stated rate were compounded monthly, and cumulative interest is repaid quarterly, then the formulas would be correct only for the first three months (and subsequently in blocks of three months, after each resetting of the loan when the cumulated interest is paid). The formulas used in Chapter 12 can be generalized (providing that there is a certain regularity of both the compounding and interest-repayment profiles). Given a stated annual rate (r_s) that is compounded m times per year, an initial $1 loan would have a value at the end of the first compounding period of:

$$\left(1+\frac{r_s}{m}\right)$$

Now, if full payment of the cumulated interest is made n times per year (such as four, for quarterly payments), then the number of times that compounding occurs before a payment of the interest is:

$$\frac{m}{n}$$

For example, with monthly compounding (m=12) and quarterly repayments (n=4), there are three (i.e. 12/4) compounding periods between each payment. Therefore, just before the cumulated interest is first paid, the compounded loan balance is:

$$\left(1+\frac{r_s}{m}\right)^{\frac{m}{n}}$$

Since the original loan value was $1, the amount of cumulated interest is:

$$\left(1+\frac{r_s}{m}\right)^{\frac{m}{n}} - 1$$

This is therefore also the effective periodic interest rate for the period between each payment.

As the loan balance is reset to $1 after each payment of interest, the process repeats, so that this amount of interest is paid n times per year, and the effective annual interest rate is simply the above figure multiplied by n:

$$r_{eff} = n\left[\left(1+\frac{r_s}{m}\right)^{\frac{m}{n}} - 1\right]$$

Figure 13.1 shows the calculation of this formula in which compounding is done four times per year (i.e. every quarter), while the interest cumulated is repaid twice per year (i.e. every six months). For a stated rate of 12% p.a., the effective rate is 12.18% (i.e. the interest on a notional $1 loan is approximately $0.1218).

(By contrast, without any repayment, the effective interest rates as 12.55% p.a., as was shown in Figure 12.1.)

Figure 13.1 **Use of the Derived Formula to Calculate an Effective Rate Given Repayments**

	A	B	C	D
1				
2		Stated rate (% p.a)	12.0%	
3		Compounding p.a.	4	
4		Periodic rate (% per period)	3.0%	C4=C2/C3
5		Interest Repayments p.a.	2	
6		Interest Paid Per $1	0.1218	C6=C5*((1+C4)^(C3/C5)-1)

Figure 13.2 **Explicit Calculation of the Effective Rate Given Repayments**

	A	B	C	D	E	F	G	H	I
7									
8		Period	Loan Start	Cum Interest-Start	Interest Charges	Cum Interest BEFORE Repay	Repayments	Cum Interest AFTER Repay	Loan End
9								0	100
10		1	100.0	0.0	3.0	3.0	0.0	3.0	103.0
11		2	103.0	3.0	3.09	6.09	-6.09	0.0	100.0
12		3	100.0	0.0	3.0	3.0	0.0	3.0	103.0
13		4	103.0	3.0	3.09	6.09	-6.09	0.0	100.0
14	Total Calculated				12.18 E14=SUM(E10:E13)				

Of course, as well as evaluating the formula, one may wish to check that it is correct by calculating the interest and payments explicitly. Figure 13.2 shows the direct calculations for the same case using a notional starting loan balance of $100 for convenience of presentation. Cell E14 shows the total interest paid ($12.18) during the year. A corkscrew structure is used not only for the loan balance, but also for the cumulated interest that has not yet been paid. This is calculated (in column D) at the start of each period, as well as at the period end but prior to any repayments (in column F), and at the period end after any payments (in column H). Column G shows the profile of payments of interest.

An important case to be aware of is when the interest payment and compounding time points are identical (e.g. both are done monthly, or both are done quarterly, and at the same time). In this case, m and n are the equal and so the above formula reduces to:

$$r_{eff} = r_s$$

That is, since interest is repaid as soon as it would otherwise compound, the interest charges in subsequent periods are not affected by interest charges in earlier periods. The situation is as if the compounding process did not exist, and the stated rate and the effective rate are the same.

13.3 ALIGNING MODEL PERIODS WITH INTEREST REPAYMENTS

The formulas in the previous section are important from a modeling perspective for several reasons:

- If the time axis can be chosen so that it aligns with the dates at which loan interest payments are made, then only the periodic effective rate is required as a model input. There need be no explicit reference to a stated rate or to the compounding frequency. For example, if payments were quarterly and compounding is monthly, then only the effective rate for the quarter needs to be used as a model input, even if this were implicitly calculated from a compounding formula. For this reason, some models may describe the input using only the term "interest rate," without explicitly stating whether it is an effective or stated rate.

- If model periods do not align with the payment dates for the interest, then the modeling could become much more complex. For example, if a model's axis were calendar months, but interest is repaid on the 23rd day of each month, then it would be quite complex to track the correct interest and loan balances with full accuracy. Where interest amounts are small and the loan calculations are an incidental part of a much larger model, these issues could potentially be overlooked (indeed, they are often not even considered at all in many cases). However, if high precision of the interest charges (and loan balances) are essential to the modeling situation, then such issues would need detailed consideration at the design stage, so that the model can be built in the most appropriate way. For example, the time axis could be made more granular, or advanced approaches to the calculations (such as using VBA macros or user-defined functions) may be needed. These are beyond the scope of this text.

13.4 CONSTANT REPAYMENT LOANS USING THE PMT FUNCTION

Excel has an in-built set of functions relating to loans. This section demonstrates the core principles of these. The functions assume that the interest rate and the payment is constant over time and use the effective rate per period as an input. In such a context, the core (five) items that describe the situation are:

- The initial amount of the loan.
- The ending loan amount (if it is to not all be repaid).
- The number of periods (over which the initial amount changes to the ending amount).
- The effective interest rate per period (which must be constant).
- The (constant) amount that is paid each period (and the timing of these, i.e. whether at the end or the beginning of each period).

These items form a "self-contained" set. That is, given the value of any four, the value of the fifth can be calculated (and the assumed timing of payment in one would be the same as that in another). They also correspond to the functions PV, FV, NPER, RATE and PMT. This section describes these functions, focusing on the PMT to demonstrate the core points (which are analogous for the others).

The PMT function calculates the payment that is required in each model period in order to pay the interest charges for the period as well as contributing to the gradual reduction of the loan balance. In Figure 13.3, it is used (cell C8) to calculate that a payment of $26.90 is required in each of four periods so that a loan of initial value $100 is fully repaid by the end of the fourth period, given a periodic (effective) interest rate of 3.0%.

Figure 13.3 **Example of the PMT Function**

	A	B	C	D
1				
2		Loan		
3		Start ($)	100	
4		End ($)	0	
5		Periods p.a	4	
6		Effective rate per	3.0%	
7				
8		PMT	-26.90	C8=PMT(C6,C5,C3,C4)

Figure 13.4 shows the Function Arguments dialog box. Note that the last two arguments (i.e. the ending balance and the timing of payments) are optional. If they are not specified, the default assumption is that the ending value is zero (i.e. the loan is fully repaid) and that payments are made at the end of each period.

Note that the function returns a negative value (i.e. –$26.90 in this case) to reflect that the payments are cash outflows. (This is one potential source of errors. For example, if the function is embedded within an IF statement that checks some condition, it is quite easy to inadvertently overlook that the return value is negative in the statement that checks the condition.)

Figure 13.4 **Function Arguments for the PMT Function**

Function Arguments			?	×
PMT				

Rate	C6	⬆	= 0.03
Nper	C5	⬆	= 4
Pv	C3	⬆	= 100
Fv	C4	⬆	= 0
Type		⬆	= number

= -26.90270452

Calculates the payment for a loan based on constant payments and a constant interest rate.

Type   is a logical value: payment at the beginning of the period = 1; payment at the end of the period = 0 or omitted.

Formula result = -26.90

Help on this function

OK   Cancel

Figure 13.5 **Explicit Calculation of Loan Repayment Using a Corkscrew Structure**

PMT | ✓ ⋮ ✕ ✓ *fx* | =C12+D12+E12

	A	B	C	D	E	F
9						
10		Period	Loan Start	Interest Charges	Payments	Loan End
11						100
12			1	100.0	3.0	-26.9	=C12+D12+E12
13			2	76.1	2.3	-26.9	51.5
14			3	51.5	1.5	-26.9	26.1
15			4	26.1	0.8	-26.9	0.0
16		Total Calculated			7.6	-107.6	
17						
18				D16=SUM(D12:D15)	E16=SUM(E12:E15)	

Figure 13.5 shows the use of a corkscrew structure to create the explicit calculations that confirm that the periodic payment would exactly pay off the interest and the loan over the four periods. Column D contains the interest charges per period (calculated for each period from the starting loan balance and the effective interest rate), with payment made at the end of each period.

The interest charges are decreasing from period to period, as the loan is gradually repaid. Therefore, although implicit in the calculations, the amount of the payment that is being used to repay the loan capital is increasing from period to period.

Note that the core reasons to the function are:

- To avoid having to build explicit calculations and structures. For example, for a 30-year residential fixed-rate mortgage with monthly payments, the explicit calculations would require 360 periods.
- To calculate in a dynamic way the payment amount (i.e. the value of cell E12 in Figure 13.5) or corresponding items for the other functions. If a function did not exist, this amount could be determined by trial and error or by using GoalSeek, but these procedures need to be "run" and are not dynamic (i.e. automatically calculated once the input values are specified).

Figure 13.6 shows the use of the optional parameter to specify that payments are made at the beginning of each period, rather than at the end. The required payment amount (–$26.12) is slightly reduced, since the earlier payment in each period means that interest charges per period are less.

Figure 13.7 shows the corkscrew structure that can be used to verify the effect of making payments earlier. Note that the order of the columns is altered, and that there is also an additional column that is used to calculate the interim loan balance (after the payment) and on which the interest charges for the period are calculated.

Figure 13.6 **Payment Value with Start-of-Period Payments**

	A	B	C	D
1				
2		Loan		
3		Start ($)	100	
4		End ($)	0	
5		Periods p.a	4	
6		Effective rate per period (%)	3.0%	
7				
8		PMT	-26.12	C8=PMT(C6,C5,C3,C4,1)

Figure 13.7 **Explicit Calculation When Payment Is at the Start of Each Period**

	A	B	C	D	E	F	G
9							
10		Period	Loan Start	Payments	Interim Balance	Interest Charges	Loan End
11							100
12		1	100.0	-26.12	73.9	2.2	76.1
13		2	76.1	-26.12	50.0	1.5	51.5
14		3	51.5	-26.12	25.4	0.8	26.1
15		4	26.1	-26.12	0.0	0.0	0.0
16		Total Calculated		-104.5		4.5	
17							
18				D16=SUM(D12:D15)		F16=SUM(F12:F15)	

13.5 CONSTANT REPAYMENT LOANS: OTHER FUNCTIONS

While the above discussion focused on the PMT function, there are other functions which are closely related, and use very similar principles:

- As noted earlier, the functions PMT, RATE, NPER, FV, and PV form a "self-contained" set. Given the values of any four items, the remaining item can be calculated by using the corresponding function (assuming that the timing of payment in one would be the same as that in another).

- The functions IPMT and PPMT can be used to split the constant payment (that would be calculated by PMT) into its two components (i.e. the part used to pay interest and the part used to repay the loan). The split is different in each period since interest charges reduce as the loan balance is repaid. Therefore, these functions require an extra argument (i.e. the period number) when using them. Similarly, the functions CUMIPMT and CUMPRINC (not the perhaps-expected CUMPPMT) calculate the cumulated principal and interest paid between two specified time periods (so that each requires two extra arguments to specify these).

When using these functions, it is important to remember that PMT (as well as FV, PV, IPMT, PPMT, and so on) may return values that are negative with respect to the loan amount. Therefore, when their equivalent values are used as inputs to one of the other functions, the sign of the "natural" values may need to be reversed. Figure 13.8 shows how the natural units (in column C), such as for the ending balance of the loan (if non-zero), need to be reversed to use the function.

Figure 13.8 **Reversal of Natural Values when Using PMT**

	Item	Natural Units	PMT
3	Starting Balance	100	100
4	Ending Balance (0 if omitted)	10	-10
5	Nperiods	4	4
6	Effective Rate per period (%)	3.0%	3.0%
7	Payment		-24.51
8			
9			E7=PMT(E6,E5,E3,E4,E11)

Figure 13.9 shows the verification that the amount calculated by the PMT function when the sign of the remaining balance is reversed (i.e. –$24.51) is indeed the correct amount that is required to reduce the loan value from $100 to $10 over the four periods.

The other functions work in a similar way. For each, the payment amount (and the other three required items) would be the inputs, while the function would calculate the value of the corresponding item. Figure 13.10 shows the use of these functions in each case. That is, column G shows that if a loan has a starting value of $100 (cell G3), an ending value of $10 (used in cell G4 after reversing the sign), and involves four payments (cell G5) of $24.51 (cell G7 with a reversed sign) then the effect interest rate per period (i.e. calculated in cell G6 using the RATE function) is 3.0%. Similarly, cell I5 uses the NPER function to determine that four periods are required to alter a loan balance from $100 to $10 if the periodic interest rate is 3.0% and payments of $24.51 are made per period.

Figure 13.9 **Verification of Calculations Using Sign Reversal**

	Period	Loan Start	Interest Charges	Payments	Loan End
10					
11					100
12	1	100.0	3.0	-24.51	78.5
13	2	78.5	2.4	-24.5	56.3
14	3	56.3	1.7	-24.5	33.5
15	4	33.5	1.0	-24.5	10.0
16	Total Calculated		8.0	-98.0	

Figure 13.10 **Examples of the RATE, NPER, FV, and PV Functions**

	A	B	C	G	I	K	M
1							
2		Item	Natural Units	RATE	NPER	FV	PV
3		Starting Balance	100	100	100	100	**100**
4		Ending Balance (0 if omitted)	10	-10	-10	**-10**	-10
5		Nperiods	4	4	**4**	4	4
6		Effective Rate per period (%)	3.0%	**3.0%**	3.0%	3.0%	3.0%
7		Payment	24.51	-24.51	-24.51	-24.51	-24.51

As noted earlier, when using these functions, one should take care due to the required sign reversals, especially when building complex or embedded formula which use them. Calculations should be checked and tested. Also, although it is not shown here for presentational purposes, by default the functions that return amounts (i.e. PMT, FV, PV, and so on) are formatted as currencies, rather than as natural values.

13.6 PERIODS OF DIFFERENT LENGTHS

As long as one knows the effective rate per period, the PMT function can be applied (i.e. even if one does not know whether the underlying interest rate structure is compounded or not, or with what frequency). However, as noted in Chapter 12, to be able to convert effective rates between periods of different lengths requires an assumption about the compounding frequency (including that it would need to be continuous if we wished to have no constraints about the lengths of the periods in question). To further illustrate this, Figure 13.11 shows a subset

Figure 13.11 **Rates When the Loan Period Is a Multiple of the Compounding Period**

	A	B	C	D
1				
2		Stated Rate per annum (%)	11.88%	
3		Compounding Per Annum	12	
4		Effective Rate per Compounding Cycle	0.990%	C4=C2/C3
5				
6		Loan Periods Per Compounding Cycle	3	
7		Effective rate per Loan Period (%)	3.000%	C7=(1+C4)^C6-1

of the calculations that were described in the earlier Figure 12.3. These show that if we are originally given an effective rate per quarter of 3.0%, and we wish to use PMT to calculate the payments for a monthly payment profile, then the effective rate to use within the function would be 1.0% (i.e. 3%/3) if compounding were quarterly (cell C7), but 0.990% if compounding were monthly (cell C4).

14

Discounting, Present Values, and Annuities

14.1 INTRODUCTION

This chapter covers a range of topics that relate to the use of discounting processes, including:

- An introduction to the time-value-of-money.
- The calculation of discounted cash flows for non-constant discount rates.
- The calculation of discounted cash flows for constant discount rates.
- The use of the NPV function in Excel.
- Formulas for calculation and discounting of annuities, and of perpetuities.
- The use of multi-stage formulas which combine annuities and a perpetuity.

The Further Topics sections describe the mathematical derivation of the formulas for annuities and perpetuities, as well as covering several issues relating to the assumed timing of the cash flow profiles. Note that the related topic of the cost of capital (i.e. the determination of the appropriate discount rate) is discussed in Chapter 16.

14.2 THE TIME VALUE OF MONEY

The time value of money (TVM) refers to the notion that money that is to be received in the future is typically considered to be worth less than money received today. There are many reasons for this. For example, the money could be invested in an interest-bearing account or in a variety of other projects or used for consumption purposes.

To best support a decision process, it is often necessary to reflect this reduction in value. For example, one may have a choice as to whether to invest $100 today to receive $120 in several years' time, or to do nothing today. While the future amount is, in nominal terms, $20 more than the investment, from an economic perspective it is not accurate to value this opportunity at $20. Indeed, depending on when the $120 is received (as well as any uncertainty as to the timing and the amount), it could be that the future $120 should be considered as being worth less than today's $100, so that it would make more sense to not invest at all.

In other words, where the decision criteria involve items that occur at different points in time, it is important to ensure that they can be compared meaningfully. This can be done by choosing a single time point and converting all the items into their equivalent value at that point. Most commonly, the point chosen is today, so that future values are reduced to their "present" values, using a process known as discounting. It is also possible to increase or inflate present values to a future specific date; the key issue is to have all items that are directly relevant to the decision expressed in comparable terms. However, the use of present values often has advantages over the use of future values and is more common in practice:

- It enables the results to be conceived of in a relative sense that is not as easy with future values (e.g. one immediately knows how much $100 today is worth, but it may be harder to have an immediate view on what $500 in 50 years' time is really worth).

- There are many possible future time points that could be used as reference points. Cash flows received before this point would need to be inflated, whereas those received afterwards would need to be discounted, thus adding complexity.

- The conversion of future values to present value terms highlights more clearly the possibility of risk or uncertainty that may be associated with the future values (such as a default by the counterparty or the general uncertainty associated with a business investment project). On the other hand, when inflating a known investment made today one may overlook or de-emphasize such risks. Normally an investor and lender would want to be compensated for such uncertainty.

14.3 CALCULATION OPTIONS FOR PRESENT VALUES

In a sense, discounting is the reverse process to that of applying an interest rate (or inflating or growing the items). A discount rate (or a profile of discount rates that change over time) can be used either to inflate current values to future terms or to discount future values to their present value.

Figure 14.1 shows a profile of cash flows in which each item is expressed in the nominal terms of the time point at which it occurs. For the moment, we also assume that the cash flows occur at the end of each period.

In order to be able to express these items in present (or future) value terms, we need to know the time profile of discount rates. Figure 14.2 shows a profile one-year discount rates that are assumed to apply to each period. For example, the rate 6.0% p.a. is the rate required to discount the cash flows at the end of the second period to the end of the first period, or to inflate the cash flow of the first period to the equivalent value for the second period.

The discount rates are the effective rates per period, and therefore they are to be compounded at the end of every period. (It is typically also implicitly assumed that they are continuously compounded, so that time-period conversions can be done as described in earlier chapters.)

The calculations of the discount factors are in principle very similar to those used in earlier chapters. Figure 14.3 shows the calculations in a step-by-step manner. In row 6, the one-year discount factors are calculated from the one-year rates in row 3 (that is the rate of 10% leads to a discount factor of around 0.91, which is the factor to discount the values

Figure 14.1 **The Assumed Cash Flow Profile for a Discounting Example**

			0	1	2	3	4	5
Cash Flows			-200	-50	100	150	200	250

Figure 14.2 **The Assumed One-Year Discount Rates**

			0	1	2	3	4	5
Discount Rates				5.0%	6.0%	8.0%	10.0%	12.0%

Figure 14.3 **Possibilities to Calculate the Discount Factors**

	A	B	C	D	E	F	G	H	I	J	K	L
1												
2						0	1	2	3	4	5	
3		Discount Rates					5.0%	6.0%	8.0%	10.0%	12.0%	
4												
5		Calculation Options	Method				1	2	3	4	5	
6		Discount Factor per year	Calc			1	0.95	0.94	0.93	0.91	0.89	F6=1/(1+F3)
7		Discount Factor cumulative	Calc			1	0.95	0.90	0.83	0.76	0.68	F7=E7*F6
8		Discount Factor cumulative (2)	FVSCHEDULE			1	0.95	0.90	0.83	0.76	0.68	F8=1/FVSCHEDULE($E8,$F3:F3)

Figure 14.4 **The Discounted Cash Flows and the Total**

	A	B	C	D	E	F	G	H	I	J	K	L
1												
2						0	1	2	3	4	5	
3		Cash Flows				-200	-50	100	150	200	250	
4												
5						0	1	2	3	4	5	
6		Discount Rates					5.0%	6.0%	8.0%	10.0%	12.0%	
7		Discount Factor cumulative				1	0.95	0.90	0.83	0.76	0.68	
8												
9						0	1	2	3	4	5	
10		Discounted Cash Flow - Present Value Terms	287			-200	-48	90	125	151	169	F10=F3*F7
11				C10=SUM(E10:J10)								

in year four to those in year three). In row 7, the factors are cumulated
to each point in time (by multiplication), with this process initialized to
the value of one in the first cell (i.e. in cell E7). Alternatively, the same
result for the cumulated calculations could be achieved by using the FVS-
CHEDULE function, which is shown in row 8.

To calculate the present value of each item, one multiplies the cash
flow by the cumulated discount factor. Figure 14.4 shows this, with the
discounted cash flows being calculated in row 10. Note that since the discounted items are directly comparable, they can be added up (meaningfully) by using the SUM function (cell C10).

Of course, a similar structure could be used even if the discount rate is
constant over time. For example, Figure 14.5 shows such a case, in which
the discount rate is a constant 10% p.a. (The total present value is $242,
which is less than the earlier $287 as 10% is higher than the average rate
implied in the earlier example.)

Figure 14.5 **Constant Discount Rate with Explicit Profile**

	B	C	D	E	F	G	H	I	J	K	L
1											
2				0	1	2	3	4	5		
3	Cash Flows			-200	-50	100	150	200	250		
4											
5				0	1	2	3	4	5		
6	Discount Rates				10.0%	10.0%	10.0%	10.0%	10.0%		
7	Discount Factor cumulative			1	0.91	0.83	0.75	0.68	0.62		
8											
9				0	1	2	3	4	5		
10	Discounted Cash Flow - Present Value Terms	242		-200	-45	83	113	137	155	F10=F3*F7	
11		C10=SUM(E10:J10)									

Figure 14.6 **Use of the NPV Function**

	B	C	D	E	F	G	H	I	J	K
1										
2				0	1	2	3	4	5	
3	Cash Flows			-200	-50	100	150	200	250	
4	Discounted Cash Flow - NPV	242	10.0%							
5										
6		C4=NPV(D4,F3:J3)+E3								

However, if the discount rate is constant, then the NPV function ("net present value") can be applied directly to the original cash flows. That is, there is no need to work out the discount factors explicitly, and so the structure can be made more compact. Figure 14.6 shows this.

Note that the formula in cell C4:

- Applies the NPV function to the range rightwards starting from column F (i.e. to F3:J3).
- Adds the value from cell E3 to this, in order to give the total net present value.

The exclusion of cell E3 from the NPV function is in order to discount correctly for the assumed timing of the cash flows (i.e. that they occur at the end of each period). The time point associated with "present" value in this model is the end of period zero (since there is no forecast in this period). The –$200 cash outflow (in cell E3) is assumed to be a definite investment that is required to initiate the project (and therefore should not be discounted). However, the NPV function discounts from its first input. That is, if the function were applied to the range E3:J3, then the result would be approximately $220 (rather than $242), since every item would be discounted by another year (at a rate of 10%).

14.4 ANNUITIES AND PERPETUITIES

An annuity is a stream of cash flows that arrive regularly over time and are either constant in nominal terms or are determined by a constant growth rate. The valuation of an annuity (in present value terms) depends on four factors:

- The payment in the first period. (All future payments are in proportion to this, so that it can often be convenient to consider this as $1 or $100.)

- The number of periods over which the payment is made. A perpetuity is a special case where the amount is paid indefinitely into the future (i.e. the number of periods is infinite).

- The growth rate per period in the payment amount.

- The discount rate per period.

Figure 14.7 shows an example of a 10-period annuity, with a growth rate of 6% per period and a discount rate of 10% per period, for a notional $1 payment in the first period. The explicit cash flows are calculated in the range E6:N6, and the NPV function is applied in cell C6.

Figure 14.7 **Valuing an Annuity by Explicit Calculation of the Cash Flows**

A	B	C	D E	F	G	H	I	J	K	L	M	N
1												
2	Growth rate	6.0%										
3	Discount rate	10.0%										
4												
5		NPV to beginning P1		1	2	3	4	5	6	7	8	9	10
6	Cash Flows (and NPV)	7.739		1.00	1.06	1.12	1.19	1.26	1.34	1.42	1.50	1.59	1.69
7		C6=NPV(C3,E6:N6)											

Of course, the explicit calculation of the cash flows could become cumbersome (or not possible) if the number of periods becomes large (or infinite). In fact, the annuity can be valued directly using the algebraic relations:

$$A_n = \frac{1}{d-g}\left(1-\left(\frac{1+g}{1+d}\right)^n\right)$$

When d and g are equal, one must instead use:

$$A_n = \frac{n}{1+d}$$

These formulas give the present value at the beginning of the first annuity period (or end of the period prior to the first payment), on the assumption that the cash flows are received at the end of each period. (Other aspects of the terminology should be clear: The periodic rate is g, the discount rate is r, and the number of periods is n.) The formulas can be adjusted if the assumed timing of payments is different (such as if the cash flows were assumed to occur at the beginning of each period; see the Further Topics II section for more).

Figure 14.8 shows the implementation of these formulas directly, which of course do not require that the cash flow profile is calculated explicitly.

Figure 14.8 **Application of the Annuity Formulas**

	A	B	C	D	E
1					
2	Annuity Formula				
3	Growth Rate		6.0%		
4	Discount Rate		10.0%		
5	Number of Periods		10		
6					
7	Annuity Value (of $1 nominal in Period 1)				
8	General		7.739		C8=(1-((1+C3)/(1+C4))^C5)/(C4-C3)
9	With g=d check		7.739		C9=IF(C3=C4,C5/(1+C4),C8)

Note that above formulas are derived using algebra only (see the Further Topics I section). That is, they apply generally to any finite period, and without needing additional assumptions. However, if one wishes for the number of periods to become infinite (that is to create a perpetuity), then one must require:

$$g < d$$

(an economic interpretation is that the value of an asset cannot grow faster – at all points in time – than the cost of financing it, otherwise there would be a permanent opportunity to make an unlimited amount of money with essentially no risk nor cost).

With this assumption, the "perpetuity" value is given by:

$$A = \frac{1}{d-g}$$

For example, using the same input values for the discount rate and growth rate, gives a value of $25.

14.5 MULTI-PERIOD APPROACHES AND TERMINAL VALUES

Since an annuity formula is for a finite period, it is possible to value a series of annuities that occur one after the other. Similarly, it is possible to value a series of (finite life) annuities that is followed by a perpetuity. There are several possible uses of this, but an important common one is to calculate the "terminal value" when valuing a corporation using the cash flow method. That is, the implicit assumption is that the business will continue indefinitely (rather than have a finite life). However, the time axis of the Excel model which forecasts the cash flows in each period explicitly (that are to be discounted for the valuation) is necessarily only finite. The value created beyond this "explicit" forecast is known as the "terminal value."

The terminal value can be calculated by using a perpetuity, or by splitting it into a combination of one or more annuities and a perpetuity. The advantage of splitting it is to deal with the restriction that the growth rate needs to be less than the cost of capital for the perpetuity part. That is, during the annuity period(s), the growth rate may be assumed to be higher than the cost of capital, even as this is not allowed for the perpetuity part.

Therefore, a robust valuation model for an ongoing business could require several components:

- Explicit forecast: Short-to-medium-term. This calculates the relevant line items in each period explicitly. It can be used to capture any specific aspects of the business that one wishes, most notably items that reflect specific aspects or management plans, such as the effect of restructuring programs or other major business changes.
- Annuity value: Medium-to-long-term. This is the value generated in a period(s) in which growth is above the discount rate, but where one does not build a detailed explicit forecast of the business. There could be several such periods (one starting after the other). For example, the growth rate in the first annuity period may be high and it then tapers down in steps from one period to the next, even as the growth rate(s) may all be higher than the discount rate.
- Perpetuity Value: Long-term. This is the value generated in a period of infinite length but whether the growth rate must be less than the discount rate.

Note that when using the multi-phase approach to the terminal value (i.e. at least one annuity and a perpetuity) the "present" values produced by directly using the earlier formulas in fact give the values at the beginning of each phase (i.e. the beginning of the annuity and that of the perpetuity). These values must be further discounted to reflect their present value at the start of the explicit forecast period of the model (i.e. to be expressed in today's present value terms): The annuity value needs to be discounted based on the length of the explicit forecast, whereas the perpetuity is discounted for a period that is the sum of the length of the explicit forecast and that of the annuity period.

Figure 14.9 shows an example of the input parameters required to calculate the terminal value using the two-phase approach. Note that the explicit forecast is not shown here, as it is covered in detail in Chapter 18. However, the information taken from that forecast that is relevant for the annuity and perpetuity calculations is shown. That is, cell C3 captures that the explicit forecast was performed for five periods and that it calculated an ending cash flow of $1000 (cell C4). The assumptions for the annuity and perpetuity phases, and for the discount rate, are shown in the range C7:C10.

Figure 14.9 **Input Assumptions for Two-Stage Terminal Value Calculation**

	A	B	C	D
1				
2		**Explicit Forecast**		
3		Number of Periods	5	
4		Ending Cash Flow	1000	
5				
6		**Terminal Value Assumptions**		
7		Discount Rate	10.0%	
8		Annuity Periods	10	
9		Annuity Growth Rate	12.0%	
10		Perpetuity Growth Rate	4.0%	

Figure 14.10 **Implementation of Two-Stage Terminal Value Calculation**

	A	B	C	D	E
11					
12		**Annuity Part**			
13		Start Time	6		C13=C3+1
14		Cash Flow in First Period	1120		C14=C4*(1+C9)
15		Cash Flow in Last Period	3106		C15=C14*(1+C9)^(C8-1)
16		Value: beginning of annuity period	11057		C16=C14*IF(C9=C7,C8/(1+C7),(1-((1+C9)/(1+C7))^C8)/(C7-C9))
17		**Value: beginning of model**	6865		C17=C16/(1+C7)^(C13-1)
18					
19		**Perpetuity Part**			
20		Start Time	16		C20=C13+C8
21		Cash Flow in First Period	3230		C21=C15*(1+C10)
22		Value: beginning of perpetuity period	53835		C22=C21/(C7-C10)
23		**Value: beginning of model**	12888		C23=C22/(1+C7)^(C20-1)
24					
25		**Terminal Value**	19753		C25=C17+C23

By applying the annuity and perpetuity formulas and taking into account that the initial cash flow for each phase is derived from the ending cash flow of the previous phase (after applying the growth rate), the calculations could be structured and implemented as shown in Figure 14.10.

This terminal value is shown in cell C25, being the sum of the values in C17 and C23. For the final valuation, this terminal amount would be added to the value calculated for the explicit forecast period to give the total value (see the example in Chapter 18).

Note also that the values from the explicit forecast period, the annuity, and the perpetuity are closely linked since:

- The starting value for the first annuity payment will generally be derived from the ending value from the explicit forecast model. For example, it would normally be calculated by applying one period of growth to the ending figure, at the assumed growth rate for the annuity period. (Note that the formula in cell C14 of Figure 14.10 is linked to cell C4 in Figure 14.9.)

- The starting value for the first perpetuity payment is derived from the last annuity payment in a similar way.

Thus, although the value created in the explicit period is typically a small proportion of the total, the ending value from the explicit forecast period (e.g. for the cash flow) is a major determinant of overall value in absolute terms. For example, if the cash flow at the end of the explicit forecast is overestimated by 10%, then so is the entire terminal value.

14.6 FURTHER TOPICS I: MATHEMATICS OF ANNUITIES

To derive the annuity formulas, one first defines the item which sums the first n powers of a number (x) starting from the zero-th power i.e.

$$S_n = 1 + x^1 + x^2 + \cdots + x^{n-1}$$

If x is equal to one, the sum is simply n. Otherwise, the expression can be multiplied by x:

$$xS_n = x^1 + x^2 + \cdots + x^n$$

so that

$$(1-x)S_n = 1 - x^n$$

This gives the fundamental formula for the summation of the powers of a number (when x is not equal to one):

$$S_n = 1 + x^1 + x^2 + \cdots + x^{n-1} = \frac{1-x^n}{1-x}$$

In the case of an annuity whose value in the first period is $1, and which grows (at a periodic rate g) and is discounted (at a periodic rate d), if the cash flows are received at the end of each period, the discounted value (of n periodic payments) at the beginning of the first period will be:

$$A_n = \frac{1}{1+d}\left(1+\left(\frac{1+g}{1+d}\right)^1 + \cdots + \left(\frac{1+g}{1+d}\right)^{n-1}\right)$$

Note that the first item (and all the others) is discounted by an "extra" term, which simply reflects that the cash flows are assumed to occur at the end of each period, but the value is defined as the present value at the beginning of the first period (or end of the period prior to which the annuity starts). The formula would need to be adjusted should the timing assumptions be modified.

We can therefore use the general summation formula where:

$$x = \frac{1+g}{1+d}$$

Note that when d and g are equal (so x is equal to one), one can immediately and directly see that:

$$A_n = \frac{n}{1+d}$$

Otherwise (after conducting a small amount of algebra) the result is:

$$A_n = \frac{1}{d-g}\left(1-\left(\frac{1+g}{1+d}\right)^n\right)$$

When n tends to infinity, this gives the perpetuity formula:

$$P = A_\infty = \frac{1}{d-g}$$

It is also interesting to note that the finite-time annuity formula (with n periods) can be viewed as representing the difference between two perpetuities: One that starts immediately, and the other that starts in n periods. For the second, the starting amount reflects the growth to that time, as well as the discounting required to convert the starting value into present value terms. This second term can be considered as the "non-realized" part of a perpetuity that has been terminated early (i.e. at the end of n periods).

14.7 FURTHER TOPICS II: CASH FLOW TIMING

The assumption on the timing of the cash flow does affect the valuation. For example, with a periodic discount rate of 10%, the value alters by approximately 10% depending on whether each cash flow occurs at the end or at the beginning of the model periods.

Most of the discussion in this chapter was based on the (often implicit, and usually the default) assumption that the cash flows are equally spaced in time and that they occur at the end of each model period. For example, this assumption is implicit when using the NPV function, and was also the default for the loan-related functions (PMT etc., covered in Chapter 13).

If the true timing of cash flows is different than this, there are several approaches that could be used, including:

- Building a more granular model (such as quarterly instead of annual).
- Using an additional discounting (or inflation) factor, for example to discount for an extra half-period of the model.
- Use the XNPV function to work out discounted values. This allows the dates of the cash flows to be specified.

15

Returns and Internal Rate of Return

15.1 INTRODUCTION

The return on an investment is perhaps the most important measure in economic-based decision-making. Without the ability to measure or forecast returns, the reasons to invest would be less clear, and doing so could jeopardize one's capital or reduce one's wealth. This chapter covers the following:

- Measuring the return when there is a single investment and payback.
- Measuring the average return when the investment or payback occurs over several time periods (i.e. the internal rate of return)
- Some core principles in making investment decisions.
- A summary of the main properties of the net present value and of the internal rate of return.

15.2 SINGLE INVESTMENTS AND PAYBACKS

- When a project has a single initial investment, which is followed by a single payback, the calculation of returns is straightforward, and essentially requires no explanation. Nevertheless, the following simple example is used to set the context for the more general calculations that are covered later in the chapter.
- Figure 15.1 shows an example of a single investment followed by a single payback that occurs at a later (currently unspecified) point in time (and where there is no income earned nor costs incurred

Figure 15.1 **Percentage Returns Calculated Explicitly in a Simple Case**

	A	B	C	D	E	F	G
1							
2					Investment	Payback	
3							
4		Cash Flows			-100	120	
5							
6		Return Total (%)		20.0%			
7							

between the two time points). The initial investment of $100 (shown in cell E4 with a negative sign to reflect that it is a cash outflow) results in a payback of $120 (cell F4) in some later period. That is, the absolute amount that is returned (i.e. $120) is $20 more than the investment amount (i.e. $100). The percentage return is 20% over this period (cell D6).

It can be useful to consider the 20% return as the growth factor that is required for $100 to grow to $120. In addition, it is the periodic discount rate that is required so that $120 would discount to $100.

Note that returns are usually expressed in percentage terms, so that projects of different sizes or which occur at different time points can be compared more easily. (Also, the above method of measuring returns is the classical or traditional method. As per the discussion in the Further Topics section in Chapter 5, it is also possible to measure returns using logarithmic approaches, but this is not the focus of this text.)

The return calculated above is a percentage over the investment horizon, which has not been specified so far. As for growth, interest, and discount rates, returns should be expressed either in annual terms, or in terms that are specific to the period length of a model. The conversion from one period to another requires formulas (and assumptions) that are essentially identical to those used earlier in the text in the discussions on growth, interest rates, and discounting (i.e. in Chapter 5, and Chapters 12–14). Figure 15.2 shows that if the payback were to occur only in the second period (rather than the first), then (while the total return may be thought of as being 20%), the average return per period is approximately 9.5%. This value can be calculated using the standard formulas discussed earlier. That is, the periodic return figure reflects the average

Figure 15.2 **Returns Expressed on a Per-Period Basis**

A	B	C	D	E	F	G
1						
2				Investment	Payback	
3					Period 1	Period 2
4	Cash Flows			-100	0	120
5						
6	Return Total (%)		20.0%			
7	Return Average Per Period (%)		9.5%			

increase in value per period, so that the initially $100 investment becomes worth $120 two periods later.

15.3 MULTIPLE PAYBACKS: AVERAGE RETURNS AND THE INTERNAL RATE OF RETURN

In the above examples, each of the investment and the payback phases occurred in a single period only. This allowed for an explicit calculation of returns to be done. However, in general each phase could occur over multiple (typically consecutive) periods. Figure 15.3 shows an example in which the $120 payback is spread over two periods.

With reference to Figure 15.2, while the return has not yet been calculated, it is clear that the average periodic return should be greater than 9.5% but less than 20%. (That is, since $60 is received in the first period of the payback (cell F4), the return is higher than the value in Figure 15.2. Similarly, since $60 is received in the second period (cell G4), then the return is lower than the value in Figure 15.1.)

Figure 15.3 **Example with Payback Occurring in Two Periods**

A	B	C	D	E	F	G
1						
2				Investment	Payback	
3					Period 1	Period 2
4	Cash Flows			-100	60	60

While there may seem to be no obvious way to determine the precise return, Figure 15.4 shows that if a factor of approximately 13.1% per period is used either to inflate (grow) each cash flow into its equivalent future value at the end of the model (rows 6–7) or to discount (deflate) the future values to their present value at the beginning of the model (rows 9–10), then the sum of these values is zero in either case (cells C7 and C10 respectively). In other words, the periodic return is 13.1%.

Figure 15.4 **Inflating or Discounting Cash Flows to Achieve a Total Value of Zero**

	A	B	C	D	E	F	G
1							
2					Investment	Payback	
3						Period 1	Period 2
4		Cash Flows			-100	60	60
5							
6		Inflation to End of Model (Factor)		13.1%	1.28	1.13	1.00
7		Inflated Cash Flows	0.00		-128	68	60
8			C7=SUM(E7:G7)				
9		Discount Factor to Beginning of Model		13.1%	1.00	0.88	0.78
10		Discounted Cash Flows	0.00		-100	53	47
11			C10=SUM(E10:G10)				

This value (13.1%) can be determined by using the IRR function. It uses an iterative "search" process, since in general the value cannot be determined through an explicit calculation. Figure 15.5 shows its use (cell D4); the input to the function is simply the range containing the cash flows (i.e. cells E4:G4).

Note that the IRR function implicitly assumes that the cash flows are equally spaced in time. It provides the effective per-period return (not

Figure 15.5 **Using the IRR Function**

	A	B	C	D	E	F	G
1							
2					Investment	Payback	
3				IRR		Period 1	Period 2
4		Cash Flows		13.1%	-100	60	60
5				D4=IRR(E4:G4)			

Figure 15.6 **IRR with Several Periods of Investment and Payback**

	B	C	D	E	F	G	H
1							
2				Investment		Payback	
3			IRR	Period -1	Period 0	eriod 1	Period 2
4	Cash Flows		11.4%	-20	-80	60	60
5			D4=IRR(E4:H4)				
6	Inflation to End of Model (Factor)		11.4%	1.38	1.24	1.11	1.00
7	Inflated Cash Flows	0.00		-28	-99	67	60
8		C7=SUM(E7:H7)					
9	Discount Factor to Beginning of Model		11.4%	1.00	0.90	0.81	0.72
10	Discounted Cash Flows	0.00		-20	-72	48	43
11		C10=SUM(E10:H10)					

the annual return): If needed, the annualized return would need to be derived from the periodic return using the methods and assumptions discussed in earlier chapters.

Figure 15.6 shows that that function can be applied even if the investment phase consists of several consecutive periods. In the example, there are two periods of investment before payback begins, and $20 of the $100 investment is made in the new (earlier) period. The IRR function (cell D4) shows that the average periodic return is reduced to 11.4% from 13.1% (as should be expected, since some investment is made earlier, so the payback occurs later in a relative sense). The calculations in row 6–7 and rows 9–10 once again confirm (through explicit calculations) that this value is the required factor so that the total of the discounted (or inflated) cash flows become zero.

The internal rate of return is normally defined as the value of the discount rate which results in the present values of the cash flows becoming zero. It corresponds to the average per period return. The following are worth noting:

- A value for the internal rate of return can only exist if there is a change in the sign of the cash flows. (Only an infinite discount rate could turn the sum of cash flows which are all positive or all negative into zero.)

- If the cash flows change sign a second time (such as there being abandonment costs that are incurred at the end of the project), then the correct measure of internal rate of return can become complex. There may (in theory) be two values for the discounted rate that would each result in a zero total for the discounted cash flows. A discussion of this is beyond the scope of this text.

- If the cash flows are not equally spaced in time, one can use the XIRR function (in which the dates must be specified). This function returns the annualized average return (unlike the IRR, which provides a return per model period).

15.4 USING ECONOMIC METRICS TO GUIDE INVESTMENT DECISIONS

This section briefly covers some core principles of making economic decisions. The discussion will implicitly be concerned with situations of "classical investment projects," which are assumed to have an initial investment phase involving cash outflows, followed by a payback phase involving positive cash inflows.

In general, some core rules of using economic analysis are:

- Ensuring that the right decision has been identified and structured (as described in Chapter 2).
- Capturing the full effect of the decision as far as possible (e.g. the effect on linked projects, external effects, cannibalization of existing products if a new one is launched, etc.).
- The analysis should also take taxes into account (e.g. being based on post-tax cash flows).
- Basing decisions on incremental cash flows, not on accounting income. Sunk costs (i.e. those already incurred before the decision would take effect) should be excluded.
- Including opportunity costs or implicit costs or benefits. For example, if a retail shop owns its premises, or is charged a rent that is below true market levels, then this should be considered: It could be that the income that could be received from renting the (owned) space is significant and would constitute a better decision that continuing in business.
- Avoiding double-counting. For example, where interest costs are captured through the cost of capital/discount rates, one should not deduct interest from the cash flows using in the decision analysis.
- Taking the time value of money into account.

Note that the breakeven and payback analysis that we described in Chapter 11 have the advantage of simplicity (from both a conceptual and a communications perspective). They can provide useful information and intuition. However, they do not generally fully reflect these principles. For example, they typically do not take the time value of money into account. Thus, a project which is more than breakeven, and which has a short payback period may still not necessarily be beneficial from an economic perspective. For example, it may not earn enough to be able to cover its cost of capital or the interest payments on any borrowings made to finance it. The net present value and the internal rate of return take the time value of money into account, and these are discussed in detail in the next Section.

15.5 PROPERTIES AND COMPARISON OF NPV AND IRR

In the following, we use the abbreviations NPV and IRR to refer to these items in their concept rather than only to the corresponding Excel functions:

- The NPV accounts for the time value of money by using an explicit discount rate. If the rate is set to be equal to the cost of capital, a project which has a positive NPV would be regarded as one that makes sense from an economic perspective. Further, a classical investment project with a positive NPV would achieve breakeven at some point and have a payback period that exists, so that the NPV criteria is generally stricter than the use of payback-based methods.

- The IRR implicitly uses the time value of money in the decision process. Although the IRR can be calculated without having assessed or assumed a value for the cost of capital, the final decision requires comparison of the IRR with one's cost of capital: If the return is greater than the cost of capital, then the project is regarded as economically viable as an investment. (Since the return is the value at which the NPV is zero, the use – as a discount rate – of a cost of capital that is lower than the return would result in a positive NPV, so the decision methods are aligned in that sense.)

There are also some differences between the use of NPV and IRR that are worth highlighting for completeness, including:

- The NPV can be calculated for any profile of cash flows, whereas the IRR exists only if there is a change in sign in the cash flows.

- The NPV can be calculated even if the discount rates for each time period are different, whereas the IRR implicitly uses (or measures) a single average rate.

- The NPV is an absolute measure, whereas the IRR is a percentage.

- The NPV scales in proportion to the size of a project, whereas the IRR is constant. That is, if there are two projects identical in all respects, except that one is 10 times larger than the other, then the NPV of the larger project is 10 times that of the smaller project, whereas the IRRs of the two projects are the same. (Similarly, if the cash flows are reversed in sign, the sign of the NPV would reverse, whereas the IRR would be unchanged.)

- The NPV decision rule implicitly assumes that there are no capital constraints. It does not measure the returns on investment directly, whereas the IRR does. If there are constraints on the amount of capital available to allocate across several investment projects, then the NPV does not provide a guide to this capital allocation problem. For example, the NPV could select the single project with the highest NPV, and which uses all of the available capital. However, this may not be the best allocation of capital to maximize the returns given the constraints.

There are some additional differences between NPV and IRR that are more subtle, and include:

- For a given discount rate, the NPV can be calculated for any profile of cash flows. However, the IRR requires that the cash flow profile changes sign at least once (and can also be problematic if there are two or more changes of sign, such as if an investment project also has abandonment costs at the end). Thus, NPV can be more suitable in contexts in which one wishes to be able to conduct sensitivity or scenario analysis on the cash flow profile (or where the profile could vary for other reasons).

- The NPV can be calculated directly, whereas the IRR requires the use of iterative methods (which are slower). In fact, by considering the inflation- or growth-based view rather than the discounting one, it is easy to see that the IRR is the rate that must satisfy a polynomial equation that has the same number of terms as there are time periods; the solution of these equations in general requires numerical methods, such as the search algorithm that is embedded within the IRR function.

- The effect of a delay in the full cash flow profile. If all cash flows are pushed out in time, the NPV (as measured today) will reduce. However, the IRR would be unchanged, since the same discount rate would result in the total discounted cash flows being zero (the interim period before the start of the project is implicitly populated with zero cash flows, which are not affected by discounting). The use of IRR by itself as a project reference measure may lead to an underestimation of the true economic impact of a time delay, and to delay decision-making (since there is no apparent loss in value by delaying).

- Replacement (implicitly or explicitly) of part of a long-term forecast with a terminal value that is calculated using a perpetuity formula. In theory, if an explicit forecast contained very many periods (such as approaching infinity), then the IRR of the overall project over its full life could be calculated. In practice, however, the explicit forecast period will be much shorter, so that a terminal value may be added on to this (i.e. as if it were a "final" cash flow for a project of finite life), and the IRR calculated based on this. The question then arises as to whether this IRR is the same as the true value (i.e. that which would arise from an infinite-life project forecast). Note that if the terminal value is calculated using cash flow methods (i.e. with annuity and perpetuity approaches), then one would need to estimate an appropriate discount rate. Also, in the typical case where the project is economically viable, the (true) IRR would be greater than the appropriate discount rate for the terminal cash flows. Thus, the terminal value will be higher than it would be if it had been determined by discounting at the true IRR (which is implicitly done when the true IRR is itself calculated). The overall effect is to increase the IRR of the finite-life project compared to that of the infinite life one. That is, the excess returns in the terminal period (i.e. the returns that are higher than the discount rate) are essentially brought forward in time, increasing the overall IRR. The new IRR is an incorrect reflection of the IRR of the whole (infinite life) project. However, it does correctly reflect the IRR of a modified project which terminates with a sale of the business at the beginning of the terminal period for a value that is equal to its future NPV (thereby also represent a transaction which has zero NPV for the buyer). In fact, the IRR of the infinite life project could be calculated from the finite-life model, by an iterative (repeated) process in which one uses the current IRR estimation as the discount rate for the terminal value, creating a new IRR each time, until the process becomes stable. For example, at the first iteration, the IRR will be higher than the true figure, meaning that the revised terminal value will be less than the true figure, resulting in an IRR that is lower that the true figure. This would reverse at the next iteration and generally settle to a stable value that is the same as if an explicit long-term forecast has been built.

Corporate Finance and Valuation

16

The Cost of Capital

16.1 INTRODUCTION

The cost of capital is an important input to investment decisions, since it is the discount rate required to calculate present values, as well as the rate against which the internal rate of return should be compared. Of course, a lender or borrower could – in accordance with their own return requirements or risk tolerances – choose to use whatever cost of capital (or return hurdle) that they wish to use to evaluate a particular investment. However, to compare projects fairly, a systematic way to determine the relevant rate(s) is needed: For otherwise, the better of two projects could be rejected simply because a higher rate was applied to it for no sound reason other than gut feel or one's mood on the day.

This chapter covers some of the core principles and common methods in determining or estimating the cost of capital. Doing so is an inexact science. This is because – while some theory and structure can be applied to the process – most of the variables are not directly observable. Therefore, it is generally necessary to estimate some items or to make additional assumptions about others. For similar reasons, while the role of risk is a fundamental part of assessing an appropriate cost of capital, it is often difficult to fully quantify.

The main topics discussed in this chapter are:

- A general introduction to the cost of capital, including the role of risk.
- An introduction to the optimal financing mix and the weighted average cost of capital (WACC).
- The properties and benefits of using debt.
- The effects of mixing debt and equity in the capital structure.

- The Modigliani-Miller formulas that relate the levered cost of equity to the debt-equity ratio.
- The Capital Asset Pricing Model (CAPM).

The Further Topics section covers the derivation of the formulas that can be used to lever or de-lever the cost of equity.

16.2 RETURNS, COSTS, AND OPPORTUNITY COSTS OF CAPITAL

The terms "cost of capital" and "returns on capital" are often used interchangeably (as being essentially synonymous). For debt, it is clear that the interest rate paid by the borrower is the same as the interest income received by (returned to) the lender, so that the cost and the return have the same value. More generally, the notion of opportunity costs links these. That is, if an investment in one asset is expected to provide a particular return, then an investor who uses their funds to invest in a different (second) asset foregoes the return that could have been earned on the first. In order to attract investors, this second asset would need to provide a return to potential investors that is comparable to the returns of similar existing assets. Therefore, at least for idealized capital markets (with a wide set of liquid investment opportunities, no transaction costs, and so on, so that asset prices adjust appropriately), the cost of capital and the returns become synonymous. (In reality, a company may earn a return which is more than or less than its cost of capital, at least for some period of time. However, such a situation cannot continue forever, as asset prices will adjust or the company will be restructured or go out of business, and so on.)

16.3 THE ROLE OF RISK IN DETERMINING THE COST OF CAPITAL

The role of risk is fundamental in determining an appropriate cost of capital. For example, suppose we are faced with a choice either to receive in one year's time either $100 as a coupon payment on a government bond or $100 as an expected dividend from a corporation. Since the benefits are the same, the preference would be for the least risky option (i.e. the bond coupon payment). Similarly, given the choice to potentially receive next year a $50 dividend from a large established company, or a $50 dividend from a struggling smaller player, one would generally prefer the first of these.

To use a discount rate methodology to capture such preferences means that in general:

- For any investor or corporation, the cost of debt should be less than the cost of equity (all other aspects being equal i.e. for the same borrower at a point in time). The obligation to repay the interest and principal gives lenders a guarantee that is not present with equity (which is a residual after other obligations and is a noncash item until dividends are paid).
- When comparing two investments, the cost of equity for each may be different (even if neither is financed with any debt). That is, the unlevered cost of equity will depend on (be specific to) the risk associated with each of the equity cash flows.

16.4 THE PROPERTIES AND BENEFITS OF DEBT

The core fundamental properties of debt are: First, that the payment obligation is fixed. Second, that the interest charges are treated as pre-tax expenses and so reduce taxes. (The latter point is generally true for companies as well as some personal situations.)

As a result, there are several potential benefits of using debt, in terms of providing returns to equity holders:

- The leverage effect. This refers to the concept that the presence of debt creates a disproportionate effect on equity if there is any change in the performance of the business. This is a direct result of the payments made to debt holders being fixed (in both the upside and downside cases of changes in performance). So, if the return on equity is higher than the cost of debt, then a substitution of some equity with (cheaper) debt will increase the return on equity even further (and vice versa; see later in this chapter).
- Tax savings. The use of debt reduces tax payments, and the benefit of this accrues to equity holders (since payment to debt holders is fixed).

These points are explained in more detail and illustrated in the following. We start with a simple example and then add some additional features. Figure 16.1 shows two possible financing structures (columns E–F) for a business whose operating profit is $10 per year (cells E5

Figure 16.1 **Threshold Level for Debt-Equity Substitution and without Taxes**

A	B	C	D	E	F	(	H	I
1								
2				Equity	Equity-Debt			
3	Equity			200	100			
4	Debt			0	100			
5	Operating Profit (EBIT)			10	10			
6	Interest Expense	5.0%		0	5	E6=C6*E4	F6=C6*F4	
7	Profit before tax (EBT, or PBT)			10	5	E7=E5-E6	F7=F5-F6	
8	Tax	0%		0	0	E8=C8*E7	F8=C8*F7	
9	Profit after tax (EAT, or PAT)			10	5	E9=E7-E8	F9=F7-F8	
10	**Return on Equity (ROE)**			**5.0%**	**5.0%**			

and F5). In one case (column E), the business is purely equity financed (with $200 of equity). In the other (column F) there is a 50-50 (percentage) split between equity and debt ($100 of each). For simplicity at this point, we assume that there are no taxes (the tax rate in cell C8 is zero). Note that the return on equity in the first structure is 5.0% p.a. (cell E10). If we assume that the cost of debt is also 5% p.a. (see cell C6), then use of debt (i.e. in the second structure, column F) has no effect on the return on equity (cell F10). That is, the returns that would have been paid to some equity holders have been substituted with the same amount of return that is instead paid to debt holders. This leaves the returns to the original equity part unchanged.

This example (in which the return to equity and cost of debt each have the same value) provides the intuition as to why the use of debt will increase or decrease the return to the (remaining) equity, depending on their relative values. For example, if debt were cheaper than equity, then the interest charges on any debt used would be less than the return to equity that would have been paid to the holders of the equity that has been replaced by debt. Thus, the remaining equity holders receive more. Similarly, if the returns to equity were lower than the cost of debt, then the reverse would be the case, with increasing debt reducing the return to equity. This can be explicitly seen with the numerical example in Figure 16.2. This shows two cases (each with two financing structures). In the first case (columns E–F), the operating profit is assumed to be $2 (cells E5, F5), rather than the original $10. In the second case (columns H–I), the operating profit is assumed to be $25 (cells H5, I5). In the first, the original return to equity (cell E10) is less than the cost of debt, so that the use of debt reduces the returns to equity (cell F10). In the second, the

Figure 16.2 **Threshold Level for Debt-Equity Substitution and without Taxes**

	A	B	C	D	E	F	G	H	I
1									
2					Equity	Equity-Debt	Equity	Equity-Debt
3	Equity				200	100	200	100
4	Debt				0	100	0	100
5	Operating Profit (EBIT)				2	2	25	25
6	Interest Expense		5.0%		0	5	0	5
7	Profit before tax (EBT, or PBT)				2	-3	25	20
8	Tax		0%		0	0	0	0
9	Profit after tax (EAT, or PAT)				2	-3	25	20
10	Return on Equity (ROE)				1.0%	-3.0%	12.5%	20.0%

Figure 16.3 **The Leverage Effect of Debt on Returns to Equity (at Book Value)**

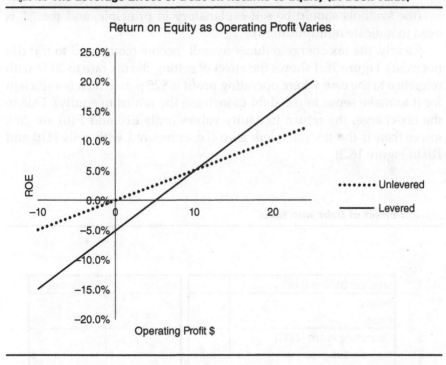

Return on Equity as Operating Profit Varies

original returns to equity are higher than the cost of debt, so that use of debt increases the returns to equity.

Figure 16.3 shows this effect in a graph that covers a wider range of values for the operating profit. For values of the operating profit which result in the pre-tax return on equity being higher than the pre-tax cost of debt, the use of debt increases the return on equity. If operating profit is below this threshold, then the effect is the opposite.

The cross-over point between the two lines in Figure 16.3 is where the returns to equity for a pure equity financed business equal the returns to equity if debt is used (with equity being the residual of the total value less the debt) i.e.

$$\frac{EBIT \cdot (1-t)}{V} = \frac{(EBIT - r \cdot D) \cdot (1-t)}{V - D}$$

This can be rearranged to give:

$$EBIT = r \cdot V$$

(the symbols should be self-explanatory in principle, and the "." is used to indicate multiplication).

Clearly, the tax charge reduces overall income (compared to if it did not exist). Figure 16.4 shows the effect of setting the tax rate to 20%, with reference to the case where operating profit is $25 p.a. (which is sufficient for it to make sense to use debt to increase the return to equity). Due to the tax charge, the return to equity values (cells E10 and F10) are 20% lower than if the tax rate were zero (i.e. compared with cells H10 and I10 in Figure 16.2).

Figure 16.4 **Effect of Debt with Taxes**

A	B	C	D	E	F
1					
2	Interest Offsettable			Equity	Equity-Debt
3	Equity			200	100
4	Debt			0	100
5	Operating Profit (EBIT)			25	25
6	Interest Expense	5.0%		0	5
7	Profit before tax (EBT, or PBT)			25	20
8	Tax	20%		5	4
9	Profit after tax (EAT, or PAT)			20	16
10	Return on Equity (ROE)			10.0%	16.0%

Figure 16.5 **Effect of Debt If Charges Were Not Offset Against Taxes**

	A	B	C	D	E	F
11						
12		Interest Not Offsettable			Equity	Equity-Debt
13		Equity			200	100
14		Debt			0	100
15		Operating Profit (EBIT)			25	25
16		Profit before tax (EBT, or PBT)			25	25
17		Tax	20%		5	5
18		Interest Expense	5.0%		0	5
19		Net Profit			20	15
20		Return on Equity (ROE)			10.0%	15.0%

The fact that interest charges are pre-tax creates a benefit compared to if the charges were not able to be offset against tax. Figure 16.5 shows the fictitious situation that would arise if interest were charged after tax (rather than before), so that interest is deducted from post-tax profit in order to calculate net profit. By comparing cell F20 in each of Figure 16.4 and Figure 16.5, one can see that effect of the tax-deductibility of interest is to increase return on equity by 1.0% p.a.

Thus, the debt creates a "tax shield" whose value is $1 per period in this case. More generally, the tax shield in the period can be written as:

$$Periodic\ Tax\ Shield = r \cdot t \cdot D$$

(This applies when the profits are sufficient to cover interest costs, so that there is a taxable post-tax profit. Tax shields may not be fully utilizable if profits are insufficient.)

16.5 THE FINANCING MIX AND THE WEIGHTED AVERAGE COST OF CAPITAL

The above discussion about the benefits of debt to potentially increase the returns on equity were done in the context of book values. If market values are used, the principle of leverage still applies. However, in efficient markets the equity value would adjust to the level of operating profits, so that the return on equity would always be higher than the cost of debt. Thus, in principle, as much debt as possible would be used.

In practice, the level of debt is constrained by a complex mix of factors, including that:

- A high level of debt increases the likelihood of financial distress (or bankruptcy).
- A high debt level requires that the business be run efficiently, whereas a low level of debt decreases the incentive of any (non-owner) managers to operate the business in the most efficient way (this is one example of "agency costs").
- A high level of debt can signal that management believes that the future opportunities for the business are strong, so that the company (equity holders) wish to keep the future gains. A low level of debt (or high level of equity issuance) could signal that management believe that the equity is overvalued (asymmetric information and signaling costs).
- The returns to investors are affected by the tax rate on interest income and dividend income. So, to attract investors, it is not only the corporate tax rate that is relevant.

In the simplest (or "reference") case(s), we assume that the financing mix is only equity and debt and take only the corporate tax rate into account. The other factors are ignored or considered irrelevant. In this case, the overall cost of capital is known as the weighted average cost of capital (WACC). It reflects the amount of each type of financing (using market values, and assuming that the optimal financing structure is used).

The WACC can be expressed as:

$$WACC = \frac{E}{D+E}k_e + \frac{D}{D+E}k_d$$

The WACC is in principle a pre-tax figure. However, often a post-tax figure is required, and is defined as:

$$Post\,Tax\,WACC = \frac{E}{D+E}k_e + \frac{D(1-t)}{D+E}k_d$$

This can also be written as:

$$Post\ Tax\ WACC = WACC - \frac{t \cdot k_d \cdot D}{D+E}$$

(again, the symbols are self-explanatory).

To avoid confusion, we will refer to the "pre-tax WACC" and the "post-tax WACC" where relevant in this text, and to WACC when the concepts discussed apply to both.

In practice, the WACC is not directly observable, and one may wish to estimate it by building it up from its components, which may have some observable aspects to them (e.g. the cost of debt, equity prices, and taxes). However, when doing so, one cannot simply "fix" a cost of equity and a cost of debt, and then use a weighted average formula to calculate the WACC. This is because the cost of equity changes according to the leverage, as discussed in the next Section.

16.6 MODIGLIANI-MILLER AND LEVERAGE ADJUSTMENTS

An important concept that was developed by Modigliani and Miller (MM) is that – in idealized circumstances (essentially perfect markets with no costs associated with financial distress, and no taxes) – the value of the operations of a business does not depend on the split between debt and equity on the funding side, but rather only on the business operations (i.e. on operational cash flows).

Therefore, for any debt/equity mix, the pre-tax WACC is constant. Further, it must equal the cost of equity for an unlevered business (since this is simply the case in which there is no debt in the mix). Since the cost of debt is constant (as debt levels vary), the cost of equity must adjust so that the pre-tax WACC stays constant. Using the formula in the last section, the cost of unlevered equity is therefore given by:

$$k_u = pre-tax\ WACC = \frac{E}{D+E}k_e + \frac{D}{D+E}k_d$$

Rearranging the left and right sides gives:

$$k_e = k_u + \frac{D}{E} \cdot (k_u - k_d)$$

Note that some practitioners instead use the formula:

$$k_e = k_u + \frac{(1-t) \cdot D}{E} \cdot (k_u - k_d)$$

Each formula is based on slightly different assumptions:

- For the first, the assumption is that the cost of the tax shield is the same as the cost of the unlevered equity (and pre-tax WACC).
- For the second, the assumption is that the cost of the tax shield is the same as the cost of debt, the debt level is constant, and that the tax shield is fully utilized.

(Given the choice, the author has a slight preference for the first, since the availability of the tax shield is closely linked to the performance of the operating earnings of the business.)

In practice, one may also (instead or as well) need to calculate the unlevered values for cost of equity from the levered value. The corresponding formulas are:

$$k_u = \frac{E \cdot k_e + D \cdot k_d}{E + D}$$

Or (as an alternative):

$$k_u = \frac{E \cdot k_e + (1-t) \cdot D \cdot k_d}{E + (1-t) \cdot D}$$

(See the Further Topics section for the derivation of these formulas.)

Figure 16.6 shows the variation in the cost of equity, debt, and post-tax WACC from a generic perspective as the debt-to-value ratio changes (using the first approach for the levered cost of equity).

That is, as debt levels rise, the post-tax WACC will initially decline (due to the tax benefit seen in the earlier formula that compares pre-tax and post-tax WACC). However, due to the potential for corporate financial distress at high levels of debt, the cost of debt, of equity, and the WACC would all start to increase. In practice – on the assumption that debt levels are sufficiently low for there to be no risk of corporate financial distress – the cost of debt is typically assumed to be known and constant, even if debt levels were to be altered slightly. Therefore, it is easy to

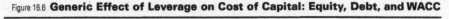

Figure 16.6 **Generic Effect of Leverage on Cost of Capital: Equity, Debt, and WACC**

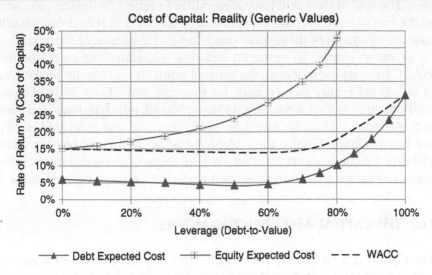

calculate the value of levered equity from the unlevered value (and vice versa) using the formulas above.

Note that – with reference to Figure 16.6 (whose values are nevertheless generic and used for illustrative purposes) – in the absence of the possibility of financial distress (i.e. where the debt-to-value ratio in Figure 16.6 is less than around 50%), then if the WACC is calculated by building it up from its components, the cost of equity is not a figure that can be fixed in isolation of the leverage: A frequent mistake made in practice is to first fix the cost of equity and then calculate various values for the WACC as the debt-equity weights change (without changing the cost of equity when doing so). This mistake is also reinforced by the common misconception that "increasing leverage reduces the average cost of capital as cheaper debt is mixed in with more expensive equity." The analysis above shows that – apart from the tax shield – any increase in debt results in the cost of equity rising in a way that exactly offsets this from an average perspective. Thus, the average cost of capital reduces only due to the tax shield, not because debt is cheaper than equity per se. (In theory, even if debt were more expensive than equity, the cost of capital would reduce due to the tax shield as leverage increases. However, such circumstances would not arise in practice, and even if they did, debt would not be used since there would be no leverage effect on the returns.) In the case of calculating the

WACC when there is the possibility of distress, the situation is more complex: The cost of debt will have a premium to reflect its default risk, and so the cost of equity would also need to be adjusted to reflect this default risk; the treatment of these situations is beyond the scope of this text.

In other words, in common practical situations, to calculate the WACC from its components, the starting point should ideally be the cost of unlevered equity (which may, for example, have been derived from methods such as the Capital Asset Pricing Model, which is discussed later in this chapter). Then, for any debt-equity mix, the cost of levered equity can be calculated. Finally, the weighted cost of capital can be calculated by bring the components together. Any subsequent change in the weighting assumptions should then be used to derive a revised cost of equity.

16.7 THE CAPITAL ASSET PRICING MODEL

The CAPM is a frequently used framework to calculate or estimate the cost of equity in a systematic way. Some of its principles can try to be used for other assets. However, the underlying assumptions used in the CAPM framework often do not correspond well to the properties of some assets. For example, the standard deviation of an asset's returns is an important general measure of risk (and is used in the CAPM). However, it is a symmetric risk measure, and is not a representative for bonds, where the risk of default is a downside, for which there is no corresponding upside. (Therefore, the cost of debt is usually estimated by other means, such as by using or estimating the market rate for debt, which can include considering the yields on investment grade bonds, e.g. US government Treasury bonds.)

Note that, given two assets that are equally risky, an investment with a 50% weighting in each will generally create a portfolio that is less risky than having a portfolio that consists of 100% of only one or other. The intuition behind this is that (simplistically speaking) a risky process could return only a high or a low value, whereas two such processes (at 50% weighting of each, and whose results are added together) will have intermediate "offsetting" cases (where one returns a high value and the other returns a low value), as well as the two extreme cases (i.e. both low or both high). Thus, the average amount of deviation considered over all possible outcomes is lower for the 50-50 portfolio (unless the two outcomes are perfectly correlated with each other, which would eliminate the occurrences of the offsetting cases). This is an illustration of the more general concept of "diversification."

The CAPM is called a "model" as it is a conceptual approach that postulates how asset prices should adjust so that the return gained by investing in any asset compensates for the risk taken. The CAPM states that an investor should not expect to be compensated for taking risk that is diversifiable, since the taking of this risk is unnecessary (due to the possibility to diversify). It assumes that asset prices adjust in order to provide a return only for non-diversifiable risk. This type of risk is known as "market risk" (the market is the set of all assets in the world that can be invested in): If one were to invest one's money in a small proportion of the market, then no more diversification is possible.

More specifically, the CAPM states that the expected return of a risky asset should be driven by a risk premium that depends on two asset-specific factors:

- The standard deviation of the asset's returns.
- The correlation of these returns with the market.

If the first item is equal to zero, then there would be no risk at all. If the second item were zero, then (although there is still variability and hence risk is present), all the risk is diversifiable, and should not be expected to earn a return. Finally, since an investment in the market must earn the market return (and is still risky, since the market is perfectly correlated with itself), the market's standard deviation acts as a scaling (normalizing) factor within the calculations. That is, the risk premium (called the beta) for the asset can be written as:

$$\beta_a = \frac{\rho_a \sigma_a}{\sigma_m}$$

Thus, the CAPM states that the expected return for the asset should be given by:

$$r_a = r_f + \frac{\rho_a \sigma_a}{\sigma_m} \left(r_m - r_f \right)$$

(where the letter rho represents the correlation, the letters sigma are – according to its respective subscripts – the standard deviations of the asset and the market, and the letter r – also according to its subscripts – is the returns of the asset, risk-free asset, or market).

Figure 16.7 **A Simple Example of the Calculation of the Expected Return**

	A	B	C	D	E
1					
2	Risk-free rate		2.5%		
3	Risk premium		5.0%		
4	Beta of asset		1.50		
5	**Expected Return of asset**		**10.0%**		C5=C2+C4*C3

The beta of an asset is often discussed or quoted as a single value (rather than being decomposed into the correlation and the standard deviations). However, the consideration of the separate components can be useful to better understand of the nature of the risk or to assist one to estimate a beta in cases where there are no published values, or where there is insufficient data to estimate it accurately using statistical measures. Note that, the beta does depend on leverage (see later), so that it can be quoted on a levered or unlevered basis.

Figure 16.7 shows a simple example of the calculations in practice (on the assumption that the parameter values are known, and the leverage is known but not explicitly stated here). It uses a risk-free rate of 2.5% p.a., a risk premium of 5.0% p.a., and a beta of 1.5. This gives an expected return of 10% p.a.

In fact, the estimation of the values of the parameters to use in these calculations is a non-trivial subject (to which whole books are devoted and remains a topic of academic research). However, it is known from statistical theory that the formula for beta is also that for the slope of the regression line of the asset's returns (y-axis) against the market's returns (x-axis). So, in theory, regression techniques can be used to estimate beta from historical data (see Chapter 20). On the other hand, when doing so, one should not forget that historical data:

- Is subject to uncertainty, so that larger data sets are required to establish reasonable intervals of confidence for the true parameters.
- May be incomplete. For example, in theory, any dividends paid need to be added to the returns data.
- May be inconsistent. The beta changes according to the levels of leverage and tax (which may not have been constant in a historical data set with many data points).

- May contain measurement error. For example, data for some geographies may be reported late due to time differences or processing issues.

Therefore, to estimate the beta for an asset with any degree of accuracy one may need to use some form of estimates or averaging in which the data from comparable assets is also used, including using industry-averaging, for example.

Regarding the effects of leverage, depending on which process (or data source) is used, one may have to either leverage it or deleverage the beta. Since the cost of equity and beta vary linearly together, the leveraging and deleveraging can be done using formulas analogous to those shown earlier for the cost of equity. For example, to leverage a beta one could use either of the formulas (in accordance with the earlier discussion regarding assumptions on the cost of the tax shield):

$$\beta_e = \beta_u + \frac{D}{E} \cdot (\beta_u - \beta_d)$$

Or

$$\beta_e = \beta_u + \frac{(1-t) \cdot D}{E} \cdot (\beta_u - \beta_d)$$

It is sometimes also assumed that the beta of the debt is zero, which simplifies the implementation. (However, it is also worth recalling that debt can be "risky" even if it is default free. For example, the value of US government debt will fluctuate as interest rates change, even though there is in principle no risk of default.)

The formulas to delever are also straightforward and can be derived from these but are not shown here for the sake of brevity.

16.8 FURTHER TOPICS: DERIVATION OF LEVERAGING AND DELEVERAGING FORMULAS

The formulas to lever or delever the cost of equity (and the beta) can be derived using a "Balance Sheet" approach. First, the value of the equity plus debt equals the value of the unlevered firm (operations) plus that of the tax shield:

$$V_u + V_{tx} = E + D$$

Second, the weighted returns (or cost) of the items on each side must also be the same (since any changes to one side must result in the other side having the same change at an aggregate level):

$$k_u \cdot V_u + k_{tx} \cdot V_{tx} = k_e \cdot E + k_d \cdot D$$

Further, multiplying every term in the first equation by the cost of unlevered equity, it can be restated as:

$$k_u \cdot V_u + k_u \cdot V_{tx} = k_u \cdot E + k_u \cdot D$$

(the terminology should be self-explanatory).

Subtracting the second equation from the restated form of the first (noting that the first term in each is the same, as so cancel each other) gives the ("difference") equation:

$$(k_u - k_{tx}) \cdot V_{tx} = (k_u - k_e) \cdot E + (k_u - k_d) \cdot D$$

Note that (to this point) no assumptions have been made as to the cost or value of the tax shield. However, assuming now that the cost of the tax shield is the same as that of unlevered equity, i.e.

$$k_{tx} = k_u$$

. . . then the left-hand-side of the difference equation is zero, and the equation can be rearranged to give:

$$k_e = k_u + \frac{D}{E} \cdot (k_u - k_d)$$

It is important to note that this formula does reflect that a tax shield is present and has been used, even if no "(1–t)" term is explicitly present. In fact, some practitioners use an alternative formula:

$$k_e = k_u + \frac{(1-t) \cdot D}{E} \cdot (k_u - k_d)$$

This can also be derived in a similar way. To do so, using the difference equation, one assumes first that cost of the tax shield is the same as the cost of debt, i.e.

$$k_{tx} = k_d$$

and second that its value is fully realized:

$$V_{tx} = t \cdot D$$

Rearranging the difference equations gives:

$$k_e = k_u + \frac{(1-t) \cdot D}{E} \cdot (k_u - k_d)$$

Note that the explicit appearance of the tax term in the latter formula is appealing, although it is not a requirement in order that taxes have been considered in the analysis.

17

Financial Statement Modeling

17.1 INTRODUCTION

The forecasting of financial statements is a common area of application in financial modeling. The forecast needs to respect fundamental accounting principles, not only so that each statement is internally consistent, but also so that the statements are consistent with each other. This chapter covers:

- A summary of the meaning of each of the main financial statements.
- An overview of the challenges involved in building financial statement models.
- A simple example to demonstrate the core principles involved in building an integrated financial statement model, including the need to have a dynamic financing adjustment mechanism.
- An overview of the types of features that real-life models may typically include, over and above those covered in the simple example.
- A summary of the main steps involved in building a general financial statement model for corporate contexts.
- Some key best practices to reduce errors and maximize transparency and efficiency.

The Further Topics section covers the subject of circularities, which are sometimes used for interest calculations.

17.2 FINANCIAL STATEMENT ESSENTIALS

The main financial statements that are most relevant from a modeling perspective are:

- Income Statement. This contains "flow" items as recognized in the accounting period. It shows sales, operating costs and profits, interest income or expenses, tax, and net income (and perhaps other items).
- Cash Flow Statement. This contains the cash items as incurred in the period. It typically also classifies the cash flows as being of an operating, investing, or financing nature.
- Balance Sheet. This consists of "stock" items. It has two sides: One summarizes the values of the assets (such as cash, equipment, raw materials, finished goods, accounts receivable, and so on) and essentially answers: "What does the business own?" or "How has the capital been deployed?" The other shows the value of the ownership or liabilities. It answers: "Who has funded the business?" or "What types of capital is employed?" It consists of equity (owners' capital), debt, accounts payable, tax liabilities, other external claims, and so on. Equity is made up of the initial equity (share) capital and cumulated retained profits (i.e. those which have not been distributed as dividends).

(Other statements or reports, such as the Statement of Changes in Equity, are usually simple to produce once a model has been completed in which the three main statements above have been created.)

The total values of each side of the Balance Sheet must be equal: Each side is simply a different way of expressing the value of the business. The fact that the Balance Sheet "balances" is often expressed through the "Accounting Equation":

$$ASSETS = LIABILITIES$$

In order to distinguish equity from non-equity claims, this is sometimes written as:

$$ASSETS = LIABILITIES + EQUITY$$

(where liabilities is then understood to be non-equity liabilities only).

This equation must hold at all points in time, including before and after any specific business transaction. For example, if a business is created with a $200 injection of cash from the owners, then the asset side has a value of $200 (since this is what the business owns) and the liability side consists of $200 of owners' equity. If the business purchased an item on credit for $50, then the asset side would total $250 ($50 for the item, and $200 in cash), while the liabilities would also be $250 ($50 in accounts payable, and $200 in equity). If the item is sold for $75, and the customer pays for it in cash immediately, and the supplier invoice is settled, then if there were no taxes, the final Balance Sheet would have assets of $225 (all cash), while the liabilities side would consist of $225 of equity in total, of which $200 is the start-up capital, and $25 is retained earnings. This last set of transactions would also impact the Income Statement (which would show sales of $75, cost of $50, and a profit of $25), as well as the Cash Flow Statement (showing net operating cash inflows of $25). The Balance Sheet also implicitly captures the effect of differences in timing between when a transaction is recognized to have occurred (in the Income Statement) and its cash flow effect (on the Cash Flow Statement).

Although the two sides are often referred to as the "left" side (for the assets) and the "right" side (for the liabilities), they are often placed one underneath the other (assets of top, liabilities underneath). This is to be able to display the Balance Sheet at various points in time in a general document or in an Excel model which (both) may have a time axis that develops horizontally.

17.3 KEY CHALLENGES IN BUILDING INTEGRATED FINANCIAL STATEMENT MODELS

The creation of a financial statement model typically involves several challenges. In principle, the individual issues are often quite simple. However, when taken together, complexity can arise. The main challenges are:

- Ensuring a sufficient understanding of the required concepts and terminology. At a basic level, the core aspects are not especially complicated. However, in general, one may need to understand specialized financing, tax, or accounting issues in order to be able to reflect these in a model.

- Determining the appropriate forecast method for each item. Some items may be treated as "independent" i.e. forecast using any method that one chooses (such as using a growth rate to forecast sales revenue). However, the forecasting of some items constrains the subsequent choices for others. For example, after forecasting sales and operating costs, the operating profit is a derived quantity. On the other hand, in some (albeit rarer) cases it can make sense to forecast the operating margin and costs as independent items, with sales revenue determined from that. Similarly, the capital expenditure and depreciation could be forecast independently, with fixed assets determined from these (using a classical corkscrew as discussed in Chapter 8). Alternatively, the value of fixed assets could be forecast independently or semi-independently (such as using a sales-ratio), so that – with an assumption on depreciation rates of existing fixed assets – the capital expenditure becomes a determined quantity (a reverse corkscrew). Thus, one must determine the forecast method for each line item, while ensuring that these are consistent. In general, there could be a large set of potential combinations and choices.
- Managing the flow. The direction of the flow of logic is a result of the choices made for the individual line items. There are many interlinked components, and it is easy to create structures which are hard for another user to follow, or to make mistakes by linking items in the wrong way, creating circularities (for example).
- Dealing with a lack of standardization across models (or modelers). Many aspects are treated differently according to individual modeler's preferences. For example, in addition to the choices that may be made as to the forecasting methods (discussed above), some models are built with many worksheets, with each financial statement (or even individual components of each statement) built on a separate worksheet. On the other hand, the integrated nature of the situation would suggest (from the author's perspective) to use as few worksheets as possible. Similarly, some modelers use named ranges for many items (also generally not ideal in the author's view), and some use circular references as a final stage to calculate interest charges and cash balances (which should also be avoided in the author's view). This lack of standardization (whatever one's views on the individual issues) as well as the potential for various flows and interactions between items means that, when reviewing or adapting a model built by someone else, it can be challenging to understand, audit, adapt or even use it at all.

- The need to create a dynamic adjustment mechanism. The initial forecast of a financial statement model should automatically have the property that the statements are consistent and that the Balance Sheet balances. However, almost inevitably, the model will need to contain an additional mechanism(s), which we call the "dynamic adjustment mechanism." This is because the forecast model generally needs to reflect additional constraints that are imposed for logical, economic, contractual, or regulatory reasons (but which are not necessary for the model to balance as such). Most typically, these are constraints on Balance Sheet items (e.g. minimal cash balances, or the financial mix such as the maximal allowed amount of debt, the minimal allowable owners' equity, or a target debt-equity ratio). In fact, such a mechanism may not be required in a very-short-term forecasting model: If the constraints are met at the beginning (i.e. based on actual values), then they are likely to still hold a short time later. However, in most models, an additional mechanism is needed. Generally, this calculates the residual financing requirement, which is often assumed to be provided by debt (sometimes it is split between debt and equity or assumed to be created by other financing instruments). The implementation of this creates additional interactions between the statements: Constraints on an interim Balance Sheet determine the financing needs which affects the Cash Flow Statement and ultimately feeds back into the final Balance Sheet. This is discussed in detail later in this chapter, as it is one of the core aspects that is required in almost any medium- or long-term model.

It is also worth noting that while modeling requires some knowledge of accounting, there are differences between the processes. First, models are statements of relationships (directionality) between the items, whereas accounting is focused on historical data. This is sometimes expressed rather simplistically by saying that – in accounting – the owners' equity is a "plug number" (adjusted as needed as a last step in the process to ensure that the final Balance Sheet balances), whereas – in modeling – it is a forecasted item (and the last step may involve debt financing, rather than equity balances, for example). Second, models are typically less detailed (granular) than accounting information in terms of the number of individual line items. (However, a model may be more detailed in terms of the granularity of the time axis, such as having quarterly time periods, whereas formal accounts may be produced only annually.) Third, some methodologies that are often applied to accounting-related contexts may be less appropriate in modeling. Notably the use of average balance (of the starting and of the ending amounts) of an item when conducting ratio analysis may be appropriate for historical analysis, whereas – if used as a forecasting method – it may create circularities and additional complexity without any material benefit (see the Further Topics section).

Finally, it is worth noting that the modeling of financial statements per se rarely requires the use of advanced Excel: The integration between the statements is largely done using simple cell references to calculations of individual line items. In most cases, advanced Excel features or functions would be needed only if the calculation of the independent items has complex aspects to it.

In general, overcoming these challenges requires having a clarity in the overall logical process and structure, and a sharp focus on integrating the components as simply and transparently as possible.

17.4 FORECASTING OF THE INTEGRATED STATEMENTS: A SIMPLE EXAMPLE

This section presents a simple financial statement model. It is deliberately designed to be as simple as required in order to demonstrate only the core elements of the links between the statements and the need for the dynamic adjustment mechanism. The example assumes that the business has the following properties:

- It is a start-up business (initially with low sales revenues that grow quickly).
- Sales revenues are generated by buying items and then immediately reselling them at a higher price.
- The fixed costs of operations are all cash costs that are incurred and settled immediately.
- There are no storage costs, no shipping costs, and the business does not own any premises or other capital items. There is no investment required.
- Suppliers are paid immediately, and customers settle immediately for their purchases (so there are no accounts receivable nor payable)

Figure 17.1 **Income Statement for Simple Model**

	A	B	C	D	E	F	G	H	I	J
1										
2	Income Statement			1	2	3	4	5		Forecast Method
3	Sales Revenue			10	50	110	510	1010		Independent
4	Product Costs			8	38	77	332	606		Independent
5	Fixed Operations Cost			60	60	60	60	60		Independent
6	Profit			-58	-48	-27	118	344		Calc: D6=D3-D4-D5

- It is financed initially with an injection of cash from the owners (i.e. which is used to cover start-up costs and losses). There is no debt financing. No dividends are paid (any profits are retained by adding them to owners' equity)
- It is not required to pay (nor calculate) taxes.

Figure 17.1 shows a simplified Income Statement. It assumes (see column J) that the operational items (sales revenue, product costs, and fixed operations cost) are all forecast independently (separately) and linked into the Income Statement. The profit (row 6) is calculated from these. Note that, due to the assumptions above, there is a single variable "Profit," whereas in general, such an item would be calculated at various stages, such as pre- and post-tax, as discussed later.

Given the above assumptions, the cash flow is directly equivalent to (derivable from) the profit. This means that cash-balance and equity-balance corkscrews can be created. Figure 17.2 shows these (rows 11–14 for the cash corkscrew, and rows 16–19 for the equity corkscrew). The values in each structure are initiated based on the initial cash (equity) injection of $200.

Finally, the Balance Sheet can be produced. Each of the asset and liability sides has only one entry (i.e. cash balance for the assets and owners' equity for the liabilities), so this can be shown directly (without a breakdown of the totals). This is shown in Figure 17.3. Note also that the model checks (row 26) that the Balance Sheet balances in all time periods. It is important to note that the balancing of the Balance Sheet is not "forced." It is simply a direct result of creating it by using the information that already exists on the Income Statement and Cash Flow Statement.

Figure 17.2 **Cash and Equity Corkscrews**

	A	B	C	D	E	F	G	H	I	J
6		Profit		-58	-48	-27	118	344		Calc: D6=D3-D4-D5
7										
8		Cash Flow Statement		1	2	3	4	5		
9		Cash Flow		-58	-48	-27	118	344		D9=D6
10										
11		Cash corkscrew		1	2	3	4	5		
12		Starting		200	142	94	67	185		D12=C14
13		(+) Total Cash Flow-Final		-58	-48	-27	118	344		D13=D9
14		Ending	200	142	94	67	185	529		D14=D12+D13
15										
16		Equity corkscrew		1	2	3	4	5		
17		Starting		200	142	94	67	185		D17=C19
18		(+) Profits		-58	-48	-27	118	344		D18=D6
19		Ending	200	142	94	67	185	529		D19=D17+D18

Figure 17.3 **The Balance Sheet for the Base Case**

	A	B	C	D	E	F	G	H	I	J
11		Cash corkscrew		1	2	3	4	5		
12		Starting		200	142	94	67	185		D12=C14
13		(+) Total Cash Flow-Final		-58	-48	-27	118	344		D13=D9
14		Ending	200	142	94	67	185	529		D14=D12+D13
15										
16		Equity corkscrew		1	2	3	4	5		
17		Starting		200	142	94	67	185		D17=C19
18		(+) Profits		-58	-48	-27	118	344		D18=D6
19		Ending	200	142	94	67	185	529		D19=D17+D18
20										
21		Balance Sheet		1	2	3	4	5		
22		ASSETS (i.e. Cash)	200	142	94	67	185	529		D22=D14
23										
24		LIABILITIES (i.e. Owners' Equity)	200	142	94	67	185	529		D24=D19
25										
26		Balance Check	TRUE	TRUE	TRUE	TRUE	TRUE	TRUE		D26=(D22=D24)

17.5 THE DYNAMIC FINANCING ADJUSTMENT MECHANISM

At first glance, one may consider that the above simple model is complete: It is integrated with logical links, with a Balance Sheet that balances, and the figures provide a basis for general business planning. In principle, one can change the value of any input assumption (e.g. to run sensitivity or scenario analysis) and the values in the model will update automatically, and the Balance Sheet will still balance.

Figure 17.4 **The Balance Sheet with a Lower Initial Capital Injection**

	A	B	C	D	E	F	G	H	I	J
11		Cash corkscrew		1	2	3	4	5		
12		Starting		100	42	-6	-33	85	D12=C14	
13		(+) Total Cash Flow-Final		-58	-48	-27	118	344	D13=D9	
14		Ending	100	42	-6	-33	85	429	D14=D12+D13	
15										
16		Equity corkscrew		1	2	3	4	5		
17		Starting		100	42	-6	-33	85	D17=C19	
18		(+) Profits		-58	-48	-27	118	344	D18=D6	
19		Ending	100	42	-6	-33	85	429	D19=D17+D18	
20										
21		Balance Sheet		1	2	3	4	5		
22		ASSETS (i.e. Cash)	100	42	-6	-33	85	429	D22=D14	
23										
24		LIABILITIES (i.e. Owners' Equity)	100	42	-6	-33	85	429	D24=D19	
25										
26		Balance Check		TRUE	TRUE	TRUE	TRUE	TRUE	D26=(D22=D24)	

The model could therefore try to be used (for example) to test whether it would be possible to set up the business by putting in less capital initially. Figure 17.4 shows the effect on the Balance Sheet of assuming that the original capital injection is only $100 (rather than $200). Note that the Balance Sheet still balances (since this is determined purely by the logic embedded within the model). However, the result is not realistic nor perhaps even possible: It would neither be practically possible to have a negative cash balance (cells E22 and F22), nor may a negative equity (cells E24 and F24) be allowed by regulatory authorities.

Thus, while the lower initial equity investment is sufficient to cover the first period, by the end of the second period, additional capital is required. Therefore, some form of adjustment mechanism is needed, and the model must be adapted to include this. As a minimum:

- The model must capture that an injection of cash is necessary, which will affect the asset side.

- It must be known whether the injection comes from the equity owners or from debt financing (or as a mixture to achieve a balance between debt and equity), which impacts the liabilities side.

The required mechanism may also reflect any other criteria that need to be met. For example, one may wish to have (at the end of any period) a minimum cash balance that is strictly positive or is above some threshold (or to achieve a target debt-equity mix). (Note that in general it is usually the case that the adjustment mechanism involves financing issues. In theory, one could try to adapt the model in other ways such as by assuming that sales revenue would increase, or costs reduce. However, such changes generally do not correspond to the reality of what would happen.)

Figure 17.5 shows the adaptation mechanism that could be used in order to ensure that there is always a minimum cash balance (defined in row 19). It calculates the cash injection required but does not assume the source of this injection (i.e. whether equity or debt). The top part (rows 9–12) uses the same cash flow figures as before. However, for clarity, these are split into the categories of operations, investing, and financing. Also (and importantly) these are treated as interim cash flow amounts (prior to the cash injection). Given the assumption of no investment, row 10 contains zero (in general, this may already contain a non-zero value that is the final investment amount). Also, since this is an interim statement from a financing perspective (i.e. prior to applying the dynamic adjustment mechanism) row 11 is also zero. The interim cash flow is used to calculate interim cash balances (i.e. what the balances would be in the absence of, or prior to, an injection). This is done with the corkscrew in rows 15–17. Also, given the specific

Figure 17.5 **Implementation of the Adjustment Mechanism**

A	B	C	D	E	F	G	H	I	J
1									
8	Interim Cash Flow		1	2	3	4	5		
9	Cash from Operations		-58	-48	-27	118	344	D9-D6	
10	Cash for Investment		0	0	0	0	0		
11	Cash for/from Financing (Initial)		0	0	0	0	0		
12	Total Cash Flow – interim		-58	-48	-27	118	344	D12-D9+D10+D11	
13									
14	Interim Cash corskscrew								
15	Starting		100	42	-6	-33	85	D15-C17	
16	Changes		-58	-48	-27	118	344	D16-D12	
17	Ending	100	42	-6	-33	85	429	D17-D15+D16	
18									
19	Minimum acceptable cash balance		5	5	5	5	5		
20	Cash Injections Required		0	11	38	0	0	D20-MAX(D19-D17,0)	
21	Cash for/from Financing (Final)		0	11	38	0	0	D21-D11+D20	
22									
23									
24	Cash Flow Statement		1	2	3	4	5		
25	Cash from Operations		-58	-48	-27	118	344	D25-D9	
26	Cash for Investment		0	0	0	0	0	D26-D10	
27	Cash for/from Financing (Final)		0	11	38	0	0	D27-D21	
28	Total Cash Flow – Final		-58	-37	11	118	344		

Figure 17.6 **Completion of Statements to Reflect the Equity Injection**

	A	B	C	D	E	F	G	H	I	J
23										
24	Cash Flow Statement			1	2	3	4	5		
25	Cash from Operations			-58	-48	-27	118	344	D25=D9	
26	Cash for Investment			0	0	0	0	0	D26=D10	
27	Cash for/from Financing [Final]			0	11	38	0	0	D27=D21	
28	Total Cash Flow - Final			-58	-37	11	118	344		
29										
30	Final Cash corkscrew			1	2	3	4	5		
31	Starting			100	42	5	16	134	D31=C33	
32	(+) Total Cash Flow-Final			-58	-37	11	118	344	D32=D28	
33	Ending		100	42	5	16	134	478	D33=D31+D32	
34										
35	Equity corkscrew			1	2	3	4	5		
36	Starting			100	42	5	16	134		
37	(+) Profits			-58	-48	-27	118	344	D37=D6	
38	(+) Financing Injections			0	11	38	0	0	D38=D21	
39	Ending		100	42	5	16	134	478		
40										
41	Balance Sheet			1	2	3	4	5		
42	ASSETS (i.e. Cash)		100	42	5	16	134	478	D42=D33	
43										
44	LIABILITIES (i.e. Owners' Equity)		100	42	5	16	134	478	D44=D39	

objective to keep cash balances above a pre-defined minimum, in row 20 the MAX function is used to determine the size of the new financing injection required, by using the ending interim balance (row 17) and the minimum required balance (row 19). (The IF function could also have been used in place of MAX.) This financing injection allows for a final cash flow statement to be completed as shown in rows 24–28 (and the cash from operations and investments is the same as in the interim statement).

The financial statement forecast can then be completed by calculating the corkscrews for the cash balance and for the equity balance (on the assumption here that this injection is from equity owners, not from debt providers). This is shown in Figure 17.6.

17.6 GENERALIZING THE MODEL FEATURES AND CAPABILITIES

In practical applications, a financial statement model is likely to require many line items and features that are not present in the simple example.

In general – especially for modelers with little experience of financial statements – it is most efficient to build a simple model which has the essential features required and to add new lines or generalities one at a time. For each new feature, one makes the necessary changes (adding the line items and the formulas to each of the impacted financial statements) and ensures that the balancing and the adjustment mechanism work before considering adding the next feature. Working in this way, one can ultimately create a sophisticated model that contains a large set of rich features.

As an example of a single step in such a process, Figure 17.7 shows the inclusion of a line item for accounts receivable. That is, we assume that there is a 30-day payment (rather than customers immediately settling their invoices). The changes that are required to be made to the earlier model are:

- Addition of rows which contain the calculation of the accounts receivable (rows 8–11). The forecast is done using the ratio methods described in Chapters 7–8, including using a reverse corkscrew (in which the net change is calculated from the balances).

- Creation of the calculation of operational cash flows to reflect the additional item (i.e. that an increase in net accounts receivable reduces cash flow) (rows 14–16).

- Creation of more line items within the asset side of the Balance Sheet, so that accounts receivable can be included (rows 51–53).

Figure 17.7 **Example of Adding an Accounts Receivable Functionality**

A	B	C	D	E	F	G	H	I	J
7									
8	Accounts Receivable		1	2	3	4	5		
9	Starting		0.0	0.8	4.1	9.0	41.9		D9=C11
10	Net Change		0.8	3.3	4.9	32.9	41.1		D10=D11-D9
11	Ending	0	0.8	4.1	9.0	41.9	83.0		D11=(30/365)*D3
12									
13	Interim Cash Flow		1	2	3	4	5		
14	Cash from Operations								
15	Profit		-58	-48	-27	118	344		D15=D6
16	Decrease in accounts receivable		-0.8	-3.3	-4.9	-32.9	-41.1		D16=-D10
17	Total cash flow from operations		-58.8	-51.3	-31.9	85.1	302.9		D17=D15+D16
18									
49									
50	Balance Sheet		1	2	3	4	5		
51	ASSETS (Total, of which)	100	42.0	9.1	29.2	147.2	491.2		D51=D52+D53
52	Cash		41.2	5.0	20.1	105.2	408.1		D52=D42
53	Accounts Receivable		0.8	4.1	9.0	41.9	83.0		D53=D11
54									
55	LIABILITIES (i.e. Owners' Equity)	100	42.0	9.1	29.2	147.2	491.2		D55=D48
56									
57	Balance Check		TRUE	TRUE	TRUE	TRUE	TRUE		D57=(D51=D55)

(Note that although it is not explicitly shown here, the observant reader will have noticed that the totals on each side of the Balance Sheet are larger than previously, i.e. before the addition of the accounts receivable functionality. This is due to the higher level of cash injection that would occur as a result of the lower operational cash flow caused by the delay in the payments of invoices.)

Of course, most realistic models would likely have several other features. For example, the Income Statement would almost always be split into more detailed components than in the simple model and would calculate "profit" at different stages. It would include:

- Sales revenue.
- Operational cost of a cash nature.
- Earnings before interest, tax, depreciation, and amortization (EBITDA).
- Depreciation and amortization (i.e. noncash operating costs).
- Earnings before interest and tax (EBIT).
- Interest income and charges.
- Earnings before tax or pre-tax profit (EBT or PBT).
- Taxes.
- Earnings after tax or post-tax profit (EAT or PAT) or net income.

(In practice, there could be other line items such as one-off charges or exceptional items, earnings relating to associated entities or minority shares in income, and so on.)

The Cash Flow Statement would usually be split into the three components noted earlier (operations, investment, and financing) with the first line on the operations part being either net income or EBITDA, depending on presentational preferences.

Other typical generalizations that affect multiple statements include:

- The interim cash flow calculations which are used in the dynamic adjustment mechanism would typically be more sophisticated. For example, new capital could be defined to be a mixture of debt and equity in order to achieve a particular debt-equity ratio over some time horizon. Similarly, cash sweeps are sometimes implemented as fixed minimum payouts or as a part of the dynamic adjustment mechanism.

- There may be different layers of seniority of the debt (with different interest rates), and so on. The associated calculations may use the waterfall structures discussed in Chapter 9.
- Tax calculations may need to reflect that cash taxes are paid in the period after which they are recognized on the Income Statement, or that there are tax loss carry-forwards, deferred taxes, and so on.
- Equity would be split between retained earnings and original share capital. Retained earnings would be calculated using a corkscrew structure (similar to that shown earlier, which was for total equity) and based on the dividends paid. Dividends paid to equity holders may often be calculated based on the post-tax profit (such as if a payout ratio is used).

These calculations will therefore affect the financing side of the Cash Flow Statement as well as the Balance Sheet.

17.7 STEPS AND PRINCIPLES IN BUILDING A FINANCIAL STATEMENT MODEL

From a practical point of view, when building a financial statement forecast, there are many things to consider: In addition to managing the challenges listed earlier, one should – even before the model is being built – consider the general issues that relate to model design (as covered in Chapter 2). Further, the model building process will likely require using many of the techniques covered earlier (Chapters 5–10).

When building a simple model for corporate financial statements, it can help to work in order in accordance with the following steps. These start with operational items on the Income Statement and gradually introduce items needed for the Cash Flow Statement and Balance Sheet:

- Sales. Create the forecast of sales revenue (typically, as an independent item, such as using a growth-based method, as discussed in Chapter 5).
- Cash costs. Build the forecast of all operational cost items of a cash nature (this may be split into fixed costs, variable costs (or more detail) and may use the ratio methods discussed in Chapter 7, for example).
- EBITDA. Calculate EBITDA from the above.

- Depreciation. Build the forecast of capital investment, assets, and depreciation. The calculation of these noncash items would require that one starts to consider the asset side of the model (which links to the Balance Sheet) as well as the capital expenditures (which links to the Cash Flow Statement). There are various assumptions and ways that the calculations of the capital expenditure, assets, and depreciation can be done (for example, see the discussions in Chapters 7–8).

- EBIT. Calculate this from above.

- Interest income and expense. A line item can be created for this but initially it can be populated with "dummy" values that will later be overwritten with formulas when the financing side is complete. The simplest methods apply the interest rate to the ending balances of cash and debt in the prior period. There may also be multiple layers of debt with different interest rates. More complex methods use average debt balances, which create circularities, and are also not fully accurate in any case (so we recommend avoiding these, as discussed in the Further Topics section).

- EBT (PBT). Calculate this from above.

- Tax. In simple cases (a business which is always profitable and stable), the taxes recognized in the period can be forecast by applying a tax rate to the pre-tax profit. In many realistic cases, the calculations of tax may require a detailed set of more complex calculations. For example, if there are start-up losses, these may be able to be carried forward to offset future taxes. Similarly, specific rules may apply which allow capital items to be depreciated in an accelerated manner. These types of situations can also create deferred tax assets and liabilities, which must be captured on the Balance Sheet. However, these types of features can be added to the model as a later step. If there is any material to complexity to the tax calculations, it can be better to simply create a placeholder until the core part of the model is complete (that is, a line item is created and populated with dummy values or with zero).

- EAT (PAT, or Net Income). Calculate from above.

- At this point, one can create the full structure for each of the three financial statements. Lines can be added for items such as accounts receivable, accounts payable, and so on.

- The interim Cash Flow Statement and dynamic adjustment mechanism can be created.

- The financing calculations can be closed by reflecting the adjustment mechanism in the cash and debt balances and calculating interest income and expense (which is then used in the Income Statement). This is a step of major importance, even though the number of calculations required may be relatively small. In principle, it is the last step in the model-building process. The calculated interest income or expense is included in the Income Statement (and hence affects taxes, net income, and cash flows). It is the step where a circularity can be created if one chooses to do so by assuming that interest items are calculated by using ending cash balances within the formulas.

In addition to ensuring that items are integrated and balance, the first version of the resulting model should generally be tested for the overall credibility of the assumptions. Notably, it is useful to calculate several ratios to ensure that these are reasonable (if not, it is in general the numerical assumptions, rather than the model logic per se that needs changing). For example, items such as the operating margins, return on capital, or the ratio of assets to sales are important indicators (ratio analysis is discussed in Chapter 19).

Several other points are worth noting:

- For reasons of transparency and flexibility, ideally one would create modular structures that are linked together. For example, each corkscrew can be built in a separate structure (such as shown for accounts receivable earlier). However, it is important to not over-fragment the overall structure. If a financial model has several worksheets, there will often be very many cross-worksheet links due to the many interrelationships since many items are closely related. Therefore, it is generally better to use as few worksheets as possible (or even one). Model navigation can be aided by the selective use of named ranges.

- Sometimes accounting conventions display cost items as negative values (or using brackets). This means that costs would be added to sales revenue to calculate profit (rather than subtracted from it). One advantage of this approach is to aid mental arithmetic: the total of a list is formed by adding all the items, rather than one having to consider whether to add or subtract a particular item. On the other hand, when using modular structures, it is more natural that items in a module would be expressed in positive terms. For example, within a module to calculate costs, the costs would be expressed in positive terms. The signs of these can be reversed (if desired) when the link to the module is made from the main model.

Finally, as noted earlier, when modeling non-corporate entities (banks and financial institutions), the required structures and processes are more specific than the general methods covered in this text: Simply put, for these entities, it is complex to distinguish operating issues from financing ones, since financial instruments (such as debt and loans) serve both purposes. The full set of modeling approaches required are therefore beyond the scope of this text.

17.8 FURTHER TOPICS: AVOIDING CIRCULARITIES

A circularity (or circular reference) arises when a calculated cell in Excel refers to itself directly or indirectly. That is, if the precedents (or dependents) of any calculated cell is traced back (or forwards) as far as is possible, then a circularity arises if the same cell is present anywhere on that path. A circularity can arise by accident when building any formula but is more likely to arise in models with poor layout and flow and if there are many interconnected components. When a circularity is created by accident, it should of course be corrected as soon as possible (i.e. the formulas adapted as needed).

Some financial statement models include circularities by intention, notably in respect of the calculations of interest expense or income. The section argues that this should not generally be done, both for reasons of accuracy and of complexity.

Note that the simplest way to calculate interest income or expense in a period is to assume that it is determined from the period-start values of debt and cash. Indeed, not only does this method correspond to how some interest calculation mechanisms work in real-life, but also its use is implicit within functions such as PMT (see Chapter 12 and Chapter 13). However, a main cause of intentional circularities in financial statement models is where one instead calculates periodic interest based on the average balance of debt or cash during the period. That is, interest expense for period N is calculated using a formula such as:

$$IE_N = r \frac{(D_{N-1} + D_N)}{2}$$

(where D represents the debt at the associated points in time).

A circularity arises since the role of the dynamic adjustment mechanism is to calculate the residual financing requirement, and this requirement takes interest into account. That is, any new residual financing affects the ending debt balance and therefore changes the interest expense (calculated based on the average balance), which changes the residual financing requirement again. From a theoretical perspective, this logical circularity is resolvable as long as the periodic effective interest rate is less than 200%. In this case, it is also numerically resolvable using the Excel Calculation Options which allow for iterations to be performed until a set of converged values is achieved within the model. (In practice, there could be various tranches of debt with different interest rates, but the principles still apply to that situation as well.)

From a superficial (and perhaps intuitive) perspective, this process seems to provide more accuracy to the models. However, there are two drawbacks. First, the method is not an exact calculation of interest expense. In fact, it does not correspond to any way that interest is calculated in real life (unlike using starting balances). It is therefore always an approximation (and always truly correct). Second – and of much more significance – it creates substantial complexity and significantly reduces model auditability. This is because the circular path runs through all financing items (and all the three Statements), and so is typically quite long. (A very short circular path that were much more contained would be much less problematic.)

It is worth clarifying whether the purpose of using the average balance method (with the above formula) is to try to treat the interest as if it were a continuously compounded process, or to reflect the timing aspect of the cash flows within each period, or for some other reason(s). (Note that the formula uses the interest rate as if it were a simple rate, but the iterative calculations could potentially be equivalent to the rate being continuously compounded.) In fact:

- The use of the method combined with an iterative calculation does not replicate a continuously compounded process. An easy way to see this is to consider the case where the starting debt amount is zero, and where new debt is taken on only at the end of the period. In that case, a continuously compounded rate would be applied to the initial amount (of zero), and interest expense for the period would be zero. Whereas, using the average-balance method, the ending amount (new debt at period end) is non-zero, so the periodic interest expense would not be zero.

- The method does not treat the timing of the periodic cash flows as if they occur in the middle of the period, rather than at the period end. To see this, note that the circularity results in interest at one iteration being charged (or earned) on interest from the previous iteration. However, if the interest calculation applied the interest rate to the (non-interest) periodic cash flows as if they occurred in the middle of the period (or half the interest rate to the full value of such case values), then interest on these new cash flows occurs only once. Thus, more interest is earned with the average balance method. Note that it is generally the case that models (using discrete time periods in Excel) implicitly assume that cash flows occur either at the end (or the beginning) of the periods. Further, most financial functions in Excel (NPV, PMT, etc.) assume that cash flows occur at period end (with some, such as PMT, allowing one to switch this assumption to be the period beginning by using an optional parameter). None of the functions assume that cash flows are mid-period. Therefore, an assumption that cash flows are to be treated as occurring in the middle of the period may be inconsistent with many assumptions that have been made (whether implicitly or explicitly).

Nevertheless, if one wishes to capture interest that may be earned during the period on (non-interest-related) cash flows, one can do this in several ways:

- Increase the time-granularity of the model. For example, by halving the length of the model periods, one can implicitly create a situation which is as if the cash flows occurred in the middle of the original periods.
- Calculate the interest by applying the rate to the average of the starting balance and an interim cash balance that includes all items except those that are not interest related. In fact, if the interest rate is a simple rate, then it can be shown that this is equivalent either to the assumption that cash flows occur in the middle of the period, or to the assumption that they occur continuously during the period.

In summary, noting that the average-balance method does not capture the true interest cost exactly, while generally creates an inordinate amount of complexity in the usability and auditability of the model, it does not seem to be a sensible choice to use it. Other methods can be used which result in simpler models and can be more accurate. The temptation to use the average-balance method comes from its apparent accuracy and because the step to close the financial statement model can be done very quickly, without having to consider or implement alternatives.

(If circularities are nevertheless used, they should be implemented with a broken circular path, whose values are iterated by using a VBA macro rather than using the Excel iterative options; see the author's *PFM* for details.)

18

Corporate Valuation Modeling

18.1 INTRODUCTION

The valuation of a corporation (both at the enterprise and the equity level) is an important topic in corporate finance. This chapter covers:

- An overview of valuation methods.
- The core principles of cash flow valuation.
- The calculations of enterprise value using the post-tax WACC method and the APV (adjusted present value) method.
- The role of an explicit forecasting period in cash flow valuation.
- An example of a valuation model that uses an explicit forecast combined with an annuity and a perpetuity for the terminal value.

The Further Topics sections briefly discuss the derivation of the formulas for enterprise valuations based on free cash flows, and the use of value-driver formulas to enhance annuity and perpetuity-based terminal value calculations, as well as the use of market prices to assess the implied cost of equity.

Note that this chapter assumes a good knowledge of the concepts and methods that were covered in Chapter 14 and in Chapter 16, so a reader may choose to first revisit these, as necessary.

18.2 OVERVIEW OF VALUATION METHODS

The methods used in corporate valuation fall into one of three main categories:

- Asset-based. These use measures such as the book value of the assets, or their replacement cost, or the value that could be achieved by liquidating them in an orderly way.

- Comparables (or relative valuation or multiples). These apply scaling factors (metrics, or "multiples") based on a set of similar assets or companies whose value is already known. For example, a real estate property may be valued using the per-square-meter price achieved by similar properties in recent transactions. In corporate contexts, the ratio of equity value to net income (or to dividends) is often used, as is the enterprise value to sales revenue or to EBIT or to EBITDA.

- Cash flow methods. These forecast a stream of cash flows that would accrue to either the equity holders or at the enterprise level. These are discounted at the appropriate cost of capital. Within the enterprise cash flows methods, there are two alternatives: The post-tax WACC approach, and the pre-tax WACC approach (or the adjusted present value, or APV, method).

(The use of option-based approaches to corporate valuation is not discussed, as these are generally of little use in most common practical applications.)

In general, the quantitative analytic techniques required in the asset-based or comparable methods are straightforward (usually involving some basic data analysis and calculations). From a modeling perspective, it is mostly the cash flow methods that are relevant for detailed discussion. The focus of this chapter is on enterprise level valuation (for reasons partly discussed in earlier chapters, as well as those covered later). Note that for all methods, it is in principle possible to convert an enterprise valuation to an equity valuation (and vice versa) by considering the value of the debt and any cash (other adjustments may be necessary in more complex cases, such as accounting for deferred taxes, associate companies, or minority interests; however, these adjustments are beyond the scope of this text).

18.3 PRINCIPLES OF CASH FLOW VALUATION

The cash flow methods generally make the implicit assumption that the business is an ongoing entity. If this is not the case, other methods may be considered instead or as a complement (such as asset-based liquidation value). Therefore, the methods are based on:

- Creating an explicit forecast of the relevant cash flows of the business for a finite period, and valuing these by discounting them at the appropriate rate. When calculating equity valuation directly, it is net income or dividends that are most relevant. These would be discounted at the appropriate rate for equity, considering the leverage (i.e. the debt-equity mix) and the tax rate. When calculating the enterprise value directly, the relevant cash flow is the free cash flow after tax. This is the cash that is available to all sources of financing (rather than only to equity holders) and is described in detail later in this chapter.

- Calculating the terminal value (i.e. the value associated with the post-forecast period). This is usually done with annuity or perpetuity formulas. However, sometimes this is instead done by using the multiples (comparables) method.

In principle, one would expect the methods to provide essentially identical results, i.e. that the equity value derived via an enterprise valuation (adjusting for debt etc.) would be the same as if an equity method were used directly (and that the enterprise value derived directly would be the same as if it were derived indirectly from an equity value). In practice, the conditions required for this to hold are rather complex, and require a set of idealized assumptions that may not fully apply in practice (a complete discussion of this is beyond the scope of this text, but includes items such as a constant leverage ratio, that the face value of debt should be equal to the market value, that the coupon on the debt is the same as the cost of debt, and that the cost of capital and leverage formulas are used completely correctly).

In general, enterprise methods are generally more robust (even to value equity indirectly). The disadvantages of equity methods include that:

- The cash flow to equity (based on net income) is a residual after several items are subtracted from enterprise cash flows. As a result, it is more sensitive to the cumulative effect of any estimation processes, assumptions, or approximations that are used. Also, dividend payments are discretionary.

- The discount rate for levered equity varies significantly depending on the leverage. This makes it harder to estimate accurately and would require that the rate be changed whenever the leverage changes (which can be in each model period). This issue is further compounded in practice, where the financial structure is likely to not be a mix of equity and simple debt, but also have

other components (such as debt with different levels of seniority, convertibles, or preferred shares). On the other hand, the
pre- and post-tax WACC is constant or much more stable (see
Chapter 16).

18.4 FREE CASH FLOW FOR ENTERPRISE VALUATION

For the enterprise method(s), the relevant cash flow is known as "free
cash flow." This is the post-tax cash flow that is available to equity and
debt holders. It is calculated by subtracting (net) investment needs from
an item called NOPAT ("net operating profit after taxes"):

FCF = NOPAT – Capital Investment – Increase in Working Capital
    + Depreciation and Amortization

(changes in working capital may also include the effect of deferred
taxes).

NOPAT is an "artificial" item that is calculated by applying the tax
rate directly to EBIT (without deducting interest). However, the fact that
it is the correct cash flow measure to use in the context of enterprise valuations is described in detail in the Further Topics I section at the end of
this chapter.

In fact, NOPAT corresponds to the post-tax profit that the firm would
have if it were financed purely with equity (so that there would be no
interest expenses):

$$NOPAT = EBIT \cdot (1 - z)$$

The tax rate to use when calculating NOPAT from EBIT (indicated
with the symbol z in the above) is the ratio of the forecasted actual tax
payment (taking actual interest charges into account) to the forecasted
actual EBT (or PBT). In a stable tax situation, this rate would be the same
as the regular tax rate. If the tax context is not stable (in the sense that
actual taxes are different, for example due to tax breaks or loss carry-
forward), then the rate to use would also be different to the normal rate;
an example of this is shown later in this chapter.

The FCF can be used in two core ways for enterprise valuation
purposes:

- In the direct method, it is discounted using the post-tax WACC.
- In the APV "adjusted present value" approach, the value is split into two components: The value of the operations and the value of the tax shield. The FCF is discounted at the pre-tax unlevered cost of equity (which is higher than the post-tax cost of capital if debt is used) to give the value of operations. The value of the tax shield is added to this and is calculated by applying the tax rate to the interest charges and discounting these also at the cost of unlevered equity (the tax rate to use is that as described above).

Although the post-tax WACC method is still more commonly used by many practitioners, the APV method is generally slightly superior: First, it can capture the effect of non-constant tax shields (or a tax rate that is not constant). Tax shields may not be fully utilizable due to changes in operating profit, leverage, or due to tax losses that can be carried forward or other specific reasons. Second, it explicitly separates the operational from the tax component, which creates more transparency (this is often stated as the key characteristic of the APV method; it is arguably less important than the first point).

Note that some practitioners discount the tax shield at the cost of debt rather than that of unlevered equity. However, the use of the cost unlevered equity to discount the tax shield has the advantage that the enterprise valuations derive from the (direct) post-tax WACC method would be the same as that when the APV method is used (under the assumption that the growth rate and the tax rate are constant).

The Further Topics I section shows explicitly how the use of FCF in the above way will result in an enterprise valuation, as well as showing the equivalence of the post-tax WACC and APV methods (given the assumptions for constant growth and tax rates).

18.5 THE ROLE OF THE EXPLICIT FORECAST

As noted earlier, the valuation is composed of the value created in the explicit forecast period, and that created in the terminal period. In general, unless the explicit forecast period is very long, a large proportion of the value is created in the terminal period. However, this does not mean that the quality of the forecast in this period is unimportant. In fact, the reverse is true: As discussed in Chapter 16, the ending cash flows of the explicit forecast in general directly impact all the annuity and perpetuity cash flows (in a linear way). That is, if the cash flow at the end of the explicit forecast is overestimated by 10%, then so is the entire terminal value.

The role of the explicit forecast is therefore to:

- Forecast to the time point where the business is stable, both operationally and financially.
- Create a realistic value for the starting cash flow of the annuity.

Operational stability means that there are no more structural changes in the line items, and that the change in the business from one time point to the next can be described by using only a constant growth rate, and a constant cost of capital. The assumption that stability will be reached at some point makes sense: For example, it is unlikely that one has a better idea of what the business situation will be in 15 years than what it will be in 10 years, so the explicit forecast period (in such a case) would not need to be more than 10 years in that case (or it could be shorter). Note also that the explicit forecast can be used to reflect any important bespoke aspects of the business that cannot typically be captured with the comparable or asset-based methods.

Financial stability means that the relative leverage (debt-equity ratio) and the cost of capital can be assumed to be constant from the end of the explicit period onwards. That is, the effects of changes due to financial restructuring (e.g. after a leveraged buyout) have been worked through. Also, the time frame may need to be sufficient for one to be able to assume that the yield curve is essentially flat from that point, since the cost of capital depends indirectly on the risk-free interest rate.

If a long explicit forecast period is used, then it may be sufficient to use only a perpetuity formula for the terminal value. Otherwise, a combination of (one or more) annuities and a perpetuity may be preferable (as discussed in Chapter 14). On the other hand, if the business could be considered as already being stable at the model start time, then an explicit forecast (model) may not be needed at all (or at least only for one period); a perpetuity formula could be used directly based on the values in a single period or recent historical data (if one implicitly assumes a flat yield curve or constant cost of capital). This is essentially what is being done – albeit implicitly – when using some multiples (such as price-to-earnings or Enterprise Value-to-EBITDA). Of course, even for a stable business, an explicit forecast may also be needed for purposes other than valuation, such as cash flow planning, discussions with creditors, or potential business partners, or other external investors (and so on).

18.6 EXAMPLE: EXPLICIT FORECAST WITH TERMINAL VALUE CALCULATION

This section shows an example of an enterprise value using the APV method. A core input to the enterprise methods is EBIT, since this is used to calculated NOPAT. The depreciation is also needed, in order to be added back to NOPAT, and an investment forecast is also required. (In some cases, the net investment can be forecasted directly, without separation of investment and depreciation.) However, items such as sales revenues or cash operating costs are not needed as such. Similarly, a full Balance Sheet is also not strictly necessary, even as it can be useful to provide cross-checks (such as to conduct ratio analysis on items such as the return on capital) or to estimate changes to working capital more accurately. The level of debt is needed in order to calculate interest calculations (which affect the tax rate, even if not part of the free cash flow).

Figure 18.1 shows an example of the first part of the calculations of an explicit forecast. The EBIT forecast, interest expense (based on the level of debt and the cost of debt), as well as the taxes are used to calculate the NOPAT. There is a tax loss carry forward (cell C20), which reduces the actual (effective) tax rate in the early part of the forecast.

Figure 18.1 **Forecast to the NOPAT line**

	A	B	C	D	E	F	G	H	I	J
1										
2	EBIT			1	2	3	4	5		
3	EBIT			100.0	112	125	140	157		
4	Growth rate			12.0%	12.0%	12.0%	12.0%	12.0%		
5										
6	Debt			1	2	3	4	5		
7	Beginning			250	270	292	315	340		
8	End		250	270	292	315	340	367		
9										
10	Cost of debt			1	2	3	4	5		
11	Cost of debt		5.0%	5.0%	5.0%	5.0%	5.0%	5.0%		
12										
13	Actual Tax Rate			1	2	3	4	5		
14	Interest expenses			12.5	13.5	14.6	15.7	17.0	D14=D7*D11	
15	PBT			87.5	98.5	110.9	124.7	140.3	D15=D3-D14	
16	Notional tax rate		30.0%	30%	30%	30%	30%	30%		
17	Losses Brought Forward (-ve for a loss)			-200	-113	-14	0	0	D17=C20	
18	Pre-Tax Profit for Tax Calc			-113	-14	97	125	140	D18=D15-D17	
19	Tax Charge			0	0	29	37	42	D19=MAX(D18*D16,0)	
20	Losses to Carry Forward (-ve for a loss)		-200	-113	-14	0	0	0	D20=MIN(0,D18)	
21	Actual marginal tax rate			0%	0%	26%	30%	30%	D21=D19/D15	
22										
23	NOPAT			1	2	3	4	5		
24	NOPAT (Using marginal tax rate)			100.0	112.0	92.6	98.3	110.1	D24=D3*(1-D21)	

Figure 18.2 **Calculation of the Value in the Explicit Forecast Period**

	A	B	C	D	E	F	G	H	I	J
22										
23		NOPAT		1	2	3	4	5		
24		NOPAT (Using marginal tax rate)		100.0	112.0	92.6	98.3	110.1		D24=D3*(1-D21)
25										
26		Free cash Flows (NOPAT less investment)		1	2	3	4	5		
27		Total Investment		115.0	112.2	104.0	107.9	112.1		
28		Depreciation		55.0	55.0	55.0	55.0	55.0		
29		Net Investment		60.0	57.2	49.0	52.9	57.1		D29=D27-D28
30		Cash Flow to Enterprise (Free Cash Flow)		40.0	54.8	43.6	45.4	53.0		D30=D24-D29
31										
32		Cost of equity (unlevered)		1	2	3	4	5		
33		Cost of equity (unlevered)	10.0%	10.0%	10.0%	10.0%	10.0%	10.0%		
34		Cumulated discount factor	100%	90.9%	82.6%	75.1%	68.3%	62.1%		D34=C34/(1+D33)
35										
36		Discounted Free Cash Flow		1	2	3	4	5		
37		Discounted Cash Flow	178	36.4	45.3	32.7	31.0	32.9		D37=D30*D34
38										
39		Tax shield at cost of equity		1	2	3	4	5		
40		Tax shield		0.0	0.0	3.8	4.7	5.1		D40=D7*D1*D21
41		Tax shield discounted at cost of equity	9	0.0	0.0	2.9	3.2	3.2		D41=D40*D34
42										
43		Value in Explicit Forecast Period	188							

Figure 18.2 shows the calculation of the FCF. (For simplicity of focusing on the core points relating to valuation, the investment profile is assumed to be known, and to contain within it any changes to working capital.) In the APV method, the FCF is discounted at the cost of unlevered equity to give the value of operations in the forecast period (cell C37), and the tax shield is also explicitly calculated and discounted at the same rate (cell C41).

Figure 18.3 shows the terminal value calculations. These use an annuity and a perpetuity, based on the formulas in Chapter 14 (some rows containing the intermediate calculations are hidden to simplify the presentation). The main new point worthy of note is that the discount rate used is the post-tax WACC: Since the business is now stable, there is no need to split the tax shield separately. This WACC is calculated using the levered value of equity, and therefore requires an assumption on the long-term debt-to-equity ratio (which should correspond to that in the optimal capital structure).

Figure 18.4 shows the calculation of the total enterprise value, as well as that of the equity that results from subtracting the initial level of debt.

Figure 18.3 **Terminal Value Calculation**

	A	B	C	D	E
22					
44					
45		Terminal Value Assumptions			
46		D-E Ratio long-term (optimal)	40%		
47		Cost of Equity (levered)	12%		C47=C33+C46*(C33-C11)
48		Discount Rate (WACC, post-tax)	6.9%		C48=C46*C47+(1-C46)*(1-C18)*C11
49					
50		Explicit Forecast			
51		Number of Periods	5		
52		Ending Cash Flow	53		C52=H30
53					
54		Annuity Part			
55		Annuity Periods	10		
56		Annuity Growth Rate	8.0%		
61		Value: beginning of model	402		C61=C60/(1-C48)^(C57-1)
62					
63		Perpetuity Part			
64		Perpetuity Growth Rate	5.0%		
68		Value: beginning of model	2325		C68=C67/(1-C48)^(C65-1)
69					
70		Terminal Value	2726		C70=C61+C68
71					

Figure 18.4 **Total Enterprise and Equity Value**

	A	B	C	D	E
71					
72		Enterprise Value Components			
73		Operations in Explicit Forecast	178		C73=C37
74		Tax Shield in Explicit Forecast	9		C74=C41
75		Annuity	402		C75=C61
76		Perpetuity	2325		C76=C68
77		Total EV	2914		C77=SUM(C73:C76)
78					
79		Equity Value			
80		Beginning debt	250		C80=C$8
81		Equity Value implied	2664		C81=C77-C80
82					

18.7 FURTHER TOPICS I: ENTERPRISE VALUE BASED ON FREE CASH FLOW AND EQUIVALENCES

This section demonstrates explicitly how the discounting of free cash flows leads to an enterprise valuation. It also proves the equivalence of the post-tax WACC and APV methods given some assumptions. The core steps involve the conversion of an operating view of free cash flows into a financing one and the switching of equity values with an annuity-based formula involving the cost of equity. That is, using the definition of free cash flow (and using self-evident terminology):

$$FCF = EBIT - TaxesWithoutShield - Net\ Investment$$

This can be written as:

$$FCF = EBIT - (Taxes + t \cdot k_d \cdot D) - Net\ Investment$$

By simultaneously adding and subtracting some items to the right-hand side and regrouping the terms:

$$FCF = (EBIT - k_d \cdot D - Taxes + g \cdot D - Net\ Investment) + (1-t) \cdot k_d \cdot D - g \cdot D$$

Note that the terms within the first bracket on the right are (in total) equivalent to the cash flow to equity. This means that:

$$FCF = CF_e + (1-t) \cdot k_d \cdot D - g \cdot D$$

Using the assumption of constant growth, the equity value is given by:

$$E = \frac{CF_e}{k_e - g}$$

So

$$FCF = (k_e - g) \cdot E + (1-t) \cdot k_d \cdot D - g \cdot D$$

i.e.

$$FCF = k_e \cdot E + (1-t) \cdot k_d \cdot D - g \cdot (E + D)$$

The right-hand side can be thought of as a "financing equivalent" of free cash flow.

For the enterprise value using the post-tax WACC method, we note that the last equation can be written as:

$$FCF = (E+D) \cdot \left(k_e \cdot \frac{E}{E+D} + (1-t) \cdot k_d \cdot \frac{D}{E+D} - g \right)$$

That is (using the definition of post-tax WACC from Chapter 16):

$$FCF = (E+D) \cdot (WACC - g)$$

So that:

$$E + D = \frac{FCF}{WACC - g}$$

Similarly, for the APV method, in the "financing" equivalent formula, the tax term can first be moved to the left side

$$FCF + t \cdot k_d \cdot D = k_e \cdot E + + k_d \cdot D - g \cdot (E+D)$$

Then (by factoring the terms in a similar way to above, also noting the formulas in Chapter 1 in relation to the unlevered cost of equity):

$$FCF + t \cdot k_d \cdot D = (k_u - g) \cdot (E+D)$$

So that:

$$E + D = \frac{FCF}{k_u - g} + \frac{t \cdot k_d \cdot D}{k_u - g}$$

Note that the core assumptions used are that the growth rate, tax rates (of the tax shield), and leverage are constant. Further, it is assumed that the interest charges are calculated as the product of the cost of debt with the value of debt; this is essentially equivalent to assuming that the market value of the debt is equal to its face value (which would typically not fully hold if the yield curve was not constant, for example).

18.8 FURTHER TOPICS II: VALUE-DRIVER FORMULAS

One of the main weaknesses of using the annuity formulas directly for the terminal value is that the cash flow in the numerator implicitly includes the investment needs. In theory this means that it is not correct to perform a sensitivity analysis by changing the growth rate used for the terminal period: If the terminal growth rate were higher, then the investment needs would also be higher, and the cash flow reduced. However, this is not captured by the formulas as presented, since the numerator does not adjust as the growth rate is varied (i.e. the investment needs are not changing in accordance with the growth).

In principle, it is in fact preferable to use the "value-driver" formulas for the terminal values. For these, one makes an additional assumption on the return on capital (ROCE) during the terminal phase. Noting that, at stability, any additional growth in EBIT must also be equal to the return on capital multiplied by the net new capital, one can write:

$$\text{Net investment} = \text{Earnings} * g \ / \ \text{ROCE}$$

Then, this concept can be used in the terminal value formulas. For example, if there were only a perpetuity, the associated value (before discounting to the beginning of the model period) would be:

$$NOPAT \cdot (1 - g \ / \ ROCE) \ / \ (WACC - g)$$

The ratio g/ROCE is known as the reinvestment rate.

Note that if a sensitivity analysis to the growth rate were performed based on this formula, then an increase in the rate reduces both the numerator and the denominator, whereas for the standard formulas, only the denominator is reduced. Also, if the ROCE is set equal to the WACC, then the formula becomes simply:

$$NOPAT \ / \ WACC$$

This confirms the economic logic that if new investment only earns its cost of capital, growth has no effect on value, so that the value can be calculated by "capitalizing" the NOPAT at the cost of capital.

Note that the value driver approach can also be used to create multi-phase terminal value calculations (that is, with one or more annuities and a perpetuity). To do so involves:

- Setting the values for the ROCE in each phase (the growth rates having been assumed to already have been defined from an initial use of a multi-phase approach).
- Calculating the reinvestment rate for each phase.
- Calculating the value of NOPAT in the first period of each phase (using the assumed growth rates, as shown earlier).
- Adjusting the numerator of the annuity formulas to reflect that the annuities are for finite time periods (i.e. for the factor which represents the future "non-realized" part of the theoretical perpetuity value, as discussed in Section 14.6).

18.9 FURTHER TOPICS III: IMPLIED COST OF EQUITY

Market values and other information or assumptions can be used to determine a market-implied cost of equity (which may be considered as a complementary method to the CAPM, for example). For example, using a perpetuity formula for the equity method based on dividends received gives:

$$Equity\ Value = \frac{Dividends}{k_e - g}$$

When expressed in per share terms and rearranging gives:

$$k_e = g + \frac{1}{DPS}$$

An alternative formula is to use the value-driver approach for the same situation. In this case, the starting point is:

$$Equity\ Value = \frac{Earnings \cdot \left(1 - \dfrac{g}{ROE}\right)}{k_e - g}$$

Noting that earnings divided by equity value is the inverse of the price-earnings ratio, gives:

$$k_e = g + \frac{1}{P/E} \cdot \left(1 - \frac{g}{ROE}\right)$$

In these equations, to reduce statistical noise and the consequences of imperfections in the data, the estimates of earnings, return on equity, sustainable growth rates, and so on may need to be normalized, or use forward estimates or industry averages, and so on (similar to estimating beta with the CAPM).

19

Ratio Analysis

19.1 INTRODUCTION

The ratio of two financial quantities (such as operating profit divided by sales) can be used to compare performance in a relative sense. Generally, the analysis is performed with items that are found on the financial statements, or to market-related information about valuation. Most aspects of ratio analysis pose little challenge from a strict modeling perspective: Division of two quantities is straightforward. However, sometimes corrections to the underlying input data are needed in order to make the calculations as meaningful and accurate as possible.

This chapter covers the following topics:

- An overview of the uses of ratio analysis and some key principles in creating and calculating ratios.

- A discussion of common ratios that relate profitability and valuation, operations and efficiency, and leverage and liquidity.

- The use of DuPont analysis, and of "variations analysis" within this framework.

The Further Topics section briefly mentions some further uses of ratio-based methods for asset selection and portfolio construction, notably Piotroski F-scores.

19.2 USE AND PRINCIPLES

Typical uses of ratio analysis are:

- To analyze the performance of a company, including the comparison with its competitors or with industry averages. This can also be relevant to credit analysis and lending decisions.
- For valuation using the multiples method (i.e. relative valuation or comparables with similar companies).
- To act as credibility check on forecasting models. For example, over the time-period of an explicit forecasting model used for valuation, relevant ratios (such as the return on capital employed, or investment as a percentage of sales) should gradually converge to (or end up close to) their long-term equilibrium value (that is implicit in the annuity or perpetuity phases).
- To aid investment decisions for assets or portfolios, by looking for assets which meet or exceed specific performance criteria defined by ratios and other metrics.

It is sometimes necessary to adjust the raw data to ensure that the items used are consistent and comparable:

- Consistency refers to the idea that it makes sense to divide the items in the numerator by those in denominator. Generally, this means that "enterprise" level items are used together, and the equity-related items are used together (and without mixing between the two).
- Comparability refers to adjustments that may be needed to ensure that – when applied to the data for two companies – the numerator and denominator are calculated in the same way for each company. For example, a company that leases its premises may have less assets on its balance sheet than a company that owns its premises, even as the true physical asset base for each (i.e. the size and quality of the premises) could be the same. Similarly, the use of leases rather than purchasing an asset with debt alters (reduces) the debt-equity ratio. Ideally, adjustments would be made for this type of situation, although to do so requires that the information be available, and that one has the time and knowledge to make them. In addition, even if two companies are essentially identical, it could be necessary to perform some adjustments to historical data to remove exceptional or one-off issues that may have affected only one of them. Frequently, ratios are also quoted on a forward-looking basis, i.e. based on forecast earnings, which generally exclude such one-off items.

19.3 RATIOS FOR PROFITABILITY AND VALUATION

Some important ratios relating to operating profitability are:

- EBIT/Sales (i.e. the operating profit margin as a percentage of sales).
- EBIT/Assets (i.e. the return on operating assets).
- EBIT/Capital employed (i.e. the return on capital).

In the first point, each of the numerator and denominator is a flow quantity defined over the same period. Thus – to the extent that the business is stable – the length of the period used would not affect the ratio significantly. On the other hand, the second and third points divide a flow item by a stock item, and so the results depend on the period length used for the flow item (annual, quarterly, and so on); most often ratios are quoted with reference to annual data unless otherwise stated. Where an item is of a stock nature (such as assets, inventory, or debt), it is often the case that the value used for the item is the average of the starting and ending balance. For example, the ratio of operating profit to assets may be calculated based on the average assets. To the extent that the ratio is based on historical information only, this cannot create a circularity and may provide some additional accuracy. (This is different to the case of forecasting models, where average balances can create circularity if items within the numerator and denominator are on the same calculation path, such as is the case if interest charges are calculated based on average debt balances.) These points apply to ratio analysis in general and so are not explicitly mentioned in the rest of this chapter.

Similar ratios can be calculated in which the numerator is altered from EBIT to NOPAT:

- NOPAT/Sales.
- NOPAT/Assets.
- NOPAT/Capital.

EBITDA could also be used in the numerator:

- EBITDA/Sales.
- EBITDA/Assets.
- EBITDA/Capital.

Valuation-related metrics at the enterprise level include:

- EV/Sales (revenue multiple).
- EV/EBIT (operating earnings multiple).
- EV/EBITDA (EBITDA multiple).
- EV/NOPAT.
- NOPAT/Capital. By comparing this with the post-tax WACC (i.e. subtracting one from the other) one gains a measure of the economic profit (i.e. the returns earned above the cost of capital).

At the level of net income, important ratios include:

- P/E (price-earnings, i.e. price per share/earnings per share, for a quoted company).
- Net income/shareholders' equity (return on equity or ROE).
- Net income/shares outstanding (earnings per share, or EPS).
- Dividends/net income (dividend payout ratio).

19.4 RATIOS RELATING TO OPERATIONS AND EFFICIENCY

Some important ratios that relate to general operations (and to their efficiency, if there is a benchmark against which to judge them) include:

- Sales/Assets (i.e. asset turnover or capital efficiency).
- Sales/Accounts receivables (accounts receivable turnover).
- Cost of goods sold/Inventory (inventory turnover).
- Working capital/Sales (sometimes called a working capital ratio, but not to be confused with the "current ratio" that is covered in the next section).
- Accounts payable/Cost of goods sold (Payables ratio).

(As discussed in Chapter 7, some of these types of ratios can be expressed in "days' equivalent" terms, rather than as pure ratios.)
Ratios that relate to capital investment amount include:

- Capital investment/Sales.
- Depreciation/Capital investment.
- Depreciation/Sales.

19.5 RATIOS FOR LIQUIDITY AND LEVERAGE

Liquidity measures are aimed at assessing the ability of a company to pay its short-term obligations. Gearing and solvency ratios are often used to assess the credit health of a company. Key ratios include:

- D/E: debt-to-equity (or net debt-to-equity, after cash has been netted from the debt).
- (Net) Debt/Capital or Equity/Capital.
- Net debt/EBITDA.
- EBIT/interest expense (the interest coverage ratio or "times interest earned").
- EBITDA/interest expense, which represents the cash interest coverage ratio (pre-tax). EBITDA could be replaced by the sum of NOPAT plus depreciation to give a post-tax measure of interest coverage.

Some other measures are:

- Current assets/current liabilities (the working capital ratio or the "current ratio").
- The "quick" or "acid-test" ratio. This is rather like the current ratio, except that the numerator includes only the most liquid current assets (typically cash, marketable securities, and short-term investments, while finished goods inventories are excluded. Receivables are sometimes included and sometimes excluded from the numerator).

Finally, operational gearing (or leverage) is analogous to financial leverage, focusing on the extent to which outlays are fixed (i.e. that the cost structure contains fixed costs rather than variable ones):

- Fixed costs/Sales (operational leverage).
- EBITDA/Cash fixed costs (the cash fixed charge coverage ratio).
- EBIT/Fixed costs (the fixed charge coverage ratio).

19.6 DuPont ANALYSIS

DuPont analysis refers to a technique developed by DuPont Corporation in the 1920s. It involves breaking down a single ratio into several components (each of which is a ratio) which are multiplied together to give the original value (the denominator of one cancels the numerator of the next). For example:

- EBIT/Sales = (EBIT/Assets) . (Assets/Sales).
- EV/EBIT = (EV/Sales) . (Sales/EBIT)
- EBIT/Assets = (EBIT/Employees) . (Employees/Assets).
- Depreciation/Sales = (Depreciation/Assets) . (Assets/Sales).

(Similarly, EBITDA may generally be used instead of EBIT in the above.)

It is possible to create chains that have more than two components, such as:

- EBIT/Sales = (EBIT/Employees) . (Employees/Assets) . (Assets/Sales).
- ROE = (Net Income/Sales) . (Sales/Assets) . (Assets/Equity).

The latter was one of the core formulas used by DuPont originally, and can also be expressed as:

"Return on Equity equals Profitability times Capital efficiency times Leverage"

(Such formulas can be thought of as providing "drivers" as to how to improve performance. For example, to increase return on equity, one can increase either the profitability, the capital efficient, or the leverage.)

When the right-hand side has only two components, one can use graphs. Figure 19.1 shows an example of the use of a graph to display the comparison between a set of companies. The x-axis plots the asset turnover (Sales/Assets), and the y-axis plots the operating margin (EBIT/Sales). The product of the x and y values is therefore the value of EBIT/Assets (pre-tax return on assets). Note that since the equation "$x.y$ = constant" would result in a hyperbola if plotted graphically, the "isoquant" lines (where EBIT/Assets is constant) are hyperbolas. An example is shown, indicating that the companies each earn approximately the same return on assets, even as one does this by being a "luxury" producer (with low turnover of assets but higher margins), while another follows a "commodity" business model (high turnover of assets and low margins).

Figure 19.1 **Generic Example of DuPont Analysis Using Linear Scales**

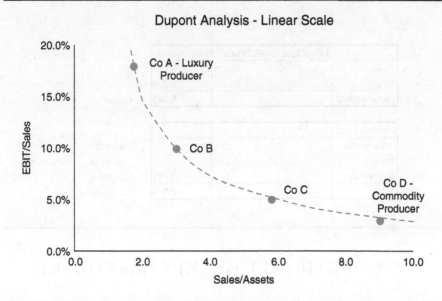

(The isoquant line will be straight if the axes are set in Excel to use logarithmic scales. This alters the presentation of the axis while the values displayed are the actual (natural) values. Alternatively, one can manually calculate the logarithm of the values and plot these on a linear scale; the isoquant line is also straight, but the values displayed on the axis are the logarithmic values not the natural ones.)

19.7 VARIATIONS ANALYSIS WITHIN THE DuPont FRAMEWORK

Where an item is the product of two others, the variation between its values can be broken into the variation of each component. (The variation may be due to the measurement at different points in time for the same company, or at the same point in time for two companies, as well as other possibilities). For example, if sales revenue is expressed as the product of price and volume, then a difference (variation) between two values of the sales revenue can be decomposed into a component caused by a difference in the price, and another caused by a difference in the volume, as well as an interaction term. That is:

Figure 19.2 **Variations Analysis Using Component Parts**

	A	B	C	D	E	F	G	H
1								
2			Sales/Assets	EBIT/Sales	EBIT/Assets			
3		Co A	1.8	18.0%	0.315			
6		Co D	9.0	3.0%	0.270			
7		Variance A–D			0.045		E7=E3-E6	
8								
9		Components						
10		Differences	-7.3	15%			C10=C3-C6	D10=D3-D6
11		Scaled	-0.218	1.350			C11=C10*D6	D11=D10*C6
12		Interaction			-1.088		E12=C10*D10	
13		Total			0.045		E13=C11+D11+E12	
14								

$$P_1 \cdot V_1 - P_0 \cdot V_0 = (P_1 - P_0) \cdot V_0 + (V_1 - V_0) \cdot P_0 + (P_1 - P_0) \cdot (V_1 - V_0)$$

(Such analysis can be generalized when an item is the product of three components, but graphical displays are not as easy to produce, and there are more interaction terms which add complexity to the interpretation.)

Figure 19.2 shows the analysis applied to the values for companies A and D in the above Figure 19.1. In cell E7 the direct variation in the aggregate value is shown. The variation of 0.045 (i.e. 4.5%, in cell E7) corresponds to the calculation on the left side of the above formula. It can be broken down into the three components on the right-hand side: A variation of −0.218 due to the change in asset turnover (cell C11), a variation of 1.350 due to a change in operating profit margin (cell D11) and −1.088 due to the interaction between these two (cell E12). The sum of these (cell E13) is equal to the total variation as calculated directly in cell E7.

Variations analysis can be used to complement Dupont analysis, where the components are ratios (rather than price or volume, as in the example).

19.8 FURTHER TOPICS: PORTFOLIOS AND THE PIOTROSKI F-SCORE

Ratio analysis (as well as the associated tools of DuPont analysis and variations analysis) also have applications in asset selection and portfolio analysis. These are very briefly discussed in the following.

The Piotroski F-Score is sometimes used to select stocks (by searching for undervalued investments). The score (from 0 to 9) is calculated as the number of criteria in the following list that are met:

- The return on assets for the last financial year (FY) is positive.
- The return on assets for the last FY is greater than the return on assets in the FY prior to that.
- Cash from operations for the last FY is positive.
- Cash from operations is greater than income after taxes for the last FY.
- The debt-to-assets ratio for the last FY is less than it was in the FY prior to that.
- The current ratio for the last FY is greater than the current ratio for the prior FY.
- The average shares outstanding for the last FY is less than or equal to the figure in the prior FY.
- The gross margin for the last FY is greater than the gross margin for the prior FY.
- The asset turnover for the last FY is greater than the asset turnover for the prior FY.

Variations analysis can be used in portfolio analysis by applying it to the individual elements which compose the portfolio. Thus, for a portfolio of investment assets, the performance of each asset can be broken into its components, and the performance of the portfolio analyzed by considering the weighting of each asset. This can be used to judge a portfolio manager's performance by splitting the aggregate performance into those which are due to the manager (such as the weighting of assets) versus those which are due to the general market. (Details of how to do this specifically are beyond the scope of this text.)

Part Six

Data and
Statistical Analysis

20

Statistical Analysis and Measures

20.1 INTRODUCTION

There are many potential roles for data and statistical analysis within modeling contexts. These include estimating appropriate values for model inputs (such as for a growth rate assumption so that it is consistent with recent actual performance), or to determine the nature of the relationships between two items (such as with regression analysis), or to analyze the outputs of models (such as to verify that they are in a realistic range or to use statistical methods to determine how likely a specific output value is).

Frequently, in addition to the analysis of data, one must first prepare it (i.e. to source, clean, manipulate, and integrate it). There are many possible variations of the structures, formats, and definitions of data that one may come across, as well as many forms of statistical analysis that could be conducted. The scope of the topics is potentially extremely large, and so the requirements and complexity of these processes can vary significantly. Therefore, this text aims to focus on the essentials that most closely relate to classical modeling in Excel.

This chapter covers some core aspects of data and statistical analysis, on the assumption that the data sets are clean (i.e. in the form required for the analysis to be carried out directly). Chapter 21 covers some of the key methods that can be used to manipulate data in Excel (i.e. to bring it into the required form).

This chapter provides an overview of statistical measures that relate to one or to several variables. These broadly fall into the following categories:

- Sums, averages, centrality.
- Spread and volatility.
- Conditional aggregations.
- Correlations, covariance, and regression.

In addition, the Chapter covers data structures in Excel and how these are related to the available functionality, as well as Excel Tables and PivotTables. The Further Topics section briefly covers some concepts in related topics including moving averages, serial correlation, and confidence intervals.

20.2 DATA STRUCTURES IN EXCEL AND THE IMPACT ON FUNCTIONALITY

Statistical measures can be defined purely using mathematical formulas, that is without reference to any specific data set, nor to how any data sets are structured. On the other hand, some Excel functions or functionality do require data to be structured in particular ways, and some do not. The following provides an overview of the main data structures that impact the types of Excel functions and functionality that is available:

- Unstructured or ad hoc data. Where the data is not laid out in a systematic way (typically with only a few data points that could be present far from each other in a model), many functions and operations can nevertheless be applied by picking out the individual items as needed. For example, the arithmetic operations (addition, multiplication, etc.) as well as many of the core functions (IF, SUM, AVERAGE, MAX, MIN, etc.) can be used in this way. That is, the data need not be in a particular form (and may also not be labeled systematically, or even at all).

- Column- or row-form arrays (with labels not used). Some functions essentially require that data be structured in a contiguous and a consistent way (i.e. in a contiguous row or column, or in a two-dimensional tabular form). For example, the conditional aggregation functions such as SUMIFS, AVERAGEIFS, MAXIFS fall into this category. (The earlier Figure 6.2 showed an example of the SUMIFS function in which the input ranges (i.e. Sum_range and Criteria_Range1) were in a row). Note that these functions did not use the labels of the data sets (i.e. the row labels or column headers) for the calculations (neither explicitly nor implicitly), so that such labels are in a sense only cosmetic (but important for transparency). Other functions which can be used in either data structure include the lookup and reference functions, such as XMATCH and XLOOKUP. (Examples of these were shown in Figure 6.3, as well as in Figure 11.7 and Figure 11.8.). Some statistical functions also behave in this way (such as the PERCENTILE-type and RANK-type, which are discussed later in this chapter).

- Column-form array (with headers not used). Some Excel functions require that the data be structured into columns, even though the column field header is not used in the calculations (explicitly nor implicitly) and as such are "cosmetic" labels. Examples include the AGGREGATE and SUBTOTAL (see later), as well as SORT and SORTBY.

- Column databases (headers are used). Some Excel functions are specifically designed to act as database functions. These include DSUM, DCOUNT, DCOUNTA, DMAX, DGET and so on (see examples later in this chapter). The single row immediately above the data values (or records) must contain field headers and these must be unique and not repeated within the data set (to avoid creating ambiguously defined items). The drop-down menu filter functionality also requires data to be structured in this way.

- Excel Table. A Table is a columnar structure like a database. However, it has some further properties: First, a Table must have a name (or is given one by default). Second, the range that defines it is automatically extended when data is added in a new row or column that is contiguous to the original Table. Third, a formula entered in the top cell of a column (first record below the header) which uses values from other fields in the same row as its inputs will automatically be copied to all rows of the Table in the same column. Excel Tables are usually presented in a banded form with alternate rows being of the same color and shading. Tables are often created automatically when a data set is imported from an external source (see Chapter 21). A data set that is initially structured as a database (as described previously) can be converted to a Table using the Excel menu Insert/Table or the shortcut CTRL+T (or Home/Format as Table, as well as by right-clicking to access the context-sensitive menu). In this text we use the term "Table" (with a capital letter) to refer to such Tables, whereas the word "table" is used for two-by-two general ranges and similar related areas.

- Relational Tables (relational databases). This is where several databases are joined together using logical (rather than physical) links to identify items that relate to each other. It is possible to achieve this using the Excel Data Model (and PowerPivot). While beyond the scope of this text, it is briefly mentioned in the Further Topics section of the Chapter 21.

Thus, while some Excel functions can be used when data is in either row or column form (or not structured at all), the more advanced functions and functionality do require a columnar form. Therefore, the examples shown in this chapter will generally be structured in column form, even though this is not strictly necessary in all cases.

20.3 AVERAGES AND SPREAD

There are many ways in which the "central" value of a set of data (about a single variable) can be measured, as well as various ways to express the range or spread of the values. Some of the important ones are:

- The mean (average or weighted average). This is simply the sum of all the items divided by the number of items, and where items that occur several times (or with given weights) are counted in accordance with that. Excel functions that can calculate this include AVERAGE (if each item is individually listed) or dividing the result of the SUM with that of COUNT (also if each item is listed individually) or using SUMPRODUCT to calculate the weighted average (if the frequency of each item is listed). It is also called the "expected value," even though it may not be a likely or even possible outcome (for example, when rolling a die, the average is 3.5, which is not an outcome that can occur, so one should not expect to see it!).

- The mode, modal, or most likely value. This is the most frequently occurring item. If all the items have values that are different to each other, then there is no single modal value (so that the mode does not exist uniquely). If it does exist, it is arguably the value that one should "expect" (if forced to choose a single outcome), although this terminology is not used generally (since it is reserved to describe the mean, as an expectation from a mathematical perspective). Excel has several related functions, such as MODE.SNGL (this will return #N/A if there is no single modal value).

- The median value is that for which half the items are below and half are above when listed in value-ranked order (with appropriate rounding or interpolation where the number of points is even rather than odd). The MEDIAN function can be used, as can the PERCENTILE-type functions (see below) at the 50% percentile.

- The FREQUENCY and the COUNTIFS functions can be used to establish the frequency of points within bins (ranges) that one predefines. (When using the COUNTIFS function, one can create two criteria ranges that relate to the same data, to count the number of items whose value is between the lower and upper limit of each bin range.)

- The full range can be found using the MIN and MAX functions, or the SMALL and LARGE functions. These latter functions can also be used to find the second or third smallest or largest values, and so on. (They are distinct from the RANK-type functions which returns the order of an item within its data set, i.e. first, second, third, and so on.)

- The spread can also be measured by using the standard deviation, with functions STDEV.S (when the data is a sample, and the function corrects for the sample size bias) or STDEV.P (when the data is regarded as consisting of the whole population). The standard deviation is a core general measure of risk (often called volatility) in many financial market applications.

- There are various functions to calculate the percentiles of a data set, including the legacy PERCENTILE and the more updated version PERCENTILE.INC. Percentiles are often used to express the values associated with scenarios of a defined probability (such as a value-at-risk measure).

From a mathematical perspective, the mean of a set of (N) individual data points can be written as:

$$\mu = \frac{1}{N}\sum_{i=1}^{i=N}x_i$$

or, equivalently, if the data values are presented according to their percentage frequency or weighting:

$$\mu = \sum_{i=1}^{i=N}p_i x_i$$

The variance of a population of N points is defined as the average of the squared distances from the mean:

$$Variance = \sum_{i=1}^{i=N} p_i (x_i - \mu)^2$$

(If the data set is a sample of a larger population, then this formula can be used to provide a de-biased estimate of the population's variance by multiplying it by N and dividing by $N - 1$.)

The standard deviation is the square root of the variance. Therefore, it is expressed in the same units as the variable (x). For example, if the data set is in dollars, then so is its standard deviation. (It is often thought of as the average deviation from the mean, although this is not fully correct, since the deviations are first squared before the overall square-root is taken.)

Figure 20.1 shows the data set that will be used to demonstrate many of the functions. The raw data consists of the month-end value of an asset over a seven-year period, as shown in column B and column C (with rows 7–60 hidden for presentation purposes). Column D is a calculated column that shows the changes (returns) in the value of the asset each month.

(Note that as discussed in the Further Topics section of Chapter 5, it can sometimes be more appropriate to calculate the changes using the logarithmic method, as this allows items to be correctly averaged or summed when using functions such as AVERAGE or SUM. However, the differences in this case would be rather small, so this is not done here for convenience of the presentation.)

Figure 20.1 **Raw Data for Input to the Statistical Functions**

	A	B	C	D	E
1					
2		Month End	Values	Changes	
3					
4		Mar-24	589	-0.8%	D4=C4/C5-1
5		Feb-24	594	-0.8%	D5=C5/C6-1
6		Jan-24	599	4.5%	D6=C6/C7-1
61		Jun-19	356	-8.7%	D61=C61/C62-1
62		May-19	390	1.0%	D62=C62/C63-1
63		Apr-19	386	-1.8%	D63=C63/C64-1
64		Mar-19	393		

20.4 THE AGGREGATE FUNCTION

The AGGREGATE function is a "wrapper" function that has several underlying function choices embedded within it. Therefore, rather than using the individual statistical functions directly, many of the results can be generated by using only AGGREGATE with the appropriate choice of underlying function (which one must specify by populating the first argument of AGGREGATE). The function also allows one to specify how items (such as errors) are to be treated (which one must specify through the second argument), and therefore it is more flexible than many of the underlying functions. The data itself is used as the third argument of the function (and a fourth argument is required for some of the underlying function forms; see later in this chapter).

Figure 20.2 shows the application of the AGGREGATE function (in column I) to calculate a range of statistical measures relating to values in column D. The underlying function is specified through the values defined in column F, and the name of the corresponding function is shown in column G. For example, cell K4 shows the formula for the function that is used in cell I4, and this function uses a reference to cell F4 (as its first argument) in order to define that the AVERAGE function is used as the underlying function. The second argument is in this case set to the

Figure 20.2 **Examples of the Use of AGGREGATE**

A E	F Function_num	G Name	I Value	J	K Formula
1					
2					
3	Function_num	Name	Value		Formula
4	1	AVERAGE	0.87%		I4=AGGREGATE(F4,6,D$4:D$63)
5	2	COUNT	60		I5=AGGREGATE(F5,6,D$4:D$63)
6	3	COUNTA	60		I6=AGGREGATE(F6,6,D$4:D$63)
7	4	MAX	14.9%		I7=AGGREGATE(F7,6,D$4:D$63)
8	5	MIN	-14.4%		I8=AGGREGATE(F8,6,D$4:D$63)
9	6	PRODUCT	0.0%		I9=AGGREGATE(F9,6,D$4:D$63)
10	7	STDEV.S	6.28%		I10=AGGREGATE(F10,6,D$4:D$63)
11	8	STDEV.P	6.23%		I11=AGGREGATE(F11,6,D$4:D$63)
12	9	SUM	52.1%		I12=AGGREGATE(F12,6,D$4:D$63)
13	10	VAR.S	0.39%		I13=AGGREGATE(F13,6,D$4:D$63)
14	11	VAR.P	0.39%		I14=AGGREGATE(F14,6,D$4:D$63)
15	12	MEDIAN	0.06%		I15=AGGREGATE(F15,6,D$4:D$63)
16	13	MODE.SNGL	#N/A		I16=AGGREGATE(F16,6,D$4:D$63)

fixed value of six, which excludes from the calculations of any error values in the input field (i.e. within the range D4:D63). The options for this second parameter are:

- Option 0 (or omitted) is to ignore SUBTOTAL and AGGREGATE functions.
- Option 1 is to ignore hidden rows, nested SUBTOTAL and AGGRE-GATE functions.
- Option 2 is to ignore error values, nested SUBTOTAL and AGGRE-GATE functions.
- Option 3 is to ignore hidden rows, error values, nested SUBTOTAL and AGGREGATE functions.
- Option 4 is to ignore nothing.
- Option 5 is to ignore hidden rows.
- Option 6 is to ignore error values.
- Option 7 is to ignore hidden rows and error values.

Note that Option 6 is particularly useful, as it allows for errors within its input range to be ignored, which is different to many Excel functions.

Figure 20.3 shows the use of the fourth argument, which is an additional parameter that is required for some of the function choices. For example, if using the equivalent to the PERCENTILE-type functions, one must specify the percentage associated with this.

Figure 20.3 **Using AGGREGATE with its Fourth Argument**

	Function_num Name	k parameter	Value	Formula
17	14 LARGE	2	13.68%	I17=AGGREGATE(F17,6,D$4:D$63,H17)
18	15 SMALL	3	-8.72%	I18=AGGREGATE(F18,6,D$4:D$63,H18)
19	16 PERCENTILE.INC	25%	-3.3%	I19=AGGREGATE(F19,6,D$4:D$63,H19)
20	17 QUARTILE.INC	1	-3.3%	I20=AGGREGATE(F20,6,D$4:D$63,H20)
21	18 PERCENTILE.EXC	75%	4.9%	I21=AGGREGATE(F21,6,D$4:D$63,H21)
22	19 QUARTILE.EXC	3	4.9%	I22=AGGREGATE(F22,6,D$4:D$63,H22)

Note also that the AGGREGATE function:

- Requires that the data be in column format.
- Does not use or require field headers. That is, the function refers to the data set in the range D4:D63, where cell D4 is the first data point. (In order to emphasize this, in Figure 20.1 the field headers were used in row 2, with row 3 containing no content.) This contrasts with Database functions and Tables, which are discussed later in this chapter.

Finally, while the AGGREGATE function embeds many common statistical measures of a single variable, it does not contain every possible measure. For example, the functions GEOMEAN and HARMEAN calculate the geometric and harmonic means of a set of data and are occasionally needed in financial analysis. Similarly, the AVEDEV function calculates the average deviation from the mean when measured in absolute terms, so that deviations on either side are directly included at their values (whereas the standard deviation squares the deviations before taking the square root of the overall total). Further, some types of measures of risk or variability are not available as Excel functions, and so may need to be calculated explicitly. For example, whereas the standard deviation is a two-sided measure, the semi-deviation is an analogous measure in which only the deviations on one side (above or below the mean) are considered. While a full discussion of this is beyond the scope of this text, the calculation steps required to determine its value are straightforward.

20.5 CONDITIONAL AGGREGATIONS

Excel has several functions that calculate values relating to a single variable, but in which only specific items are included based on defined criteria. The main ones are SUMIFS, AVERAGEIFS, COUNTIFS, MINIFS, and MAXIFS. (In general, it is preferable to use the -IFS forms, even if only one criterion is to be applied – for example to use SUMIFS rather than SUMIF – as the parameter order for the -IF form is different, and therefore one loses flexibility if an additional criterion is desired to be applied.)

Figure 20.4 shows the same data set as used above, but which has applied the MONTH and YEAR functions (in columns C and D) to the dates (in column B) to split out the month and year numbers.

The conditional functions such as AVERAGEIFS function could then be used to analyze some of the statistical aspects of the data, on a monthly or an annual basis. (That is, the total, average, minimum, maximum, or number of data points could be established.)

Figure 20.4 **Augmented Data Set with Month and Year Information**

	Month End	MONTH	YEAR	Values	Changes
	Mar-24	3	2024	589	-0.8%
	Feb-24	2	2024	594	-0.8%
	Jan-24	1	2024	599	4.5%
	Dec-23	12	2023	573	-3.4%
	Nov-23	11	2023	593	-1.0%
	Oct-23	10	2023	599	8.7%
	Sep-23	9	2023	551	7.4%

Figure 20.5 **Use of the AVERAGEIFS Function**

	Month	Average Returns	
	1	3.2%	I4=AVERAGEIFS(F$4:F$63,C$4:C$63,H4)
	2	-0.7%	I5=AVERAGEIFS($F$4:$F$63,$C$4:$C$63,$H5)
	3	-2.1%	I6=AVERAGEIFS($F$4:$F$63,$C$4:$C$63,$H6)
	4	2.3%	I7=AVERAGEIFS($F$4:$F$63,$C$4:$C$63,$H7)
	5	0.1%	I8=AVERAGEIFS($F$4:$F$63,$C$4:$C$63,$H8)
	6	1.5%	I9=AVERAGEIFS($F$4:$F$63,$C$4:$C$63,$H9)
	7	-2.5%	I10=AVERAGEIFS($F$4:$F$63,$C$4:$C$63,$H10)
	8	-0.1%	I11=AVERAGEIFS($F$4:$F$63,$C$4:$C$63,$H11)
	9	2.1%	I12=AVERAGEIFS($F$4:$F$63,$C$4:$C$63,$H12)
	10	2.4%	I13=AVERAGEIFS($F$4:$F$63,$C$4:$C$63,$H13)
	11	6.5%	I14=AVERAGEIFS($F$4:$F$63,$C$4:$C$63,$H14)
	12	-2.2%	I15=AVERAGEIFS($F$4:$F$63,$C$4:$C$63,$H15)

Figure 20.5 shows an example of the use of AVERAGEIFS to analyze the information by month. The function refers to the raw input data that is to be aggregated (which is in column F in the augmented data set shown in Figure 20.4), as well as using the range in column C as its criteria range, against which the criteria value (in each associated cell of column H) is checked.

Note (see the formulas displayed in column K) that the functions refer only to the ranges that start from row 4, so that the header fields are not used or required.

20.6 DATABASE FUNCTIONS

Database functions include DAVERAGE, DSUM, DCOUNT, DMIN, DMAX, DGET, and DSTDEV. For example, DAVERAGE could be used to conduct a similar type of conditional analysis to that in the last Section with AVERAGEIFS. However, when using these functions (in contrast to those in the last section), the data set must not only be in columnar format, but also have unique header fields for each column that are contiguous with the raw data. Also, these functions require one to define a separate "Criteria Range" that defines the criteria and the values to be used.

Figure 20.6 shows an example of the earlier dataset, but which has been adjusted so that each column has a unique field header that is contiguous with the raw data (i.e. in comparison with Figure 20.4, the row with the original labels (field headers) has been moved down by one).

Figure 20.6 **Data Set with Field Headers**

	A	B	C	D	E	F	
1							
2							
3		Month End	MONTH	YEAR	Values	Changes	
4		Mar-24	3	2024	589	-0.8%	
5		Feb-24	2	2024	594	-0.8%	
6		Jan-24	1	2024	599	4.5%	

The criteria range for the database functions is a separate range that uses the same field headers (or a subset of them), as well as at least one row underneath these, into which the values of each criterion are entered. Figure 20.7 shows an example, which is set so that the analysis would use only the data from March (i.e. from month three).

The DAVERAGE function would then be entered in a cell. The inputs required are the full database, the name of the field that one wishes to analyze, and the full criteria range. Figure 20.8 shows an example of the Functions Argument dialog. Note that the first and third arguments (i.e. the definition of the database and of the criteria range) include the header rows. The field to be analyzed is defined using the second argument to point to a header field within the database. In this case the use of cell F3 as the field header means that it is the "Changes" data (from cell F4 downwards) that is to be analyzed (i.e. whose average is to be calculated for the March records).

Figure 20.7 **Example of a Criteria Range for a Database Function**

	A	G	H	I	J	K
1						
2						
3			MONTH	YEAR	Changes	
4				3		
5						

Figure 20.8 **Function Arguments for the Database Functions**

Function Arguments

DAVERAGE

Database	$B3:$F64	⬆
Field	$F3	⬆
Criteria	$H3:$J4	⬆

Naturally, one would expect that the results produced by the functions would be the same as if the corresponding conditional function were used. Figure 20.9 shows the results of applying the DSUM, DCOUNT, and DAVERAGE functions with the arguments defined as in the above figures. Thus, the value in cell N4 (which is the average for the month of March) is the same value that was calculated using the AVERAGEIFS functions (in cell I6 of Figure 20.5).

The main disadvantage of Database functions is the complexity of using the same criteria multiple times (i.e. as the value tested for a specific criterion is varied). That is, when using the AVERAGEIFS function (Figure 20.5), the formula was simply copied down the rows to create the analysis for each of the twelve months. However, with a database function this would not be possible. It would be necessary either to – for each month – create a new criteria range associated database functions – or to retain a single criteria range but run the multiple values (i.e. of the month) using a sensitivity analysis. (This is discussed in detail in *PFM* where it is shown how to use VBA macros to do so.)

On the other hand, the main advantages of the Database functions are that:

Figure 20.9 **Results of Applying the Database Functions**

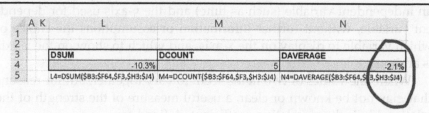

A K	L	M	N
1			
2			
3	DSUM	DCOUNT	DAVERAGE
4	-10.3%	5	-2.1%
5	L4=DSUM($B3:$F64,$F3,$H3:$J4)	M4=DCOUNT($B3:$F64,$F3,$H3:$J4)	N4=DAVERAGE($B3:$F64,$B3,$H3:$J4)

- The functions allow for the identity of the criteria (rather than the values for each criterion) to be rapidly changed. That is, once a (database) criteria range is set up, the simple entry of a value in the range underneath a field header means that that criterion will be invoked. For example, to change the analysis from monthly to annual (referring to Figure 20.7), one can simply clear cell H4 in and enter the required year in cell I4. By contrast, when using functions such as AVERAGEIFS, the changing of the identity of a criterion involves relinking the function to the underlying data (since the criteria range for these functions is within the data set), which is time-consuming, cumbersome and error prone.

- The database functions are more transparent when several criteria are to be checked, since a visual inspection of the criteria range is simple. On the other hand, the conditional functions require, for each criterion, a new input argument that is linked to the full data set to identify its criteria range.

- The database functions also provide some functionality that is not present in the conditional functions, including DSTDEV and DST-DEVP (which can be used to calculate the standard deviation of a subset of the data, such as by month or by year), as well as DGET (which allows one to pick out the value of a unique record that matches the specific criteria defined, rather like some of the lookup functions).

20.7 CORRELATIONS, COVARIANCE, AND REGRESSION

When exploring the possible relationships between two items, the creations of an X-Y (or scatter) plot a is a useful starting point. Doing so may allow one to form a view of the general relationship between the items such as whether they seem to be independent of each other, or tend to increase (or decrease) together.

While it is often the case that the x-axis of a chart tends to be used for an independent variable (such as time) and the y-axis used for dependent variable, without further information or assumptions the choice of which variable to display on the x-axis, and which to show on the y-axis is arbitrary.

Where the values of two items seem to vary together, but for reasons that may not be known or clear, a useful measure of the strength of the relationship is the correlation coefficient, defined as:

$$\rho = \frac{\sum_i (x_i - \mu_x)(y_i - \mu_y)}{\sqrt{\sum_i (x_i - \mu_x)^2 \sum_i (y_i - \mu_y)^2}}$$

(where x and y represent the individual values of the respective data sets, and μ_x and μ_y are their means).

This is known as the "linear" or Pearson correlation coefficient. It can be calculated using either of the functions CORRREL or PEARSON. The numerator captures the effect of any relationship between the items: Each of its individual components is the product of the deviation of each item from its own mean value. Each product term is positive only when the specific x and y values are either both above or both below their means (otherwise the contribution is negative, or zero). The denominator is essentially a scaling factor that ensures that the result is between minus one and one (in fact, it is the square root of the product of the variances, i.e. the product of the standard deviations). Thus, the correlation captures the extent to which the items tend to vary simultaneously or not (each relative to its own mean). It is a symmetric measure, in that no variable is given preference over the other, and the values of the two data sets could be interchanged without affecting the result.

If a linear regression analysis is conducted, with the regression line displayed on the X-Y scatter chart, there is a relationship between the correlation coefficient and the standard deviations of the values, that is given by:

$$\text{Slope} = \rho \frac{\sigma_y}{\sigma_x}$$

Note that – as seen from the ratio term on the right-hand side of the formula – the slope would depend on which item is used on the x-axis and which on the y-axis (even as the correlation coefficient would be unchanged due to its symmetry property).

Figure 20.10 **Data Set for Correlation and Regression Analysis**

	A	B	C	D	E	F	G	H
1								
2								
3		Month End	MONTH	YEAR	V_Mkt	V_Asset	Chg_Mkt	Chg_Asset
4		Mar-24	3	2024	13,400	589	-1.4%	-0.8%
5		Feb-24	2	2024	13,650	594	-2.2%	-0.8%
6		Jan-24	1	2024	13,950	599	1.4%	4.5%
7		Dec-23	12	2023	13,760	573	1.3%	-3.4%
8		Nov-23	11	2023	13,590	593	1.6%	-1.0%

Figure 20.11 **X-Y Scatter Plot with Trendline Displayed**

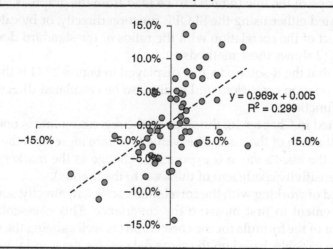

In practice, the item which is considered "more independent" or "more fundamental" may be chosen to be displayed on the x-axis. For example, when comparing the changes in the value of an individual stock or asset with the changes in the value of the overall market, one would typically choose to use the x-axis for the market-related data.

Figure 20.10 shows a data set similar to that used earlier, but in which the values of the market (column E) and the changes (returns) in the values are calculated (column G).

The returns data (in columns G and H) can be plotted on an X-Y scatter plot, with the market data as the x-axis. When doing so in Excel, the option to display the (regression) trendline is available by right-clicking on any of the data points (and the option to show the equation of the line is also available). This is shown in Figure 20.11.

Figure 20.12 **Calculation of Slope, Correlations, and Standard Deviations**

	A	G	H	I	J	K	L	M
1								
2								
3		Chg_Mkt	Chg_Asset		SLOPE	0.969		K3=SLOPE(H4:H63,G4:G63)
4		-1.4%	-0.8%					
5		-2.2%	-0.8%		Item	Result		
6		1.4%	4.5%		CORREL (returns)	54.7%		K6=CORREL(G4:G63,H4:H63)
7		1.3%	-3.4%		STDEV (market returns)	3.5%		K7=STDEV(G4:G63)
8		1.6%	-1.0%		STDEV (asset returns)	6.3%		K8=STDEV(H4:H63)
9		3.2%	8.7%		CORREL*STDEV/STDEV	0.969		K9=K6*K8/K7

The slope of the line (which can be read from the graph as 0.969) can be calculated either using the SLOPE function directly, or by calculating the product of the correlation with the ratios of the standard deviations. Figure 20.12 shows these methods.

(Note that the R-squared value displayed in Figure 20.11 is the square of the correlation coefficient and could also be calculated directly using the RSQ function.)

As noted in Chapter 16, the slope of the regression line is one way to estimate the beta of the asset. This value therefore represents the amount by which the asset's value is expected to change as the market changes (i.e. the sensitivity coefficient of the asset to the market).

Instead of working with the correlation coefficient directly, sometimes it is convenient to first measure the covariance. This is essentially the numerator of the formula for the correlation (as well as being the variance of a single variable, based on the same data set for the x and y values):

$$Covariance(X,Y) = \sum_i (x_i - \mu_x)(y_i - \mu_y)$$

or

$$Covariance(X,Y) = \rho \sigma_x \sigma_y$$

The covariance can be calculated directly using the functions COVARIANCE.P for the full population of COVARIANCE.S (to estimate the population covariance from a sample). This topic was briefly mentioned in the Further Topics section of Chapter 4 in relation to portfolio optimization.

20.8 EXCEL TABLES

Excel Tables are column-based structures that use field headers, rather like a database. In addition, they must have (or be given) a name. Their main property is that the range (rows or columns) is automatically extended if a row or column of data is entered immediately underneath or to the right of an existing table. Also, any formula that is entered into the first cell underneath a header will be copied downwards to all cells in that column. Tables are usually formatted in banded form.

Tables are important structures, not only due to the property that their range is extended automatically in these ways, but also because data sets that are brought into Excel from external sources very often use a Table structure by default.

Figure 20.13 shows the Create Table dialog that results from selecting a cell anywhere in the data set and using CTRL+T (which is a shortcut for the Table option under the Insert menu tab).

Figure 20.13 **Creating a Table**

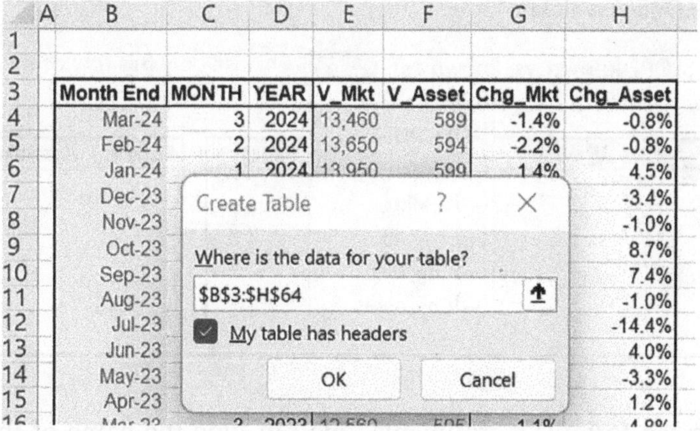

Figure 20.14 shows that after setting the range definition (and then pressing OK), the Table Design tab will appear. It allows one to define the name of the Table (which is otherwise allocated by default) or to convert the Table back to a normal Excel range. The structure will typically appear in a banded-row format (that can be altered on the Table Design menu).

If one wishes to create a formula that requires a whole column of data, such as to calculate the correlation between the asset changes, then when

Figure 20.14 **The Table Design Tab**

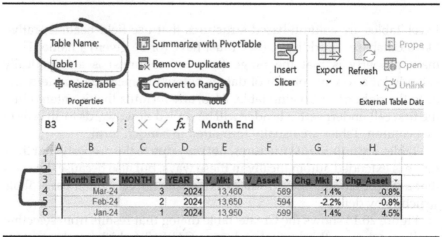

Figure 20.15 **Entering a Formula That Will Refer to a Table**

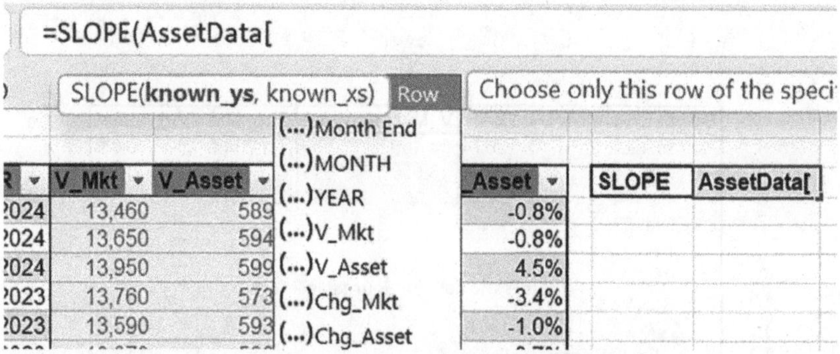

entering the formula's arguments, one can type the name of the Table followed by an opening square bracket, so that the list of column field headers will appear from which the formula can be built. Figure 20.15 shows an example in which the Table has first been named as "Asset-Data" (using the Table Design menu) and the SLOPE function used in cell J3 in a way that references the Tables data.

(Note that when using the SLOPE function, it is important to enter the order of the two data sets correctly i.e. the first argument to the function is the data for the y-axis.)

A further discussion of Tables takes place in Chapter 21, in the context of using the PowerQuery functionality to link to external data sources and manipulate data, as well as when using the Excel Data Model (PowerPivot).

20.9 PIVOT TABLES

A PivotTable is a way to create flexible summary reports based on a dataset which is structured either as a database or as a Table (i.e. with a columnar structure and unique and well-defined field headers for each column). The word "pivot" is used because the row and column structure of the table are defined by the user (and are taken from the column headers of the data set) and so the structure can be altered easily. The resulting table contains a summary of a specific item (chosen by the user) that is presented in this row-column structure, and in accordance with a specified type of analysis.

Figure 20.16 shows an example of a completed PivotTable in which only a row structure has been used (i.e. the month of the items is used as the category for the rows), and the report created shows the average returns of the asset per month (whose values are therefore the same as the results shown in the earlier Figure 20.5).

Figure 20.16 **Completed PivotTable with a Row Structure**

	A	B	C
1			
2			
3	Row Labels ▼	Average of Chg_Asset	
4	1	3.2%	
5	2	-0.7%	
6	3	-2.1%	
7	4	2.3%	
8	5	0.1%	
9	6	1.5%	
10	7	-2.5%	
11	8	-0.1%	
12	9	2.1%	
13	10	2.4%	
14	11	6.5%	
15	12	-2.2%	
16	Grand Total	0.9%	
17			

Figure 20.17 **First Step to Insert a PivotTable**

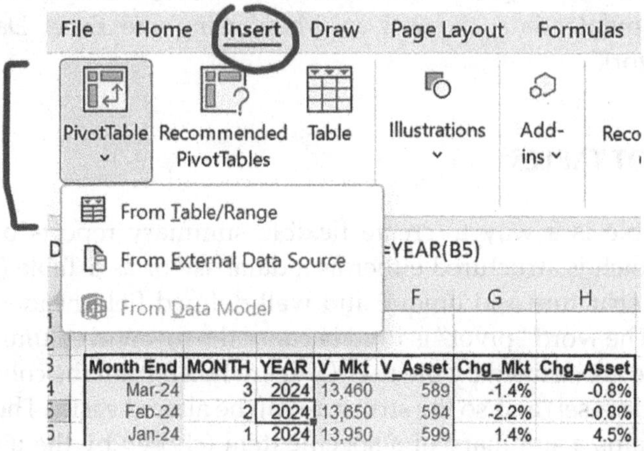

Figure 20.17 shows the first step in the process of creating a PivotTable by using the step-by-step menu on the Insert tab of Excel. The input range currently is a regular Excel database. (The menu allows for data to be obtained from an external source, which is discussed in Chapter 21.)

Figure 20.18 shows the next part of the step-by-step process. Often it is preferable to place the PivotTable in a new worksheet. Note that the option to "Add this data to the Data Model" is not used here (and is discussed briefly in the Further Topics section of Chapter 21).

Figure 20.19 shows that once a PivotTable has been created in a generic sense, the next step is to define the specific items required. This is done using the PivotTable Fields menu (which displays a list of all database column headers) to select which item is to be used for the structure of the PivotTable (i.e. for the row and/or for the column), as well as which item is to be analyzed, and the nature of the analysis (e.g. forming the totals, or the averages and so on).

In fact, the types of analysis that are possible with "classical" Pivot-Tables is rather limited. A much wider and more powerful set of possibilities exists if one uses the PowerPivot functionality (and the Excel Data Model). This allows for a user to define "measures" (i.e. specific types of calculations) as well as being able to link tables in a relational way. A detailed treatment of this is beyond the scope of this text, however some of the core aspects are discussed briefly in the Further Topics section of Chapter 21.

Figure 20.18 **Completion of Step-by-Step Creation of a PivotTable**

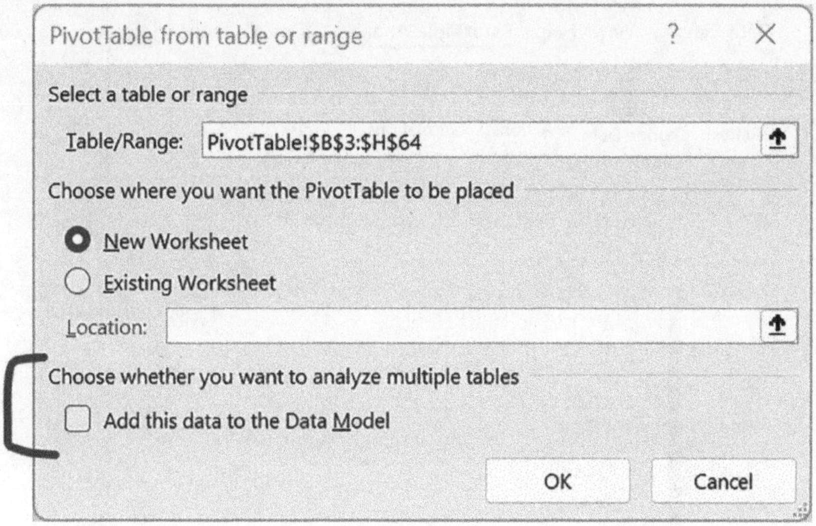

20.10 FURTHER TOPICS: MORE ON AVERAGES, CORRELATIONS, AND CONFIDENCE INTERVALS

This Section briefly mentions some slightly more advanced topics that are related to the discussion in this chapter, namely:

- Moving Averages.
- Serial Correlation.
- Confidence Intervals.
- An introduction to the LINEST function.

A moving average is simply the average value of a data set over a fixed number of periods. For example, given monthly data, the six-month moving average is the average of the last six months. These averages are smoother than the original series (since, for example, if there is an abrupt change in the value of an asset in a particular month, only one-sixth of this is reflected in the moving average, although this is then included for six months in total). Moving averages can also be smoothed in a non-equal way, for example so that more recent data is weighted more strongly, with the weighting of the older data gradually reducing until it

Figure 20.19 **Population of the PivotTable Structure**

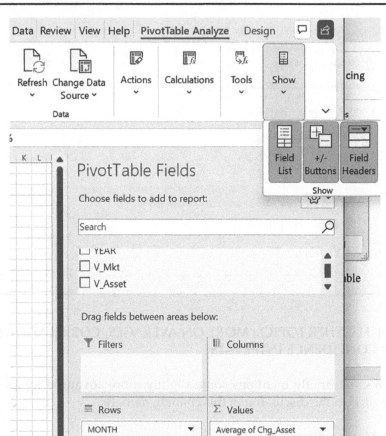

implicitly becomes zero once it is no longer within the period over which the moving average is calculated. The calculation is straightforward. For example, the weights to use can be defined in a fixed input range, and the SUMPRODUCT function used to each time point to calculate the moving average, where one input range is the fixed weights, and the other is the range of data for the relevant number of previous periods.

Serial correlation refers to the situation where the changes in the value of a variable in one period are correlated with those of an earlier period (or periods). In principle, where all known information about the value of an asset is immediately reflected in an asset's price, then asset values should not display serial correlation (assuming that new information arrives randomly and independently of previous information). The measurement of the correlation between the changes in one period and the changes in another should essentially be zero (apart from statistical error). In practice, serial correlation may be found in some cases. One simple way to research whether it exists is to copy the column containing the data on the asset's return to another column but moved down by one row (or time-period), and again by two rows (or time periods) and so on. This reflects a "delay" in the data. Then one can calculate the correlation between the original data and each of the "delayed" series and look for items whose magnitude may seem to be significant (i.e. quite different from zero).

When data sets correspond to a sample (rather than the full population), the calculation of items such as the mean or standard deviation provide only estimates of the true values for the population (which remain unknown). For example, the theoretical average value when a die is rolled many times is 3.5 (since the values 1, 2, 3, 4, 5, and 6 are equally likely). However, if this were not known, and a die-like item were rolled 100 times, with the outcomes added up, one may find a total of (say) 340. In other words, given only the experimental results (i.e. 340 from 100 rolls of the die), there is a range of possible values. Of course, in the absence of any information, one can only say that the true range is (with 100% confidence) between minus infinity and infinity. However, statistical theory allows one to use the standard deviation of the experiment to estimate with much more precision (but with lower confidence, such as 95%) the possible range of possible true values. A simple example can be demonstrated using the LINEST function, discussed in the following paragraph. (More precise details and general background are beyond the scope of this text but can be found in many other texts focused on statistics.)

The LINEST function provides several statistical values relating to the regression line between two variables. Its results are in two columns, with the first relating to the slope of the regression line and the second to the point of intercept of the line with the y-axis, as well as providing other information. Figure 20.20 shows an example of its results. The first two

Figure 20.20 **Results of the LINEST Function**

LINEST	
0.969	0.50%
0.195	0.69%
0.299	5.30%
24.750	58
0.070	0.163

entries in the left column are the slope and the standard error. The third entry is the R-squared figure. In the second column, the fourth entry (the value 58) is the number if degrees of freedom associated with the data set. This value is required (as is the confidence interval desired, such as 95%) as an input into an inverse T-distribution, which returns the required number of standard deviations for this confidence level. In this case, the T-figure is approximately 2.0 (similar to that for a normal distribution). Thus, the 95% confidence band for the slope is a range which is +/− the standard error (i.e. 0.195) multiplied by 2.0. Therefore, the two-sided range is approximately +/− 0.390, so that the estimate of the beta (slope) is that it is centered at 0.969 with a 95% confidence range that is between 0.579 and 1.359.

(The function can also be used to create multiple regression analysis for several variables; see the *PFM* for an example.)

Data Preparation: Sourcing, Manipulation, and Integration

21.1 INTRODUCTION

Chapter 20 covered some core analysis techniques that can be applied to data sets which are already in Excel and are "clean." This chapter covers topics that relate to the preparation of data that may be required prior to being able to analyze it. The main areas covered are:

- Data-related issues that should be considered when one is first engaging in a modeling process.
- An overview of the stages in the general data preparation and analysis processes.
- The cleaning and manipulation of data sets that are already in native Excel.
- The integration of Excel data sets into a single structure or "flat table" in Excel.

In fact, the overall Excel functionality in this area is rather large and is regularly augmented. The Further Topics sections of this chapter introduce PowerQuery and PowerPivot (the Excel Data Model). These have functionality that is potentially important for those needing to build models which use significant amounts of data or require manipulation before it can be analyzed.

21.2 MODELING CONSIDERATIONS

Early in a modeling process, it is worth reflecting on the core characteristics of the situation from a data perspective, since the tools and techniques required can vary significantly. Some key items to consider are:

- The overall role and importance of data to the model.
- The number of data sets.
- Their location or source.
- Their structure.
- Their size.
- Their quality and accuracy.
- The frequency with which they will be updated (if the model would also need to be updated or not).

In the simplest models, there may be only a small amount of input data (or values defined based on the modeler's judgment), with the model used for a one-off purpose. In others, although there is a small amount of data (or judgmental estimates), there may be many formulas (a "formula-dominated" model). In these cases, one may not even consider the topic of data preparation as an explicit process at all; data is simply entered directly into the relevant cells or ranges in the model. In more complex cases, there may be large data sets but relatively few formulas (a "data-dominated" model). In the most complex cases, the modeling requirements are not only for both a significant amount of data preparation but also for subsequent model formulas to depend on the results of the data analysis. Therefore, it is imperative to consider the above issues at the model planning stage and before engaging in significant model building or implementation activities.

21.3 OVERVIEW OF DATA MANIPULATION PROCESS

In general, one can think of data manipulation and analysis as potentially requiring several stages (even as in any specific situation some of these may not be necessary or be extremely simple to perform):

- Sourcing and Connection. This is the process by which the data or a data source is connected to Excel. It can range from the simplest process of direct entry in cells, to the copy/paste of data that is in another workbook, to the establishment of a connection to non-Excel sources (such as an internal computing network or an external website).

- Cleaning or Manipulation. This is the process to treat the data so that it can be processed further. For example, data that is sourced from a non-Excel environment could contain invisible (non-readable) characters, or excess spaces, or may use text datatypes for fields that should be treated as numbers, and so on. It may be necessary to split items which are joined together, such as data that may have been imported in a .csv-formatted file. Multiple data sets may need to be manipulated so that they have identical structures or in other ways so that they can be used together.
- Integration. This is the process to combine multiple data sets appropriately. It can consist of needing to append data (such as to add into a columnar structure data that relates to the most recent month underneath the data for the previous months), or to combine data sets which contain complementary information. These combinations can sometimes be done "structurally" (i.e. physically joining them together as one in Excel to create a "flat table") or only "logically" (i.e. keeping the data sets separate, having a mechanism to define that the items in each data set is related to those in another). Typically, to combine data sets one will often need to create identifiers or keys, so that related items in two different sets can be identified as being so.
- Analysis. This stage is the production of the analysis and final output or reports. The core aspects of this were discussed in Chapter 20, and so are not discussed further.

21.4 CLEANING EXCEL DATA SETS

There is a large variety of ways that data may need to be cleaned to render it into a form that can then be subject to integration and analysis. The types of methods available include:

- Manual. These are where one inspects a data set visually and makes any relevant changes to the items by using mouse and keyboard operations directly. For example, there may be a small number of spelling mistakes that can be corrected manually, or a small number of items that should be deleted, or the name of a field header should be altered, and so on. Of course, this method is effective for ad hoc or non-systematic types of changes or correction, and if they are only a few. (It is not covered further in the text since it is largely self-explanatory.)

- Excel operations. This refers to manual (or one-off) steps, but which use specific Excel operations to inspect or manipulate a larger number of data items than is possible with a pure manual approach (see later in this section for examples).

- Excel functions. The use of functions to manipulate data means not only that the operations are repeatable (if a new or updated set of raw data is used), but also that some or all of the steps can be easily replicated in another data analysis context. There are typically a small number of types of operations that are regularly required (see later in this section for examples).

- Using PowerQuery. This can be used to link to external data sets, to manipulate data that is in tabular form, as well as to create summary reports that can be presented as Excel Tables. When using this, the individual operational steps are recorded, so that these are reused automatically if the user refreshes the data. Some key aspects are covered in the Further Topics sections.

- Using VBA macros. These can be used to record operations in Excel (that would otherwise be done on a one-off basis) so that they can be used again. Further there are a small number of functions in VBA that are not available in Excel and can sometimes be useful in data manipulation. This topic is beyond the scope of the text (the author's *PFM* covers macros in detail).

Examples of Excel operations that may be used on a one-off basis include:

- The Find/Replace functionality, which may (for example) be used to correct some spelling mistakes. (This is accessible on the Home tab or with the shortcuts CTRL+F or CTRL+H).

- The Conditional Formatting options (also on the Home tab) can be used to highlight certain values, such as errors, duplicates, and positive or negative items.

- The Data tab contains functionality such as Text-to-Columns (which may be used to split each data item into its components, assuming that these are defined with a delimiter or are of a fixed width) and Remove/Duplicates (to create a unique list of a larger set of items).

- The Sort and the Filter functionalities (on the Data tab) can also be useful to inspect data and to look for anomalies and errors so that they can be corrected. For example, if one applies the Data/Filter option to a database, the drop-down menus for each field show the list of unique items in that field and which are presented in order (ascending or descending). This can be used to see potential errors (such as an item being spelled in two similar but different ways, or for negative numbers in fields that should only contain positive items). The Advanced Filter functionality may be able to be used to isolate fields that can be deleted all at once, and so on.

- Similarly, the creation of a PivotTable (or other forms of reports) can sometimes highlight errors or spelling mistakes in the underlying data.

- The GoTo/Special (F5/Special) menu provides a range of ways to highlight specific types of items (such as blanks, constants, formulas, and the last cell used in a worksheet).

Common Excel functions that are useful to clean or manipulate data include:

- The functions CLEAN and TRIM can be used in sequence as a first step when data is brought in from a non-Excel environment. The CLEAN function can be used first to remove non-readable (non-printable) characters, followed by the TRIM function, which removes extra spaces (such as converting a double space to a single).

- Identifying the precise nature of an item using ISNUMBER, ISTEXT, ISLOGICAL, ISBLANK, or ISERROR. For example, sometimes it is necessary to know whether a numerical-looking item is a number or a text field.

- Searching for the position of a delimiter using SEARCH (or FIND).

- Replicating an item with a text field, such as the part between two delimiters, by using the MID function. The LEFT and RIGHT functions are also sometimes useful (although they are essentially special cases of MID), and the LEN function is useful to find out the length of a text field.

- REPT can be used to repeat an item.

- TEXT can be used to convert a number into a numerical-looking text field. One useful application is to create dynamic chart labels or titles. That is, the label of a chart is linked to a cell in Excel, and this cell contains a formula that uses the TEXT function to refer to a model's input value. Thus, the label (or title) of the chart will also show the scenario that the chart describes. For example, if cell B9 contains the value 10% (or the number 0.1), then a chart label such as "NPV at a discount rate of 10%" could be created by using (for the label) a cell reference to a cell into which the following formula has been entered: = "NPV at a discount rate of " & TEXT(B9, "0%").

- The REPLACE or SUBSTITUTE functions can be used to find a text field within a (larger) one and replace some text with alternative text.

- The & symbol as well as the functions TEXTJOIN (or the legacy CONCATENATE) are useful to join text items together in a particular order. This can be useful to create unique keys to be able to match items in two data sets that are related to each other. (Generally, when doing so a delimiter should be used so that the item can later be further manipulated if necessary.)

- Functions such as UNIQUE, SORT, SORTBY, and FILTER are useful to create unique lists, or to dynamically sort or filter. (Recall that an example of the UNIQUE function was shown in Figure 3.8.) The TRANSPOSE functions can also be useful to switch rows to columns and vice-versa.

Figure 21.1 shows the context for the example that will be described using some of these functions. The situation is that the data is originally available in the form shown in column B (cells B3 downwards), however one wishes to transform this so that it is presented as in column D. That is, the first part of the text field is removed (leaving the country name), and the last part is altered so that it is a five-digit number.

There are often several ways that the transformation of the data could be carried out. The following shows one of these, using a step-by-step process to split the data based on the delimiters, to add the required number of zeros, and to recombine parts of the new fields into the desired form.

Figure 21.1 **Raw Data and Desired Transformation**

	A	B	C	D
1				
2		Original		Desired Format
3		Cust-UK-17		UK-00017
4		Cust-USA-26		USA-00026
5		Cust-Spain-23		Spain-00023
6		Cust-Italy-18		Italy-00018
7		Cust-UK-27		UK-00027

Figure 21.2 **Calculation Steps for One Item, Shown in a Column**

	A	B	C	D	E
1					
2					
3		Original	Cust-UK-17		
4					
5		Delimiter	-		
6		Split 1	5		C6=SEARCH(C5,C3,1)
7		Remaining	UK-17		C7=MID(C3,C6+1,LEN(C3)-C6)
8		Split 2 Rel	3		C8=SEARCH(C5,C7)
9		Split 2 Abs	8		C9=C6+C8
10		Part 2	UK		C10=MID(C3,C6+1,C8-1)
11		Part 3	17		C11=RIGHT(C3,LEN(C3)-C9)
12		Len Part 3	2		C12=LEN(C11)
13		To Add	000		C13=REPT(0,5-C12)
14		Result	UK-00017		C14=C10&"-"&C13&C11

Figure 21.2 shows the step-by-step calculations that would be applied to each item. Here, for convenience of presentation of the formulas, the steps are presented in a column form (using the first data item as the input in cell C2) only. When applied to the file shown in Figure 21.1, the calculations would be built along each row (as shown later).

The first step (cell C6) uses the SEARCH function to find the position of the first delimiter. This position is then used as one of the inputs to the MID function (in cell C7) to isolate the part of the text field that occurs from that point. The function also uses the LEN function embedded within it (although this step could also be broken out separately), since the MID function needs to be told the required length of the text field that it should create (i.e. which is the length of the original field minus the length of the part up to the first delimiter). Similarly, the second and third parts are broken out by applying the MID function (in cell C10) and the RIGHT function (in cell C11). (Note that the MID function could also be used for this third part; here we are using the RIGHT function simply to demonstrate the use of a wider set of functions.) Then, the LEN function is used (cell C12) to calculate the length of the third part, and the REPT function is used (cell C13) to create a text field which consists of zeros only, and whose length is that which is required so that the total length of these zeros and the original right-hand part would be five. Finally, the & operator is used to combine the relevant fields in the correct order (cells C10, C13, C11) to give the desired form.

Figure 21.3 illustrates the layout that would result when the calculations are laid out in each row (i.e. in a transposed form).

Figure 21.3 **Row Form of the Calculations and Results**

A	B	C	D	E	F	G	H	I	J	K	L	M
1												
2	Original		Delimiter	Split 1	Remaining	Split 2 Rel	Split 2 Abs	Part 2		Part 3	Len Part 3	To Add	Result
3	Cust-UK-17		-	5	UK-17	3	8	UK	17	2	000	UK-00017
4	Cust-USA-26		-	5	USA-26	4	9	USA	26	2	000	USA-00026
5	Cust-Spain-23		-	5	Spain-23	6	11	Spain	23	2	000	Spain-00023

21.5 INTEGRATION OF EXCEL DATA SETS

It is very often necessary to be able to access data records that are in another data set. For example, one data set could contain a list of transactions that are made in several local currencies, whereas another contains the currency exchange rates that are required to turn the local currency values into dollar equivalents. In principle, to access the value of a related item(s) in another data set, there needs to be some form of mechanism (or key) that shows (or defines) that two items are related. In some cases, such a record may already exist within each data set. For example, there could be a unique key which is common to each data set. In other cases, such keys may need to be created by using (or manipulating) the items in each data set. For example, the methods described in Section 20 which split and recombine data, may be needed to do so.

As long as related items in data sets can be identified, then there are in principle two main approaches to combining the data sets:

- The "flat table" approach is where a new database is created by starting with the most detailed original data set (such as the transactions data) and then both looking up and integrating the required values from the less detailed data set, using a "many-to-one" lookup process.
- The "relational table" approach is where the original data sets remain separate and there is an additional logical step which specifies how the items in the data sets are related. This is the most effective approach for very large data sets. However, to do this in Excel requires the use of the Excel Data Model and of PowerPivot. This is introduced within the Further Topics sections.

In the following, we show an example of the flat table approach, which is the one traditionally used in Excel when the size of the data sets is reasonable. It is often sufficient for many practical purposes that relate to traditional financial modeling.

Figure 21.4 shows an extension of the original data set (i.e. of that shown in Figure 21.1) but which also contains a column showing the value of a corresponding transaction in column C. (For the rest of this section, we shall refer to this as the "main" table).

Figure 21.4 **Data Including Transaction Values in Local Currency**

	A	B	C	D
1				
2		Original	Value in Local Currency	
3		Cust-UK-17	119	
4		Cust-USA-26	121	
5		Cust-Spain-23	46	
6		Cust-Italy-18	113	
7		Cust-UK-27	74	
8		Cust-USA-30	138	
9		Cust-USA-4	95	
10		Cust-Spain-10	54	
11		Cust-Italy-3	82	
12		Cust-UK-1	100	
13		Cust-Germany-3	66	
14		Cust-France-12	128	
15		Cust-Spain-1	45	
16		Cust-USA-22	55	
17		Cust-UK-10	129	
18		Cust-Germany-24	48	
19		Cust-France-26	64	
20		Cust-Spain-11	107	
21		Cust-Italy-15	46	
22		Cust-UK-28	106	

Figure 21.5 shows two additional data sets. On the left (columns E and F) is a table which maps each country to the currency that it uses. On the right (columns H and I) is the mapping of the currency to its dollar value.

Note that in the earlier Figure 21.3, column I (labeled "Part 2") in fact shows the name of the countries that correspond to each transaction. Therefore, by starting with the table (in Figure 21.4) and applying the same process that was used earlier (i.e. start with Figure 21.1 and using Excel functions to generate Figure 21.3), one can create an augmented main table which shows the country names. Figure 21.6 shows the result of doing this (in column R, with intermediate calculated columns hidden).

Figure 21.5 **Tables with Additional Information That Need to Be Referenced**

AD	E	F	G	H	I	J
1						
2	Country	Local Currency		Local Currency	Currency per $	
3	UK	Pounds		Pounds	0.74	
4	USA	Dollar		Dollar	1.00	
5	Germany	Euro		Euro	0.87	
6	France	Euro				
7	Italy	Euro				
8	Spain	Euro				
9						

Figure 21.6 **Augmented Main Table Showing Country Names**

AD	K	L	R
1			
2	Original	Value in Local Currency	Part 2
3	Cust-UK-17	119	UK
4	Cust-USA-26	121	USA
5	Cust-Spain-23	46	Spain
6	Cust-Italy-18	113	Italy
7	Cust-UK-27	74	UK
8	Cust-USA-30	138	USA
9	Cust-USA-4	95	USA
10	Cust-Spain-10	54	Spain
11	Cust-Italy-3	82	Italy
12	Cust-UK-1	100	UK
13	Cust-Germany-3	66	Germany
14	Cust-France-12	128	France
15	Cust-Spain-1	45	Spain
16	Cust-USA-22	55	USA
17	Cust-UK-10	129	UK
18	Cust-Germany-24	48	Germany
19	Cust-France-26	64	France
20	Cust-Spain-11	107	Spain
21	Cust-Italy-15	46	Italy
22	Cust-UK-28	106	UK

Note that in Figure 21.6, each country name (column R) appears several times. On the other hand, in the table on the left in Figure 21.5 (i.e. column E), each country name appears only once. Therefore, the table (in Figure 21.6) can be further extended by using an XLOOKUP function (or a combination of the XMATCH and INDEX functions), to map the currencies associated with each transaction. Figure 21.7 shows the top part of the result, in which column S contains the looked-up names of the local currencies.

Finally, the same process can be applied to use to match the currency names (in column S of Figure 21.7) with those in column H of Figure 21.5, and thereby to look up the exchange rates (in column I of Figure 21.5). If this is done, the values can then be converted into (common) dollar values. The result is the "flat" table shown in Figure 21.8 (with intermediate steps hidden).

Figure 21.7 **Main Table with Further Augmentation**

AD	K	L	R	S	V	W
1						
2	Original	Value in Local Currency	Part 2	Local Currency		
3	Cust-UK-17	119	UK	Pounds		S3=XLOOKUP(R3,$E$3:$E$8,$F$3:$F$8)
4	Cust-USA-26	121	USA	Dollar		S4=XLOOKUP(R4,$E$3:$E$8,$F$3:$F$8)
5	Cust-Spain-23	46	Spain	Euro		S5=XLOOKUP(R5,$E$3:$E$8,$F$3:$F$8)
6	Cust-Italy-18	113	Italy	Euro		S6=XLOOKUP(R6,$E$3:$E$8,$F$3:$F$8)

Figure 21.8 **The Completed Flat Table**

AD	K	L	U	V
1				
2	Original	Value in Local Currency	$ Value	
3	Cust-UK-17	119	161	
4	Cust-USA-26	121	121	
5	Cust-Spain-23	46	53	
6	Cust-Italy-18	113	130	
7	Cust-UK-27	74	100	
8	Cust-USA-30	138	138	
9	Cust-USA-4	95	95	
10	Cust-Spain-10	54	62	
11	Cust-Italy-3	82	95	
12	Cust-UK-1	100	135	
13	Cust-Germany-3	66	76	
14	Cust-France-12	128	148	
15	Cust-Spain-1	45	52	
16	Cust-USA-22	55	55	
17	Cust-UK-10	129	174	
18	Cust-Germany-24	48	55	
19	Cust-France-26	64	74	
20	Cust-Spain-11	107	123	
21	Cust-Italy-15	46	53	
22	Cust-UK-28	106	143	

From this point, one can use the data and statistical analysis processes described in Chapter 20 (such as using functions such as SUMIFS, Database functions, PivotTables, and so on).

21.6 FURTHER TOPICS I: INTRODUCTION TO PowerQuery – APPENDING TABLES

The PowerQuery functionality in Excel can be used to manipulate data, as well as to connect to external data sources. This Section provides a brief introduction using examples.

Figure 21.9 shows an example of the result of using PowerQuery to append two Tables one under the other. That is, there are two original source Tables (column B and column D), and PowerQuery has been used to create a third Table (column H) that results from appending the two Tables. Note that once this type of structure is set up once, the data in the source Tables can be updated (i.e. data values change, or new records added or items deleted) and the third Table will update when the Data/Refresh menu is used.

This appending process can be implemented in several ways, but perhaps the simplest from the point of view of getting started is the one described in the following.

Figure 21.9 **Results of Appending Two Tables to Create a Third**

	B		D		H
	Original_Data		Original_Data		Original_Data
	Cust-UK-17		Cust-France-12		Cust-UK-17
	Cust-USA-26		Cust-Spain-1		Cust-USA-26
	Cust-Spain-23		Cust-USA-22		Cust-Spain-23
	Cust-Italy-18		Cust-UK-10		Cust-Italy-18
	Cust-UK-27		Cust-Germany-24		Cust-UK-27
	Cust-USA-30		Cust-France-26		Cust-USA-30
	Cust-USA-4		Cust-Spain-11		Cust-USA-4
	Cust-Spain-10		Cust-Italy-15		Cust-Spain-10
	Cust-Italy-3		Cust-UK-28		Cust-Italy-3
	Cust-UK-1				Cust-UK-1
	Cust-Germany-3				Cust-Germany-3
					Cust-France-12
					Cust-Spain-1
					Cust-USA-22
					Cust-UK-10
					Cust-Germany-24
					Cust-France-26
					Cust-Spain-11
					Cust-Italy-15
					Cust-UK-28

The first step is to define the relevant data sets as Tables and load them into PowerQuery:

- Given the two source data sets, make sure that each has identical column headers (e.g. in this case cell B2 and D2 are spelled identically).
- Define each range as an Excel Table, such as by using the shortcut CTRL+T (and give each a name as desired).
- Although not necessary, for simplicity of doing the process the first time, one can also create a blank third Table (which also uses the same header as the other Tables, and whose content is a single blank row underneath it). This Table can be used later to facilitate one stage of the process, as shown below. (In Figure 21.9 this "dummy" Table is contained in column F, which is hidden.)
- For each Table in turn, use the icons within the Get & Transform Data tab of Excel's main Data toolbar, selecting the option to get the data from a Table/Range. (There are several ways to do this with the tab, but it is self-explanatory.)
- Each time this is done, one will be brought to the PowerQuery Editor, which is shown in Figure 21.10.

Figure 21.10 **The PowerQuery Editor**

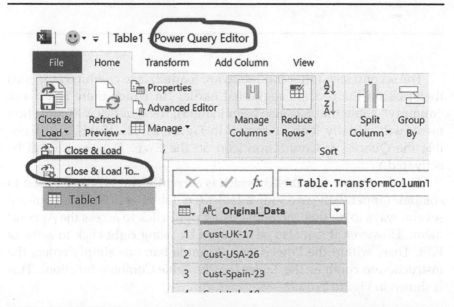

- One should initially then use the "Close and Load To" option (highlighted in Figure 21.10). This gives the option to select "Only Create Connection," as shown in Figure 21.11. (This means that the Table is not rewritten back into Excel.)

Figure 21.11 **Selecting to Create a Connection Only**

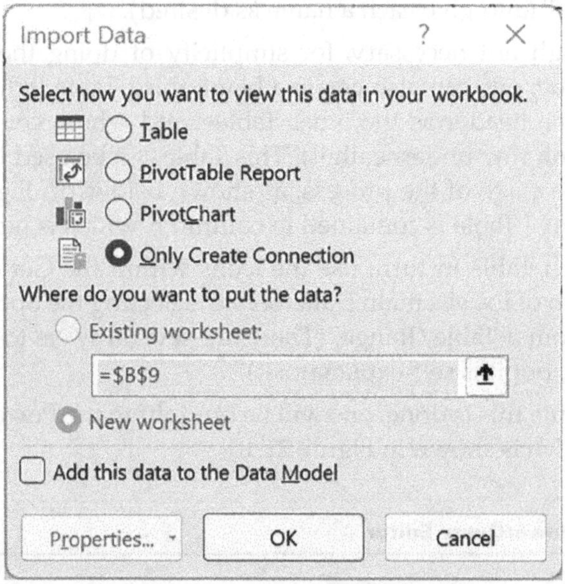

The second step (after the Tables are loaded) is to combine (append) them. Using the process suggested earlier (in which there is a blank "dummy" Table that has also been loaded), the Queries & Connection menu will initially look as shown in Figure 21.12. (If this is not visible the Queries & Connection icon on the Excel Data menu can be activated.)

The third table (i.e. Table3, which is currently empty) can be used to combine (append) the two source Tables (i.e. Table1 and Table2). There are several ways to do this, including using right-click to access the Append menu. However, it can also be achieved by using right-click to activate Edit. Then, within the PowerQuery formula bar, one simply enters the instruction to combine the Tables (i.e. the Table.Combine function). This is shown in Figure 21.13.

Figure 21.12 **Queries & Connections Before Appending**

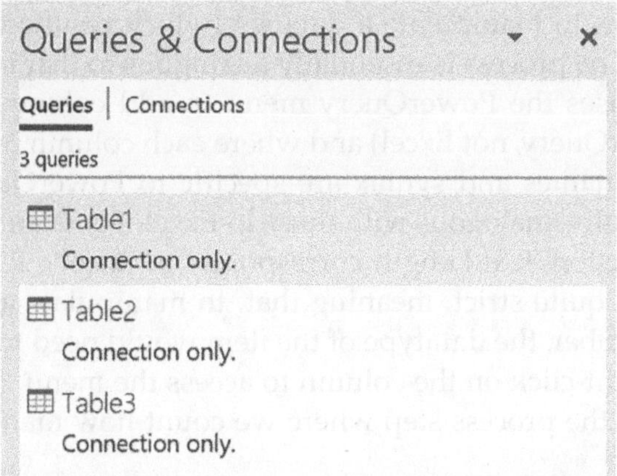

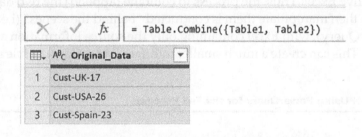

Figure 21.13 **Using the Table.Combine Operation**

The final step is to load this Table into Excel. This can be done by right-clicking on it, selecting the Load To menu, and selecting the option to create a Table in Excel (which would give the result shown in the earlier Figure 21.9).

21.7 FURTHER TOPICS II: INTRODUCTION TO PowerQuery – DATA MANIPULATION

PowerQuery can be used to manipulate data in many ways. Some of the options are visible in the menu area (and other tabs) of the earlier Figure 21.10, while right-clicking to activate the context-sensitive menu reveals many other possibilities. In fact, PowerQuery can be used to replicate the process described in the main part of the chapter which used Excel functions to manipulate a data set (which resulted in the earlier Figure 21.3). The process is essentially analogous to that in native Excel. That is, one uses the PowerQuery menu to add columns to the Table (within PowerQuery, not Excel) and where each column uses a function. The function names and syntax are specific to PowerQuery, although they are typically analogous with those in Excel. For example, the (PowerQuery) function Text.Length corresponds to Excel's LEN. The datatyping is also quite strict, meaning that, to manipulate as text an item which is a number, the datatype of the item would need to be defined as text, using right-click on the column to access the menu. (Note that this is required in the process step where we count how many digits are in each number).

Figure 21.14 shows an example of the result of such a process. That is, instead of loading the appended Table into Excel (as was done in Figure 21.9), the further manipulations required were first conducted using PowerQuery operations and functions; only the final result is present in the native Excel. Thus, the process to combine (append) the two data sets and to then manipulate them is conducted "behind the scenes" (i.e. using PowerQuery), with Excel containing only the source information and the result. This can create a much smaller interface and a more flexible model.

Figure 21.14 **Using PowerQuery for the Full Process**

	A	B	C	D	G	H
1						
2		Original_Data ▼		Original_Data ▼		Final ▼
3		Cust-UK-17		Cust-France-12		UK-00017
4		Cust-USA-26		Cust-Spain-1		USA-00026
5		Cust-Spain-23		Cust-USA-22		Spain-00023
6		Cust-Italy-18		Cust-UK-10		Italy-00018
7		Cust-UK-27		Cust-Germany-24		UK-00027
8		Cust-USA-30		Cust-France-26		USA-00030
9		Cust-USA-4		Cust-Spain-11		USA-00004
10		Cust-Spain-10		Cust-Italy-15		Spain-00010
11		Cust-Italy-3		Cust-UK-28		Italy-00003
12		Cust-UK-1				UK-00001
13		Cust-Germany-3				Germany-00003
14						France-00012
15						Spain-00001
16						USA-00022

It is worth also noting that the Get Data menu (on the Get & Transform Data tab) has many options to link to external data sets (such as may be contained in tables on websites, or in .csv files that result from querying other external databases). These can therefore be linked to an Excel workbook and manipulated by PowerQuery to create quite sophisticated and rich applications. For example, large external data sets (that may be too big to be brought into Excel) to be loaded directly into PowerQuery for manipulation. The manipulated information can be loaded into Excel, or (if the data set is too large) PowerQuery could also be used to create simple summary reports that aggregate data (see for example, the Group By option on the right-hand side of the menu bar shown in the earlier Figure 21.10). Alternatively, the manipulated data can be loaded into the Excel Data Model, and PowerPivot used to create the reports, as discussed in the next Section.

21.8 FURTHER TOPICS III: INTRODUCTION TO PowerPivot AND THE DATA MODEL

Earlier in this chapter, we used lookup processes (based on unique identifiers) to create a flat table (i.e. a table which is built at the most detailed level, and which brings in the relevant records from other data sets explicitly). If there are several large data sets, then the process of creating a single flat table would be cumbersome and inefficient, especially if the size of the data set changes when the data is updated. Also, non-Excel data sources may result in data sets that are too large to bring fully into a native Excel worksheet.

Fortunately, in Excel, each workbook can have its own "Data Model." The option to load data into the Data Model is visible in the lower part of the earlier Figure 21.11. The Data Model allows for one or more data sets (database tables) to be stored within it, and for relationships between these tables to be defined (assuming that the unique identifiers are present in the tables). The overall database is a relational database (i.e. that consists of several related tables). The statistical analysis of this is done using PivotTables that are created by the PowerPivot add-in. This allows for the PivotTables to display the results of more complex types of analysis (based on calculations known as measures that the analyst can create). The add-in is shipped with Excel and simply needs to be installed using (File)/Excel/Options/Add-ins, noting that under the Manage dropdown menu, the COM Add-ins category should be selected.

Figure 21.15 **Tables and Their Relationships within the Data Model**

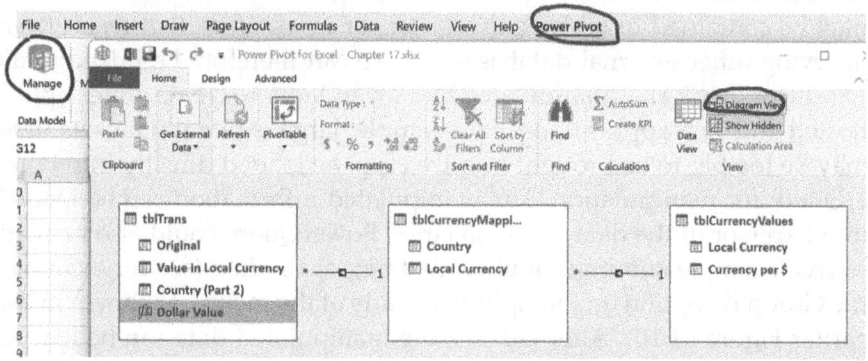

Therefore, a general data sourcing, manipulation, and analysis process (of which not all steps may always be needed) involves:

- Using PowerQuery to link to external sources.
- Using PowerQuery to manipulate the data.
- Loading the manipulated data as tables into the Data Model.
- Within the Data Model, creating the relationships between the tables.
- Creating PowerPivot measures.
- Generating PivotTables for the final reports (the values can also be converted into formulas by using the OLAP Tools menu on the PowerPivot Analyze tab).

As an example, recall that we earlier created a flat table by starting with the most detailed transactions table (see the earlier Figure 21.4) and using lookup functions to integrate the data in the two additional tables (see the earlier Figure 21.5) in turn. Figure 21.15 shows the result of first loading PowerPivot, then adding each of the three tables to the Excel Data Model (as noted earlier), then using the Manage tab of the PowerPivot menu in order to expose the Diagram View of the three tables. Finally (and importantly) the relationships between the tables were created by simply drawing (drag and drop) a line between the tables. Because the unique identifiers are already present in the data sets, when the lines are drawn, the links between the first and second table, and between the

Figure 21.16 **Creation of a Measure**

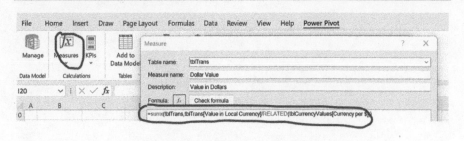

Figure 21.17 **PivotTable that Displays the Value of a PowerPivot Measure**

	A	B	C
1			
2			
3		Row Labels ▾	Dollar Value
4		Dollar	409
5		Euro	922
6		Pounds	713
7		**Grand Total**	**2044**
8			

second and third table (and hence, implicitly, the links between all three) will be created automatically.

To calculate the values in dollar terms, a measure can be created that divides the local currency value by the exchange rate that is in the related table. This is shown in Figure 21.16.

A PivotTable can then be inserted into Excel (also under the Manage menu of PowerPivot) and the row axis defined to be the currency names, with the values used being chosen to be those of the defined measure (using the PivotTable Field Settings). The result is shown in Figure 21.17.

Note that – as already noted – in addition to PowerQuery and PowerPivot, the manipulation and analysis may also require the use of VBA macros (see the author's *PFM*).

Index

Page numbers followed by *f* refer to figures.